CU00420914

I'M SO GL
ASKED Mᴇ ᴛHAᴛ
FOR THE THIRD
TIME

A Third Compilation
Of Answers

by

Robert Cubitt

Published by Robert Cubitt, Daventry, United Kingdom.

Other work by the same author:

Fiction

The Charity Thieves
The Inconvenience Store
The Deputy Prime Minister

The Magi Series (in numerical order)

The Magi
Ghengis Kant
New Earth
Cloning Around
Timeslip
The Return Of Su Mali
Robinson Kohli
Parallel Lines
Restoration

Carter's Commandos Series (in numerical order0

Operation Absolom
Operation Tightrope
Operation Dagger
Operation Carthage

The Warriors Series (in numerical order)

The Girl I Left Behind Me
Mirror Man

Non-Fiction

A Commando's Story
The A to Z of (Amateur) Golf
I Want That Job
I'm So Glad You Asked Me That
I'm So Glad You Asked Me That Again

INTRODUCTION TO THE BOOK

This is not a book that is designed to be read like a novel. However, readers may find that it takes about the same amount of time to read an answer as it does to travel between two stops on the London Underground, so it makes an ideal companion for the commuter as it doesn't require the reader to re-familiarise themselves with the plot every time they look up to identify which station or bus stop they have arrived at. It's also quite good for a quick read during a coffee break, while waiting to see the doctor or dentist, while making the kids their tea, while waiting for a bus, well, you get the idea.

Since 1993 the Daily Mail has run a column called Answers to Correspondents' Questions. Regardless of what you may think of that newspaper in terms of its editorial standards, this column is both entertaining and informative. It wasn't the first time the title had been used, as Alfred and Harold Harmsworth had first used it as a title for a weekly magazine published in the Victorian age. The questions are many and varied in nature, just as they were in the days of the Harmsworth brothers, sometimes stemming from a desire to find out about some aspect of family history, sometimes just a matter of curiosity.

Almost from the beginning, in 1993, I have contributed to the answers to the questions that are published each weekday. Many of my answers have been published, but just as many have not. Sometimes the editor would edit my answers before publication, and sometimes they were used to augment the answers of others in order to make them more complete, while answers from other contributors were edited into mine to supplement them. These were common sense editorial decisions, of course, but it did mean that some of the material I worked so hard to compile wasn't used, wasn't complete or wasn't even recognisable as being mine.

Regular readers of the Daily Mail will probably recognise my name, but as more of my contributions were published the editor took the decision to publish some of my answers under pseudonyms.

So some of my work was printed under the name Dillon (my wife's maiden name) or Sutherland (my mother's maiden name). For a period my wife's first name, Bernadette was used, also with the various last names. However, all the work printed here resulted from my own research.

This may be seen as something of a vanity project and I plead guilty as charged, but I wanted to bring all my contributions together under a single cover. The answering of these questions became something of a hobby, if not an obsession, and I am proud of what I produced. In 2013 I compiled my answers up to that point into a book called "I'm So Glad You Asked Me That". However, the urge to carry on answering the questions was not diminished and since then I have written many, many more. That resulted in volume 2 of my answers, which covered the period up until the end of 2016 and now this volume brings us up to 2020.

I must offer my thanks to the good people who run Wikipedia and those who contribute to their articles. This website is often maligned but I have found that it is usually my first port of call in answering a question and it is often the most complete source. Its reliability has been proven many times by cross referencing to other sources.

My second thank you goes to all the people who have written into the Daily Mail with their questions over the last 27 years. Without you there would be nothing for a geek like me to answer. I live in dread of the day when you all buy computers and discover the joys of surfing the internet and are able to research your own answers.

Friends have often asked me what inspired me to answer a particular question. Sometimes it was a half remembered fact from childhood, or something I learnt along the way in later life. I am an avid reader and spent a lot of my life studying for my higher qualifications and when you do that you pick up a lot of extraneous information. Professional training over three different careers has also left its mark on my memory. Certainly there was usually enough to form the basis of my answer, which was then supported and expanded upon by research on the internet. In many cases I was just interested enough in the question to want to find out the answer for myself.

There are answers which I thought I knew but which I found I was wrong about. For example, I thought that Duchies (or Dukedoms) were introduced into England by William the

Conqueror. They weren't. They didn't appear until about 300 years later (see later answer). So, I'm always learning, which is great.

I started my RAF career as an electronics fitter, specialising in communications, so I am naturally attracted to questions relating to that topic and there are several answers on that subject in this volume. I then went on to become an officer in the Supply Branch of the RAF, so Logistics is also an interest. Following a change of career I then went to work for Royal Mail so questions related to postal services are bound to attract my attention.

I am particularly interested in the military and aviation history, as will be seen from the numbers of answers related to these topics, so any questions in those areas were bound to draw me in. This stems from my own 23 years of service with the RAF which followed on from my father's 22 years in the army. My wife's Irish ancestry has inspired me to research answers to questions related to her country of birth, which often get ignored by other regular correspondents. With an insatiable curiosity, a computer, a broadband connection and a little time it's possible to answer most questions.

I am also asked if there are questions that I won't try to answer. The answer to that is yes. I usually stay clear of science and mathematics based questions as there are people far better qualified than I am to answer. The same applies to music (pop or classical) and the arts, though I will sometimes have a bash at them if I have some clue as to the answer. While I love sports I'm not a sports geek, so I will only try and answer a sports question if there is a tie in to another area of interest, such as my fondness for golf and rugby.

I'm not a train spotter and don't possess an anorak so I don't answer questions about trains and I'm not too great on questions about cars either. Other than that I'm happy to fire up the computer, type a few words into the Google search bar (other search engines are available) and see what comes up.

Have I ever been beaten and not found an answer? Yes, several times. Sometimes there just isn't much information available on a particular subject and my own knowledge isn't adequate enough to formulate a meaningful answer. Just like a fisherman, I am often taunted by "the one that got away". I'm happy to say, though, that those occasions are rare.

The dates shown for each answer reproduced in this book was the date on which I wrote the answer, which is not the same date as that on which it was published by the Daily Mail – if it was published at all. Answers are usually published about two weeks after the question is printed.

Keen observers will note that I sometimes answer several questions within a few days of each other, sometimes even two on the same day, while at other times there are lengthy gaps between answers. This is purely arbitrary and is dependent on the questions that are being sent into the Daily Mail.

When I originally wrote my answers I didn't include any personal opinions with regard to any of the things I discovered. It didn't seem to be appropriate to do so and it may have resulted in my answer not being published if my opinion was contentious. However, in this book I'm not fettered by such considerations. Interspersed with the answers I have added a few opinions, anecdotes, musings and asides to break things up. If any of my opinions don't meet with your approval then I'm unapologetic. I'm as entitled to my opinions as you are to yours. Article 10 of the European Convention on Human Rights applies, so please don't e-mail me to tell me I'm wrong, unless I'm wrong about a point of fact rather than belief or opinion.

Now for a short health warning. Every effort was made to ensure that the answers to the questions were as accurate as possible at the time they were written. However, like all researchers, I'm at the mercy of both time and my sources. Wherever possible material was cross referred to other sources to ensure accuracy, but in some cases I was only able to find one source and so was unable to be as academically rigorous as I might have liked. So, if you intend using the contents of this book to settle pub disputes, to settle bets, or as the basis for school or college assignments then I accept no liability if it later turns out that my answer was either incomplete, incorrect or is now out of date. There is no substitute for doing one's own research. Where possible I have provided updated information in my "Author's notes" if I am aware of any changes since the original answer was published.

If you wish to submit your own questions as a challenge for me to answer then please e-mail them to this address: robert.cubitt@robertcubitt.com. I can't promise I'll come up with an answer, but will guarantee to reply to you and to do some initial research.

If you are a reader of the Daily Mail I hope you will enjoy future answers to correspondents' questions, because I haven't stopped submitting them yet. Finally I hope that you find this book interesting and/or amusing. If you did then putting a review of it on Amazon will help to boost sales, which in turn will benefit Help For Heroes, so please feel free to do so. Negative reviews are not required.

Which battle in the past 500 years has seen the smallest army overcome the greatest odds?

A likely candidate for this honour would be the Battle of Kohima, which took place between 4th April to 22nd June 1944, with the Commonwealth troops involved being most heavily outnumbered during the period 3rd – 16th April. 1,500 British and Indian soldiers faced a force of between 12,000 and 15,000 Japanese.

The intention was for the Japanese 31st Division to capture Kohima and cut off the supply routes to Imphal, where the British were attempting to invade Burma. An earlier attack by the Japanese, in February, had failed to encircle the British in the Arakan region and this new thrust could be seen as an extension of that campaign.

Kohima was a ridge of land in the Nagaland area of Assam, India, dominating the main road from Burma to India, sitting on which was a telegraph station and the residence of the Deputy Commissioner of Nagaland, Charles Pewsey. At the start of the Japanese advance it was defended by a newly raised battalion of the Assam Regiment and a few platoons of the Assam Rifles. There were also some poorly trained service troops. Unsure of the Japanese intentions, Major General Ranking of 2nd Division concentrated his defence on Dimapur, the railhead for the region, regarding Kohima as no more than a 'speed bump' for the Japanese.

Late in the day the 161st Brigade was ordered to reinforce Kohima, but only the 4th Battalion, Queens Own West Kent Regiment and a single company of the 7th Rajput Regiment were able to reach Kohima before the Japanese cut the road. This brought the total military strength at Kohima to approximately 1,500 men. Arrayed against them was the battle hardened Japanese 31st Division.

Following an advance by the Japanese starting on 3rd April, the siege of Kohima started on 6th. The Japanese shelled and mortared the area, interspersed with direct attacks which threatened to overrun the ridge. The defenders were slowly forced into a small area known as Garrison Hill. There was artillery support from 161st Brigade, but they were unable, at that time, to advance and come to the aid of the defenders of Kohima. At times the British and Indian troops fought the Japanese across the narrow strip of the Deputy Commissioner's tennis court, throwing grenades and firing at each other. The defending British and Indian troops had the advantage of fighting from trenches, whereas the Japanese had to advance across open ground.

Water was in desperately short supply for the defenders, with the Japanese having captured the main supply early in the attack. The dressing station was under direct fire from the Japanese, meaning that wounded waiting for treatment were in danger of being hit again. Many were.

The Japanese, however, had problems of their own. Many of their soldiers were suffering from dysentery and there were severe supply shortages. The Japanese attacking doctrine was to carry supplies sufficient only for the first few days, then to live off supplies captured from the enemy, or to live off the land. With the stiff resistance offered by the defenders of Kohima there were no supplies for the Japanese to live off when their own ran out.

Although the Japanese captured the Deputy Commissioner's bungalow on 15th April, they didn't press home their advantage and the next day Indian troops of the 161st Brigade made the breakthrough that would bring the siege to an end after 10 days of fighting.

The British 2nd Division eventually drove the Japanese out of the area, stopping their northward advance. Fighting would continue for several more weeks as the Japanese were pushed further away from the Indian border and back into Burma, from where they would eventually be expelled.

In total the British and Indian armies lost 4,064 men killed, wounded and missing, compared to the Japanese losses of 5,764.

The battle has sometimes been referred to as the Stalingrad of the East. The Kohima War Cemetery is the last resting place for 1,420

Commonwealth soldiers who died in and after the battle. Engraved on its war memorial are the words "When you go home, tell them of us and say 'For your tomorrows, we gave our today.'" These words are repeated each year at the Royal British Legion Festival of Remembrance, held at the Albert Hall.

Two Victoria Crosses were awarded for direct involvement in the Battle of Kohima. These were to LCpl John Pennington Harman, 4th Battalion, Queens Own West Kent Regiment and Capt John Niel Randle, 2nd Battalion, Royal Norfolk Regiment, who was part of the relief force.

A very good account of the battle may be read in Fergal Keane's book, Road Of Bones.

18th January 2017

Was dentistry practised in Roman times?

In 1987, in a drain beneath a shop being excavated in the ancient Forum in Rome, 86 loose teeth were found. All were intact,but showed evidence of cavities. Those teeth were later dated to the 1st century AD and provide evidence that the premises were used as a dental practice.

The shop itself was situated in the base of the temple of Castor and Pollux and it may be that the twin Gods were associated with the art of dentistry. The temple was destroyed by fire in 14BC, so no earlier evidence is available of dental practice by the Romans.

Roman medicine, following from the Greek traditions, was quite advanced. Serious operations such as amputations and caesarean sections, catheter insertions and gynaecological examinations, were practised, so basic dentistry would be well within Roman capabilities. However, this would have been limited to tooth extraction and herbal pain relief.

Examination of the 86 teeth showed little in the way of damage resulting from their removal, leaving bio archaeologist Marshall

Becker, who examined the teeth, to conclude that the dentist or dentists that removed them were quite skilled.

The Roman Law of the Twelve Tables, created in 450BC, show that teeth were highly valued, stating that 'Whoever shall cause the tooth of a free man to be knocked out shall pay a fine of three hundred as'. Ancient recipes for toothpaste also exist, which go back as far as the ancient Greeks. It was they who first used mint as an ingredient, a practice still in use today.

It is known that the Etruscans, the forefathers of the Romans, practised cosmetic dentistry, replacing lost teeth with bridges anchored to neighbouring teeth by gold bands. The original teeth would be inserted into the bridges if they weren't too badly damaged. It was during the Roman era that dentists were first granted their own patron Saint, St Apollonia, who was born and martyred in the 2nd century AD. As part of her martyrdom she was supposed to have had all of her teeth pulled out in a most brutal fashion.

26th January 2017

What were the achievements of Regimental Sergeant Major Lord that saw him become a subject of TV's "This Is Your Life" in 1959?

Regimental Sergeant Major John Clifford Lord MBE was featured on This Is Your Life in edition 118, broadcast on 30th November 1959, hosted by Eamon Andrews. It was broadcast not from London, but from the Academy Theatre, Royal Military Academy Sandhurst. The guest list included His Majesty King Hussein of Jordan and a filmed tribute from Major General Sir Gerald Lethbury.

King Hussein's appearance marked the first time that any reigning monarch had appeared live on British Television, other than for state appearances. The King had met RSM Lord while he was a cadet at Sandhurst.

John Lord was born on 26th April 1908 in Southport. In March 1933 he joined the Grenadier Guards for a four year enlistment. Following his discharge he joined the police in Brighton.

As John Lord's Army discharge had included a term as a reservist, he was recalled when war broke out in 1939. He was posted to the Officer Cadet Training Unit at Sandhurst as a Sergeant instructor, before being promoted to Company Sergeant Major. In October 1941 he was posted to the newly formed 3rd Battalion, The Parachute Regiment, as its first Regimental Sergeant Major (RSM).

During 1942 and early 1943 RSM Lord saw action in Tunisia and Italy, before his battalion was recalled to the UK to train in readiness for the invasion of France. On 17th September 1944 RSM Lord took part in Operation Market Garden, the plan to capture bridges across the Meuse and Rheine rivers to permit the advance of ground forces to invade Germany from Holland. He parachuted into Arnhem along with the rest of the British 1st Airborne Division. The story of this disastrous operation was told in the film "A Bridge Too Far."

On 21st September, having been wounded, RSM Lord was captured by the Germans and taken to Stalag XI-B, located near Fallingbostal in Lower Saxony. He found conditions in the camp poor, with low morale among the British prisoners. He took charge and started to make changes to improve matters. He may have been a bit of a thorn in the side of his captors, because he was offered a place at a more comfortable POW camp for NCO's, but refused it. When the Germans started to move men from the camp ahead of the allied advances he hid beneath the floor of a hut until the Germans had left, being fed through a hole in the floorboards.

When Major Ralph Cobbold of the Coldstream Guards arrived to relieve the camp on 27th April 1945 he was surprised to find a well turned out British guard force wearing maroon berets. So smart were they that he assumed that somehow the British 6th Airborne Division had managed to arrive at the camp ahead of him. When he asked to meet the Guard Commander he was greeted by RSM Lord, so well turned out that he might have been on the parade ground at Sandhurst.

For his leadership at Stalag XI-B RSM Lord was awarded the MBE and he later appeared on This Is Your Life, the only serving British soldier ever to do so.

After the War RSM Lord remained in the Army, first training paratroops, then as RSM of the Royal Military Academy, Sandhurst, probably the most prestigious non-commissioned role in the British Army at that time. When he retired in August 1963 RSM Lord had held the rank of Warrant Officer First Class for 22 years, the longest term ever recorded. A popular rumour was that his initials, JC, stood for Jesus Christ.

RSM Lord died in August 1968 at his home in Camberley, Surrey. His medals may be seen at the Airborne Assault Museum, part of the Imperial War Museum at Duxford, Essex.

20th February 2017

British cinema names from a certain period seem to come from a pool that includes The Odeon, The Curzon, The Savoy, The Adelphi etc. Where did these names come from?

The origin of the names of our cinemas is varied. Many, but not all, cinema names were chosen because the name was synonymous with luxury.

An odeon was an Ancient Greek amphitheatre. When Oskar Deutsch established his first cinema in 1928 in Brierley Hill, Dudley, he decided to call it The Odeon. There were soon 250 cinemas of that name and it became a household word.

The Curzon may come from the Curzon family name. The first cinema of that name opened in 1934 and today they are best known as being small, art house cinemas. The Curzon family came to England with the Norman Conquest and take their name from the French town of Notre Dame de Courson in Normandy. The chain originally started under the name "Picture House Cinemas" and there are still 23 cinemas operating under that older name.

The Savoy cinema chain probably stems from the Savoy family, who were dominant in Italian and French politics in medieval times. They owned several luxurious palaces which led to hotels and theatres being given the Savoy name and, ultimately, to Savoy cinemas.

The Adelphi cinemas probably took their names from the Adelphi Theatre in London, which in turn took its name from the Adelphi Buildings, a group of neo-classical terraced houses built between The Strand and the Thames, which were just across the street from the theatre. The origins of the word Adelphi were Ancient Greek, meaning "siblings" deriving from a + delphi, literally "from the same womb".

The name of the Ritz cinema chain was taken from the Ritz hotel group, whose hotels were a byword for luxury. The hotel chain took its name from its owner, Swiss hotelier César Ritz (1850 – 1918).

Less prosaic in its origins was the ABC cinema chain, the initials standing for Associated British Cinemas. The chain was founded in 1927 when a solicitor, John Maxwell, merged three small independent Scottish cinema circuits. It was ABC who set up the first children's Saturday morning cinema clubs in the 1940s.

Author's note: When this answer was published, the final paragraph was omitted.

20th February 2017

Does the trawler Cornelis Vrolijk really have the right to take 23 percent of the British fish catch?

Under the EU's Common Fisheries Policy all EU countries are allocated a quota of fish that they may catch in the waters off the coast of EU countries. There are strict controls on the types and size of fish that may be caught and where they may be caught and boats found to be in breach of the rules may be intercepted and the Captain prosecuted. Large fines and the confiscation of fishing gear may result from successful prosecutions.

In order to manage the size of fishing fleets, individual countries divide their quota up and allocate it to fish producer organisations (FPO). In the UK, the Ministry of Agriculture and Fisheries divides the fishing quota into four, each administered by a different government: England, Scotland, Northern Ireland and Wales. Once they receive their quota each goverment then re-allocates it to regional FPOs. These represent individually owned vessels or collectives of vessels that operate in UK waters. There are several that cover the English fishing ports, with some overlapping into Scotland, Northern Ireland and Wales. Some FPOs specialise in particular fish types, such as shell fish, crab and lobster.

With certain types of fish being difficult to catch it has led to larger and larger trawlers being introduced so that they may remain at sea for longer, processing the fish while it is still on board and setting it ashore already frozen. The Cornelis Vrolijk is one of those trawlers. The Cornelis Vrolijk is described as a pelagic fish trawler, which means that it catches species of fish that live in the middle layers of the sea, rather than just beneath the surface or at the bottom of the sea. These species do not include either cod or flat fish. The main catch of a trawler such as the Cornelis Vrolijk in the North Sea is likely to be herring.

Although the Cornelis Vrolijk is Dutch owned it is British registered with its port of registration being Kingston Upon Hull (registration letters H171). Its owners pay tax in the UK and they state that they employ British fishermen on board. This means that it is legal for the ship to bid for a share of the British fishing quota, under licence from the Eastern England FPO. However, they do discharge their catch at the Dutch port of Ijmuiden, which is also legal. Herring is considerably more popular in North West Europe than it is in England.

According to a report in The Times, published on 4th November 2014, five foreign owned vessels hold a one third share of British fishing quotas, of which the Cornelis Vrolijk holds 23% of the English (not British) quota.

This is a game any trawler owner can play. Technically a British trawler owner could register their boat in the Netherlands in order to gain access to Dutch waters. Under EU laws it is not the nationality of the owner that is relevant, it is the port of registration of the boat.

In 2015 the Irish newspaper The Journal reported that the largest trawler in the world, the Dutch owned ANNELIES ILENA, was fishing in Irish waters, This ship was previously called the Atlantic Dawn, and its Irish owner Kevin McHugh sold it to its present Dutch owners in 2007. It is currently registered in the Netherlands. At the time it was Irish owned it held one third of the rights to catch fish from the Irish EU fishing quota. Its presence in Irish waters in 2015 suggests it still holds some fishing rights there.

27th February 2017

Why is something or someone set up as an easy target for criticism known as an 'Aunt Sally'?

This term goes back to the 17th century and refers to a game popular in pubs and at fairgrounds.

The Aunt Sally in question was a doll which was sat on a post. The doll was modelled on an old woman with a clay pipe in her mouth. The objective was to throw a stick at the doll and try to knock the pipe from her mouth without dislodging the doll. In fairgrounds prizes were awarded for success, while in pub gardens it was more of a game, with scores being kept.

From the game it is easy to see how the present day use of the term emerged, referring to someone putting an idea forward in order to see if anyone could knock it down. In that respect it is similar to another popular business term, the straw man, which is easy to re-shape or take apart.

Aunt Sally as a team game is still played in pub gardens in Oxfordshire, and in southern Northamptonshire and Warwickshire, with league structures just like those for darts. Nowadays the doll has been replaced by a 6 inch high skittle, called a dolly, and the stick has become a wooden baton. The baton (still called a "stick") is about 18 inches long and two inches thick. The stick is thrown from a distance of 10 yards. The Oxford and District Aunt Sally Association, which governs the game, was established before World War Two. It currently has 120 teams divided into twelve sections.

Early origins of the game are unclear, but some think that a live cockerel was impaled on a stick and whoever killed it got to take it home for food. Other sources claim that the game was invented by the soldiers of King Charles I during the Civil War to help pass the time. Its prevalence in Oxfordshire would fit in with such a theory, as King Charles based himself in Oxford and his army was garrisoned throughout the county. The first battle of the Civil War was fought at Edge Hill, just along the road from Banbury, which is home to one of the local Aunt Sally leagues.

In popular fiction, Aunt Sally was the female admirer of Wurzle Gummidge, the scarecrow that came to life in the books written by Barbara Euphan Todd. Aunt Sally was supposedly from a fairground sideshow and was very fastidious in her habits. On TV she was played by Una Stubbs. On the TV show Hidden Villages in 2016 Penelope Keith visits the village of Hook Norton, near Chipping Norton, where she is taught to play the game. The game is also seen being played in an episode of Midsomer Murders, Dark Autumn, aired in September 2001.

28th February 2018

Is there an obligation in the EU Lisbon Treaty for the UK to pay compensation for leaving the EU?

There is no "exit fee", or compensation system as such, for leaving the EU. However, in order to trade with the EU on a "tariff free" basis after Britain leaves the EU we will almost certainly have to make an annual financial contribution to the EU.

These arrangements are already in place for other non-EU countries such as Norway and Switzerland. How large any financial contribution might be will be a matter for negotiation as part of the leaving process.

At present Norway pays about £740 million p.a. to the EU compared to the UKs £14.5 billion to be a full EU member. However, Norway's economy and trade balance with EU is considerably smaller than Britain's, so it is a reasonable expectation that any charge to access the EU "tariff free" would be in excess of £1 billion p.a. and could go as high as £10 billion. Norway exports about £150 billion of goods to the EU (mainly oil and gas) and imports about £100 billion, compared to the UK's £600 billion and £480 billion respectively in 2016, which is approximately 4 times as much gross trade as Norway.

Those that recognise the £350 million per month net savings figure that was bandied about during the EU referendum campaign can work out that the cost of trading with the EU after Brexit dilutes that saving and if the trading charge is set any higher than £4.2 billion p.a. it is cancelled out completely.

The alternative to a negotiated agreement would be to trade under "World Trade Organisation" rules, which allows the EU to charge import tariffs on non-EU goods and services, up to a maximum level. Britain would have the right to charge similar tariffs on goods and services imported from the EU, on a 'tit-for-tat' basis. Both the EU and Britain could agree that these tariffs are set at zero, however they could go quite high on selected products and services.

WTO trade tariff levels vary widely, depending on products. The permitted maximum tariff on wine, for example, is 41% but for liquefied natural gas it's only 4.1%. The tariff for cars is capped at 9.8%. The significance of that is that Nissan cars produced on Tyneside, or Minis produced in Oxford, could be up to 9.8% more expensive to purchase in the EU compared with their European equivalents. The same could apply here for VWs, Fiats and Citroens. So, there are swings and roundabouts when it comes to the EU setting trade tariffs. Individual governments within the EU will be lobbying hard in Brussels to prevent their key industries being adversely affected. How successful they will be we will have to wait and see.

9th March 2017

How is the distance between towns and cities defined on road signs? Was it once measured as the distance between the main post office in each city?

The measurement of distances between British towns and cities pre-dates the arrival of post offices by approximately 1,600 years. It was started by the Romans, who measured distances along their roads and marked them with milestones. The origin of the term is in the Latin *mille*, or 1,000, the distance a soldier covered when marching one thousand paces. The measurement was started from a significant point within a town.

The Romans placed milestones along their roads mainly so that military commanders could plan the stopping points for soldiers on the march.

Legend has it that in the centre of Rome was a "Golden Milestone" from which all other distances in the Empire were measured. If this is true that milestone has now been lost. The first known milestones were placed along the Appian Way, the road that led South East from Rome to Brundisium (Brindisi).

In Britain from mediaeval times onward, distances from London to other towns were measured from the Eleanor Cross, which was close to the modern day Charing Cross Station. On the death of his wife Eleanor, King Edward I had her body transported to London for burial. At the place where her coffin rested each night a memorial cross was erected, the last of these being at Charing Cross.

The first Headquarters of the General Post Office in London was located near Cloak Lane (near Dowgate Hill) and was later moved to Lombard Street and then to St Martin's le Grand, none of which locations are used as measurement reference points. The modern headquarters of the Post Office (rather than Royal Mail) is in Finsbury Square, London.

Any non-Roman milestones still in existence will owe their origins to the Eleanor Cross reference point. A milestone will usually display two sets of figures. On one side will be the distance to London and on the other the distance from the previous town on the route.

Turnpike trusts were established from the 17th century through to the 19th century by Acts of Parliament and allowed local councils to build roads and to charge tolls for their maintenance. There was no standard reference point for measuring distances between towns so it was defined by the local council and will usually relate to some significant landmark within the town boundary, such as a Town Hall, Guildhall, a barter cross (buttercross) or other permanent marker, which might even include an old Roman milestone. This could include the parish church or a post office, depending on when and where the roads out of the town were constructed.

While most towns had a Postmaster from 1635 onwards, who was a government official, many didn't have a Post Office, as such, until the 19th century.

Those towns that built the best roads gained the most visitors and therefore prospered. This later led to the establishment of the coaching routes, as coaches required the best roads to travel on. Most distance measurements used today were established during that period. This can, and has, led to discrepancies between the distances marked on modern motorway and A Road signs and those marked on historic milestones.

19th March 2017

Who invented the flame thrower that was used in World War II? Were they effective? Are they still used by any military force today?

The history of the flamethrower goes back to the 5th century BC when tubes filled with burning coal or sulphur were used in a similar way to a blow gun. However, the flame thrower as we know it is a 20th century invention.

In 1901, a German engineer by the name of Richard Fielder developed two models, one large and one small, for the use of the Kaiser's army. It would take another 12 years for these to be developed to the point where they could be used safely in the field. Safely, that is, for the operator.

The *kleinflammenwerfer*, or small flame thrower, could be carried by one man. It used pressurised air to throw a stream of oil up to 60 ft. It provided about 2 minutes worth of usage, though not in a single stream. Each time the operator wanted to fire a new stream he had to replace the ignition device, which was a major inconvenience.

The *grossflammenwerfer*, or large flamethrower, needed more than one person to carry it, but could throw its stream of burning oil almost twice the distance and could also maintain a single burst for up to forty seconds.

Both weapons were introduced to the First World War in 1914, where their first use caused considerable consternation against French troops. A significant part of the effectiveness of the weapon was the psychological impact. The fear of fire is one of the hardest for humans to overcome. Its first use against British troops was at Hooge Crater in the Ypres Salient on 30th July 1915. It was just as successful as it had been against the French the previous year.

However, despite a moral boundary having been crossed, the weapon was soon in use with all the combatant armies except for the U.S. Army. As late comers to the war they hadn't developed a model of their own and didn't do so until 1940.

The British experimented with large scale models, assembling the components in the trenches. They were first used in 1916 during the Battle of The Somme. While they were extremely effective at clearing front line trenches, their lack of mobility was a considerable disadvantage. It wasn't until 1917 that the British developed a portable model.

In all the German Army used the *flammenwerfer* on at least 650 occasions during World War I. There are no records for French or British use, but their later introduction onto the battlefield would suggest much lower usage figures.

During World War II the use of flamethrowers was more widespread, with technological advances making the weapons lighter and the development of re-usable ignition devices meant they were more efficient to use. They were mainly used in the same way as they had been during the First World War, as a method for clearing fixed defences. Models were also developed for use on tanks. The Americans used them in large numbers in the Pacific theatre, where they were the most effective way of clearing the well dug in Japanese fixed defences.

The flamethrower continued in use throughout the Korean and Vietnam wars, but the increased mobility of modern infantry and a reduced dependence on fixed defensive lines resulted in them falling out of favour with most modern armies. The Convention on Certain Conventional Weapons, signed in Geneva on 10th October 1980 came into force in 1983 and put an end to their use by all signatories. By May 2016 there were 123 signatory nations, but not all have signed all five of the Convention's protocols, leaving them free to use some types of incendiary weapon.

The IRA used a smuggled military flamethrower against a British position at Derryard, near Rosslea, on 13th December 1989 and an improvised flamethrower, made from a manure spreader, against a position in Crossmaglen on 12th November 1993. These were probably the last two uses of the weapons in combat.

22nd March 2017

Why did they never use Winchester Rifles in World War I or II? They could hold about 15 rounds and were also not as cumbersome as Lee Enfield Rifles.

There are three reasons, the first two were the rate of fire that could be achieved from the different weapons and the effective range. The second was related to safety.

The Winchester rifle had a tube magazine and its bullets were round nosed. Magazine fed bolt action rifles, however, could fire a pointed bullet which was more aerodynamic. Putting a pointed bullet into a tube magazine could cause the round ahead of it to be fired by accident, causing an explosion inside the weapon. In a magazine fed weapon the bullets are stacked one above the other, removing the risk of an accidental discharge of that nature.

When the Winchester ran out of ammunition it had to be reloaded by feeding each round individually into the interior magazine. Magazines for bolt action rifles, however, could be pre-loaded and carried in ammunition pouches, making it quick and easy to swap an empty magazine for a full one.

The final issue with the Winchester was its limited range. A box magazine allowed for a larger cartridge to be used, containing more and better quality propellant, which radically increased the range of the weapon. The tube magazine and the limited scope of the lever mechanism of the Winchester left it incapable of handling such a large round.

Two early designs by Walter Hunt of New York paved the way for the Winchester Rifle. In 1848 he patented a very complex repeating rifle that used a tube magazine to hold its ammunition. He also developed the "rocket ball" projectile, which stored explosive powder in the hollow base of the bullet, which was then fired by a percussion cap. This removed the need to pour a black powder charge into the weapon every time it was loaded. However, the complexity of the weapon itself meant the design was impractical in commercial terms.

Hunt's patents were purchased by Lewis Jennings, who was able to make slight improvements to the weapon's design, which resulted in some limited production, but in 1852 the patents were sold on again, this time to Horace Smith and Daniel Wesson of Connecticut. They set up the Volcanic Repeating Arms Company, one of the investors in which was Oliver Winchester. The company produced the earliest viable repeating rifles and pistols by modifying Hunt's designs.

After the American Civil War, Winchester renamed the company the Winchester Repeating Arms Company and the first true Winchester Rifle was produced in 1866. It immediately found popularity both at home and abroad. It used cartridge ammunition, with the powder stored in a metal case into which the bullet was inserted, making a significant improvement to the Hunt design.

The French Army purchased 4,000 Winchesters which were used in the Franco-Prussian War of 1870 and the Ottomans purchased 45,000 which were used in the Russo-Turkish War of 1877. The American Army, however, largely shunned the Winchester. A few were purchased for use in the 1898 Spanish American War but they weren't introduced in large numbers until the First World War. The British did purchase a few Winchesters for use by the Royal Flying Corps, where they were used to fire special incendiary rounds to explode the hydrogen gas in German observation balloons. Their smaller size and lighter weight made them more suitable for aerial use than the Lee Enfield.

Various models of the Winchester Rifle have been produced, the latest of which is the Model 9422 which was introduced in 1972. Nowadays the weapons are mainly purchased by those with an enthusiasm for the lever action rifle.

By the late 1800s improvements were being made in the development of bolt action rifles, with the introduction into the German Army of the Mauser Gewehr 98 and into the American Army the M903 Springfield.

The Lee Enfield Mk1 Rifle was introduced into the British Army in 1898 and remained in service in various marks right up until 1957. The Lee Enfield had an effective range of up to 550 yards, but stories abound of them being used against targets up to 1,000 yards away. By comparison, the 1866 Winchester had an effective range of about 100 yards, though this was improved by the introduction of better ammunition, but limits to the size of cartridge still meant it had a much shorter range than its bolt action competitors. The British Army trained its soldiers to achieve a rate of fire of between 30 and 40 rounds per minute compared to the Winchester's 20 rounds per minute.

The Lee Enfield was replaced by the L1A1 Self Loading Rifle which was manufactured under licence from a design by the Fabrique National de Herstal arms company of Belgium. In terms of range it was less effective than the Lee Enfield, but its larger magazine and self-cocking action meant it provided an increased rate of fire of up to 700 rounds per minute in automatic mode, though the British mainly used it in single shot mode.

28th March 2017

What stops ball-type ammunition rolling out of the weapon after being loaded and the weapon is being carried with the barrel facing down, as seen in many films?

From pistols to cannons, essentially the same method of loading was used in all muzzle loaded weapons.

First the powder was poured into the barrel, then the ball was dropped in, then wadding made of paper or other material was inserted into the barrel to prevent the ball rolling out. It is this element that had to be rammed home, using the weapon's ramrod. This kept the bullet firmly pressed against the powder charge so that the none of the power of the discharge was lost. Most hand held weapons were also carried with the barrel pointed upwards as an additional precaution.

With cannon there is also an essential first step. The barrel is swabbed out using a wet sponge, in order to prevent any smouldering material or left over gunpowder inside the barrel from igniting the charge prematurely. Forgetting to do that in the heat of battle was a common cause of death amongst sailors and artillerymen.

The amount of powder in use was a critical factor; too little and the ball won't travel far enough, too much and it may cause the barrel of the weapon to shatter. For this reason, various methods of measuring the charge were used.

For naval and artillery cannons the powder was measured into calico sacks, which were inserted bodily into the barrel. Because of the friction created by the bag, these too had to be rammed home. To fire them, a quill filled with powder was inserted into the touch hole, which would pierce the bag inside the gun. The linstock would then be used to light the powder at the top end of the quill, causing it to flash down into the main charge.

From around 1586, the powder for muskets was measured into paper tube cartridges, with the ball inserted into the top of the tube. The cartridge was then sealed with wax. By the 19th century these cartridges had developed to the point that they were made of carboard and greased with animal fat to help keep out moisture.

The cartridge was opened with the use of teeth and the ball was held in the mouth while the powder was poured into the weapon, before the ball was spit into the muzzle with the cardboard case being rammed home afterwards. This was the catalyst that started the Indian Mutiny (1857) as agents provocateur spread rumours amongst Muslim troops that the grease was pork fat and amongst Hindu troops that the grease was beef fat. In fact it was neither, it was mutton fat.

29th March 2017

Following the Norman invasion, did a group of English nobles leave to fight for the Byzantine Empire?

The Varangian Guard was an elite unit of the Byzantine Army, established in the 10th century AD and continuing to the 14th century. It was made up of soldiers form Germanic tribes, such as the Norsemen. In 330 AD the Emerpor Constantine moved the seat of the Roman Empire to Byzantium, which was later renamed Constatinople after him.

Following the Norman Conquest, William the Conqueror's followers were rewarded with lands seized from Anglo-Saxon and Danish nobles. Left destitute, many of these nobles and their followers travelled to Constantinople (modern Istanbul) to join the Varangian Guard in the service of the remnants of the Roman Empire.

The Varangian Guard was founded in 874 AD by peoples from Kievan Rus, which was located in the area now known as the Baltic states and Belarus, after a period of hostilities with Byzantium. The people of this area were Norse in origin. Initially it was an obligation forced on the Rus, but following further outbreaks of hostility between 901 and 911 the commitment was made voluntary. Other contingents are known to have come from Norway, Denmark, Sweden and Iceland.

The Varangian Guard, along with other troops of the Byzatine Empire, served in several campaigns, especially against the Seljuk Turks intent on conquering Turkey and Greece.

The first record of Anglo-Saxons joining the Varangian Guard is in the 1070s, when it was thought as many as 5,000 exiles arrived in 250 ships. Byzantine historians record the new arrivals as being axe bearing warriors, which fits with them being the House Carls, or personal guard, of Anglo-Saxon nobles.

The Varangian Guard became the personal guard of the Emperor and the Anglo-Saxon contingent became the dominant part of the unit.

It is thought that the first military service undertaken by the Anglo-Saxon contingent of the guard was in the Balkans against the Italo-Norman forces of Robert Guiscard. This might have provided the Anglo-Saxons the opportunity to gain some revenge of the Normans, even at a distance.

Those Anglo-Saxons that didn't join the guard settled along the Black Sea coast of modern Bulgaria and Romania, garrisoning towns there. There is a legend that an Earl Sigund was granted title over any lands he could seize from the "heathens" that lived there and the Earl and his followers drove the inhabitants out to establish a country they called England and naming towns there London, York and similar.

On June 12th, 1942, a Bristol Beaufighter went on a solo mission to drop a huge Tricolour over the Arc de Triomphe in Paris to bolster French morale. Was it a success?

On 12th June 1942 a French Tricolour was dropped onto the Arc De Triomphe by a Beaufighter of 236 Sqn flown by Flt Lt Alfred Gatward and his navigator, Sgt Gilbert Fern.

Intelligence reports had shown that the German Army paraded down the Champs Elysees each day between 12.15 and 12.45. As a morale boosting exercise Coastal Command was tasked with dispatching an aircraft to strafe the German parade and drape the tricolour over the Arc de Triomphe. Flt Lt Gatward was a skilled low level pilot and was persuaded to volunteer for this high risk mission.

Gatward obtained a tricolour from the Navy in nearby Portsmouth and split it horizontally into two parts, one for each of two targets. He and Sgt Gilbert practised for the raid by dropping the weighted flags from a hanger roof to see how they would unfurl as they fell. An attempt to complete the mission on 13th May was abandoned due to bad weather, so it was rescheduled for June.

Arriving over Paris at about 12.27 Gatward circled the Eiffel Tower until 12.30 when he then crossed the River Seine to fly over the Arc de Triomphe. Sgt Fern ejected the flag through the aircraft's flare chute, but unfortunately the intelligence information was inaccurate and there were no troops to strafe on the Champs Elysees. The second part of the tricolour was then dropped onto the Ministry de Marine (Naval Ministry) a few seconds later and the building was strafed, scattering the sentries.

The estimated height of the aircraft during its passage along the Champs Elysees was forty feet, about second floor window height compared the height of the buildings along its route. Gatward then turned for home and landed his aircraft safely at RAF Northolt.

Intelligence later confirmed that the parade had still been assembling at the time of the attack and was abandoned in the resulting confusion. Flt Lt Gatward was awarded the Distinguished Flying Cross and Sgt Fern the Distinguished Flying Medal immediately after the raid.

Some newspaper reports state that the building that was strafed was the Gestapo HQ, but this is incorrect. The flight path of the Beaufighter meant that it didn't pass over that building, which was on Avenue Foch on the west side of the Arc de Triomphe. The Ministrie de Marine is in the Place de la Concorde at the east end of the Champs Elysees and was directly on the flight path chosen by Gatward. Sadly, history doesn't record whether or not the two flags actually hit their targets.

Flt Lt Gatward's record of the flight in his log book is very succinct. "Paris – No cover – 0 ft (feet). Drop Tricolours on Arc Triomphe <sic> & Ministry Marine <sic>. Shoot up German HQ. Little flak, no E.A. (enemy aircraft) Bird in STBD (starboard) oil radiator. Returned Northolt and on to Command 61 photos. Heavy rain over England. France fair to light. Northolt to Thorney, Thorney return base. Air Test."

The bird strike reported by Gatward happened as he was circling the Eiffel Tower and could have caused the aircraft to crash. Legend has it that the dead bird was removed from the radiator intake at Northolt and "laid to rest".

Flt Lt Gatward was later awarded a bar for his DFC following a raid on German shipping off Norway. He was also awarded a Distinguished Service Order in 1944. He went on to finish the war in command of 157 Wing and retired with the rank of Group Captain in 1964. He lived in Frinton On Sea until his death in 1998.

Was Gediminas, a former Lithuanian peasant, once the most powerful man in Europe?

Gediminas was Grand Duke of Lithuania and ruler of most of Eastern Europe from the Baltic to the Black Sea and therefore probably one of the most powerful men in Europe at the time.

He was born around 1275. The lack of written records of his early life make his origins obscure; he may have been the son of his predecessor, Vytenis, his brother, his cousin or even his stable hand. There are two versions of his life, produced long after his death.

The version produced by the Teutonic Knights, the long-term enemies of Lithuania, claim that he was a stable hand who killed his master to seize the throne. The other version, the Lithuanian Chronicles, claim that Gediminas was Vytenis's son.

The Encyclopaedia Britannica, however, states that Gediminas was the brother of Vytenis.

What is known is that Gediminas became Grand Duke of Lithuania in 1316 and ruled until his death in 1341.

The Teutonic Knights regularly raided Lithuania and its territories on the pretext of converting it to Christianity. Gediminas himself was a pagan, however he did protect Christians within the Grand Duchy and appealed to the Holy See to curb the activities of the Teutonic Knights.

The Teutonic Knights, or Teutonic Order, started off as a religious order founded by merchants from Bremen in 1189 or 90. They were dedicated to assisting sick and wounded crusaders. However, when a number of German crusaders decided to return home in 1197 an alliance of German Princes and Bishops decided to turn the nursing order into a military one.

In 1211 the order transferred their centre of operations from Palestine to Hungary when King Andrew II requested their assistance to protect his borders against eastern pagan tribes. After that they pursued any and every opportunity to capture lands in

Eastern Europe, which eventually brought them into conflict with Gediminas.

Gediminas expanded his rule from what we now call the Baltic States all the way to the Black Sea. As well as Lithuania, his lands incorporated large parts of the modern nations of Belarus, Russia and Ukraine. He also founded Vilnius, the modern capital of Lithuania and made it his seat of government. By most accounts, he was a wise ruler, by the standards of the day.

On his death in 1341, Gediminas was given a pagan cremation which included the human sacrifice of his favourite servant and several German slaves. His death probably came about as the result of a coup d'etat and he was replaced by his son, Jaunutis.

The Teutonic Knights still exist as an order and are now based in Vienna, though their activities are strictly limited to ecclesiastical and charitable work.

14th April 2017

Why were the Chinese Communist barefoot doctors so called?

The barefoot doctors pre-date Communism in China by about 25 years. In the late 1920s and early 30s the Chinese nationalist government was having difficulty in encouraging well paid urban doctors to move to rural areas where there was a great need for healthcare. Accordingly, they set about providing rudimentary medical training for rural dwellers so that they could provide a local source of medical assistance.

It was Mao's Communist government that formalised the arrangements and provided more structured training.

These trained workers were referred to as "barefoot doctors" because a large amount of China's farming and rural economy was focused on rice growing in paddy fields, where the farmers worked barefoot in water filled rice paddies. This is still a cliched image of rural China.

Typically, the barefoot doctor would be graduates of the secondary school system who had received about six months of medical training at the nearest hospital, but training could extend to up to eighteen months.

Workers were trained to treat minor ailments and injuries and to dispense both western and Chinese drugs. Many relied on herbal remedies, growing the herbs in their own back gardens. There was a considerable focus on prevention rather than cure, with the barefoot doctors carrying out immunisation projects. By itself this had a significant beneficial impact on healthcare.

The barefoot doctor scheme ended in 1981 as part of the move away from collectivism to individual entrepreneurship. Barefoot doctors were given the option to take a national exam that would allow them to study medicine more formally and become "village doctors". Many doctors now working in rural China started their careers as barefoot doctors. Chen Zsu, the current Chinese Minister for Health, is reputed to have started out that way.

The barefoot doctor scheme provided the basis for the Alma Ata Declaration, signed in 1978, which encouraged countries to set up similar primary healthcare systems in deprived rural areas.

17th May 2017

Apart from the yellow Star of David, what were the other coloured badges used in Nazi concentration camps?

The Nazis used a comprehensive system of triangular badges to denote different groups of people they regarded as "undesirable." However, the yellow Star of David was unique, as it was the only one used outside of the concentration camps. All other groups were only required to wear their symbols once they had been sent for detention or "re-education".

The Star of David was, effectively, a double symbol. One yellow triangle was inverted and placed on top of the other triangle.

All other triangles were worn inverted and the full list of colours and their meanings is:

Brown – Gypsy.
Lilac – Bible researcher (usually, but not exclusively, Jehovah's Witness).
Pink – homosexual (men only. Lesbians were regarded more as Asocial).
Green – habitual criminal.
Red – political prisoner (usually communist, but also Christian Democrats and other parties)
Asocial – included alcoholics, prostitutes, vagrants, and people who consorted sexually with other categories. This category was also used for the physically disabled and mentally ill.
Blue – Emigrant – Forced foreign labourers and Germans who left Germany without permission and who were later captured.

A red triangle the normal way up indicated an enemy prisoner of war or deserter. These were almost exclusively worn by Russians or Slavs.

If a person belonged to more than one category, they would wear all the appropriate triangles, using the six pointed star. So not all people wearing that symbol were Jews. However, the inclusion of the yellow triangle meant that they were specifically Jewish. A Jew who was also regarded as political detainee would have his star made up of a yellow triangle and a red one and the same applied to other categories of Jewish detainees.

As well as the triangles, coloured bars and dots were also used. A bar above a triangle indicated a repeat offender, ie someone who had been released and then re-arrested for the same offence. These were usually from the criminal or Asocial groups, but could be from others.

Erziehungshäftlinge (reformatory inmates) wore a white square badge with the letter E or EH imprinted in black. These were prominent citizens who were being held in "protective custody". In other words, to stop them using their influence against the Nazis but who were too powerful to be held using any of the other categories.

Other letters would be printed on triangles, such as an F on a red triangle to denote a French political prisoner. A on a black triangle indicated *Arbeitserziehung Häftling* (broadly 'workshy person') who was only being detained for labour re-education – teaching them to become a useful worker. A black dot inside a black circle, below the relevant triangle, indicated someone who was in a punishment company – in other words they had been singled out for special punishment above and beyond the normal conditions of the concentration camp. A red dot within a black circle indicated that someone was an escape risk, usually because they had made at least one escape attempt.

The system of using badges to denote categories of prisoners started around 1935/36 with individual concentration camp commanders. These became standardised during the winter of 1937/38.

The Jews, gypsies and the physically and mentally disabled were the subject of deliberate extermination strategies, however other detainees were there principally to prevent them "contaminating" Germans society and were rarely under sentence of death. When they died, as they did in their hundreds of thousands, it was mainly through neglect and ill treatment, rather than as part of a plan.

31ˢᵗ May 2017

Would a car fuel tank explode if hit by a bullet?

The short answer to this question is no, but the explanation as to why it is no comes in several parts, as there are several factors that affect the explosive nature of fuels.

Anyone who has poured cold brandy onto a Christmas pudding and then tried to light it will know how hard that is to do. However, if you heat the brandy first it will light easily. This is because it isn't the brandy that burns, it is the vapour from the brandy, which is released when it is heated. The same applies to petrol, diesel and aviation fuel.

For a petrol or diesel explosion to take place it requires three things: fuel (vapour), oxygen (air) and an ignition source (spark, flame or high temperature). If any of these three are missing then the explosion won't take place. In this instance it is the heat source that is missing, because bullets don't get hot enough to cause ignition.

You can drop a lit match into a pool of petrol and it will just fizzle out. However, hold the same lit match half an inch above the pool, where the vapour combines with air to form an explosive mixture, and it will explode. Please do not try this.

If a bullet punctures a fuel tank it will be immersed in liquid fuel, not vapour, and therefore the fuel can't explode. If the tank then leaks, the fuel starts to produce vapour when it reaches the open air and can be ignited by any spark, but that will only happen outside the tank.

If the fuel vapour is hot enough it will reach what is known as its "autoignition" temperature and will explode spontaneously. For petrol vapour this temperature is 280° C and for diesel it is 256° C. A bullet isn't hot enough when it reaches its target to heat vapour to that temperature, which is why it is necessary to use a naked flame or a spark to produce an explosion.

The only sort of ammunition that might cause an explosion in a fuel rank are incendiary bullets, which are filled with a chemical charge capable of melting the armour of a tank, but even then it wouldn't work with a full fuel tank, where there is no room for vapour to form. Incendiary bullets are large calibre, typically 12.7 mm or greater and are fired from a machine gun or other heavy weapon.

What is the meaning of the word "daylights", as in "the living daylights?

This term had a quite specific meaning in the 18th century. "Daylights" was a word used to describe the eyes. The living daylights was, therefore, the life force seen in the eyes. If you scared the living daylights out of someone, you were scaring the life out of their eyes.

   The first known citation of the word is in Henry Fielding's 1752 novel AMELIA. "Good woman! I don't use to be so treated. If the lady says such another word to me, damn me, I will darken her daylights." In modern terms he was threatening her with a black eye.

   The first usage of the term "living daylights" doesn't appear until the 1890s. In September 1890 the Decatur Morning Review, an American journal, published the quote "'I'm not going to be insulted by a miserable rabbit', and he started to club the living daylights out of the beast with his gun." By this time the term had lost its association with the eyes and now referred purely to the life force.

   By the 20th century this had mutated to become "to punch someone's lights out". This first appeared in 1956 in relation to a boxing match between Sugar Ray Robinson and Carl (Bobo) Olson, "Robinson's knockout punch turned out the lights for Bobo in the second round."

   In the 18th century the term was also used to refer to other things related to sight, such as spectacles or windows. From that we get the term "daylight robbery" which relates to the window tax that was introduced in 1696 and not repealed until 1851.

   Modern politicians like to think that they are quite clever by introducing terms such as "bedroom tax", "dementia tax" and "garden tax", but in fact they are only following in the footsteps of their predecessors.

How long have there been artificers (tiffies) in the Royal Navy and the Army? Are there any in the RAF or in the Royal Marines?

The term artificer is defined as "a person who is skillful or clever in devising ways of making things; inventor." In the armed forces of countries where the term it is used, artificer is a rank, rather than a job description.

The term was in use as early as the American War of Independence, when the was a Corps of Artificers in the Revolutionary Army, which remained in existence until after the American Civil War. In the British armed forces the origins are with the Royal Navy, dating from the earliest days of steam ships in the 1820s. To become an artificer, the sailor had to serve for many years to gain the necessary experience and qualifications. Nowadays, being awarded the rank of Artificer is more a matter of training.

The RAF was formed from the Royal Naval Air Service and the Royal Flying Corps, so it might be expected that the rank of artificer might have survived the transition, however, it seems not.

The RAF has always preferred to use the grades of Aircraftsman, Leading Aircraftsman and, from 1951, Senior Aircraftsman for its lower grades of technical tradesmen. From 1951 onwards Junior Technician, Senior Technician and Chief Technician were used for its higher technical grades. The rank of Senior Technician was removed in 1964. From 1950 to 1964 there was also a rank of Master Technician, equivalent to a Warrant Officer.

In the Royal Mechanical and Electrical Engineers (REME) there is an Artificer Sergeant Major, normally the senior non-commissioned rank in a REME unit and the rank is also used for specialist REME soldiers selected for an accelerated path to the rank of Staff Sergeant.

Given its specific technical meaning, there are no artificers in the Royal Marines, except those that may be on secondment from the Royal Navy or REME.

30th June 2017

Is it true that the average golf handicap has stayed the same for decades, despite new technology?

Statistics show that in 2014 the average handicap for male golfers was around 14.3 and for women 26.5. This compares with 16.3 and 29.7 in 1991. Some of that reduction in average handicaps may be attributable to improved golf equipment technology.

The handicap a golfer holds is a reflection of their golfing ability rather than the technology of their equipment. A good golfer will still be a good golfer playing with clubs made forty years ago, while a bad golfer will still be a bad golfer playing with the latest hi-tech offerings from the equipment manufacturers. It has often been said that "you can't buy a good golf shot".

In particular it is not the distance a player can drive the ball from the tee that will govern their handicap, it is their ability to sink a 6 foot putt. The Pro's have a saying "Drive for show – putt for dough". Putters have barely changed in their technology since they were first introduced to the game. Modern putters may look very different, but in essence they are still a flat faced bit of metal on the end of a stick. Many low handicap golfers use their old putters in preference to new ones because they feel familiar in their hands and that familiarity gives them confidence.

Most improvements in golfing technology are in the most expensive club in the player's bag, the driver. However, this is only used for about 12 shots in 18 holes, whereas the putter is used for between 18 and 36 shots (or more) in 18 holes.

Professional golfers do gain some advantage from new driver technology. Between 1980 and 1993, average driving distances on the US PGA Tour increased just 3 yards, from 257 to 260. Over the next 10 years, however, they increased by 27 yards, reaching 287 yards in 2003. Since then there has only been a small increase. During the same period in the lady's professional game there was an increase of 22 yards. Research suggests that improvements in driver technology in the 1990s accounts for a large part of the increase, however, this rate of change in driving distances has not been maintained over the last decade, so further technological improvement seems to be an illusion.

A significant amount of this increase in driving distance will also be due to improved fitness regimes and better coaching, both of which lead to better technique.

Being able to hit a ball a long way is not a guarantee of a low handicap or a winning score, as any professional will testify. It is often better for the amateur to hit the ball shorter but straighter, to stay out of trouble, and improved technology is of very little help in that respect.

Technology is probably of most use off of the golf course. The ability to video a golfer's swing on the practice ground allows a coach to identify small flaws in the golfer's technique and to correct them. However, few amateur golfers invest in that sort of coaching.

The principle reason golf handicaps remain relatively high is the lack of practice that amateurs are able to put in. Most golfers play only once or twice a week, which is insufficient for many of them to develop a consistent swing. It is noticeable that when someone retires from work and starts to play more golf, their handicap will often reduce quite quickly, before starting to climb once again as age and infirmity take their toll.

The Dad's Army script has the men carrying '.300 calibre Ross rifles'. Is this historically accurate? What is known of these weapons?

This is partly true and partly a conflation of two different weapon types. The British did purchase the Ross Rifle for use by the Home Guard. However, the Ross used .303 ammunition, the same as the British Lee Enfield rifle. As well as the Ross, the British also purchased American rifles that fired .300 ammunition.

During the Second Boer War the British had refused to licence the manufacture of their standard Short Magazine Lee Enfield (SMLE) rifle to the Canadians. This led to them developing their own version, the Ross Rifle. This was heavily influenced by the Austrian built Mannlicher 1895 rifle.

The 1905 pattern Ross Rifle had been highly successful as a target shooting weapon, but design flaws made it unsuitable for use in trench warfare during World War I. By 1916 all the Ross Rifles had been withdrawn and replaced with the Mk I SMLE.

The Ross Rifle had one significant advantage over its British counterpart, and that was its accuracy over long ranges. It therefore remained in use as a sniper's weapon.

In all about 420,000 Ross Rifles were produced, of which 342,000 had been purchased by the British to make up for World War I shortages of the SMLE.

When Winston Churchill ordered the formation of the Local Defence Volunteers (LDV), later to become known as the Home Guard, in the summer of 1940, he envisaged about 500,000 men volunteering. However, nearly 1½ million came forward and they all expected to be armed.

In addition, all the rifles lost during the evacuation of France had to replaced, as many of the survivors had to abandon their weapons in order to make their way out to the ships standing off the beaches of Dunkirk. Between the two demands it created what was known as the "rifle crisis", a shortage of weapons to arm both the army and the volunteers.

There were a number of P14, or 1914 model Lee Enfields held in reserve, and these became the earliest weapons issued to the LDV, while the army was given priority for the replacement Mk III SMLEs..

As part of the solution to the rifle crisis of 1940, Britain placed an order with the Canadian government for 75,000 Ross Rifles. Although all of these were issued to the LDV, they were eventually replaced with the SMLE.

As well as the Ross Rifles, orders were also placed with the American company Winchester, Eddystone and Remington, for the 30.06 rifle, which used .300 ammunition. About 500,000 of these were purchased and issued, making them far more common than the Ross.

20th July 2017

If a laser is fired vertically upwards, as it loses energy, will it eventually disappear?

Laser energy falls into the same category as radio waves and visible light in that it is a form of electromagnetic energy. In accordance with the first law of thermodynamics, energy can neither be created nor destroyed, it can only be converted from one form to another.

In the case of lasers, their energy is usually converted from light to heat, which dissipates into whatever medium it passes through.

Electromagnetic energy follows an inverse square law. That is to say, every time the distance travelled is doubled, the energy content is halved, the other half being converted to another form of energy. As an example, the output of a 100kw radio transmitter will be 50 kw at 1 metre from its source, 25kw at 2 metres from its source, 12.5kw at 4 metres, 6.25 kw at 8 metres, etc. However, as fans of shortwave radio can tell you, it is possible to send a radio signal around the world with radio transmitters of much lower power output than 100kw.

Using the inverse square law, it is apparent that the laser energy will continue to travel for an infinite distance, but at a certain point its remaining energy will be too small to measure using conventional measuring equipment. The actual distance at which this happens is determined by the output power of the laser transmitter and the sensitivity of the measuring equipment. However, even many light years from Earth, it would still be possible to detect the laser's light if you had equipment sensitive enough.

11th August 2017

St Patrick is said to have banished snakes from Ireland. Were there once snakes there?

At the end of the Ice Age, animals spread north as the ice retreated. First to arrive in the British Isles would have been the very heavily furred animals, such as the woolly mammoth, followed by the grass eaters: oryx, elk, deer etc which were, in turn, followed by predators such as bear, wolves and wildcats. Humans will also have migrated, following the animals that were a major source of food. Snakes, lizards, newts and frogs, being cold blooded, need a lot of warming sunlight to allow them to move and so would have been much later arrivals on our shores.

Before the Ice Age the Irish Sea was a large fresh water lake, but the erosion caused by the ice allowed it to connect to the sea as the ice melted about 10,000 years ago. Larger mammals had probably crossed the ice to Ireland before it melted, in search of new grazing, while others will have been taken there by humans as they, too, migrated. While England was still connected to the continent by a land bridge where the English Channel now lies, the melting ice left Ireland separate, meaning that some species of animal, snakes and lizards included, never arrived there.

There is no fossil record of snakes or lizards ever having inhabited Ireland.

The land bridge between England and Europe was finally destroyed about 6,500 years ago, creating the English Channel and preventing the further unaided migration of animals from the continent. One such example is the rabbit. These weren't native to our shores and were introduced by the Normans. Our native species of Lepus is the hare.

Frogs, toads and newts will have arrived in Ireland by having spawn transported stuck to the feet of migrating wading birds, but the larger eggs of snakes and lizards couldn't be carried that way. Another animal not to make the journey to Ireland was the mole, which was also kept out by the sea. It is somewhat ironic that a B&Q store in Dublin actually sells mole repellent.

The myth that St Patrick expelled the snakes in Ireland probably grew up after the Saint's death. It may be a reference to the serpent, the symbol of evil, which St Patrick would have metaphorically banished by converting the Irish pagans to Christianity. It is also a myth that St Patrick was the first Christian missionary to Ireland. Pope Celestine sent Bishop Palladius from Briton to Ireland during the Roman era, around 431 AD.

St Patrick's arrival is dated at 432 AD, but this may have been amended in later accounts to minimise the role of Palladius in taking Christianity to Ireland. It is known that the Irish traded with the Romans in Briton and it is unlikely that Christianity in the British Isles, when it arrived in the early in the 4th century AD, would have failed to cross the Irish Sea ahead of the arrival of St Patrick or Palladius.

Amongst other places that people with snake phobias can visit without fear are New Zeeland, Iceland, Greenland and Antarctica.

17th August 2017

What is the strangest thing found by Customs at a UK airport or port?

Something of which the general public is unaware is that all mail sent by air has to be x-rayed before it can be loaded onto an aircraft. The reasons are exactly the same as those for x-raying luggage. This may be expected for airmail for overseas destinations, where the security checks are carried out at Royal Mail's international distribution centre at Langley, Berks, before being moved on to Heathrow and Gatwick airports.

What is generally not known is that a sizeable quantity of mail posted within the UK for delivery within the UK is also carried by air for part of its journey and is subject to the same security measures.

This seems fairly obvious for mail travelling to and from the Channel Islands, the Isle of Man and Northern Ireland, however, a considerable amount of mail travelling from the south of England to Scotland and vice versa is also carried by air.

Royal Mail has two main air hubs in England at Stanstead Airport and East Midlands Airport, as well as smaller operations in airports at Glasgow, Edinburgh, Newcastle, Southampton, Bournemouth and a few others.

The x-ray operators are all trained Royal Mail staff and all of them have stories about the sort of items that they see pass through their machines. Drugs, weapons and ammunition (both real and replica) are quite common but there is also a steady stream of what might best be called "adult toys".

Illegal items are handed to the police for investigation, but the legal items travel through the system unimpeded. So, if your Postie gives you a knowing smile one day, it might be because they know what's in the package they're delivering.

Author's note: This answer was written as a supplement to the original answer, but was never published.

18ᵗʰ August 2017

Is it true that turtles breath through their rear ends? Do any other creatures do this?

A turtle's lungs are connected to the mouth and nose in a similar manner to those of humans and most other species of mammals and reptiles. There is no usable connection to the anus.

Even if the turtle were to have some physical connection between fore and aft, the anus of a turtle is on its underside, meaning that it is submerged whenever it is in the water, cutting off the supply of air.

There is one species of freshwater turtle, the Australian Fitzroy River turtle, that uses a technique called cloacal breathing to remove oxygen from water. The water required for this is drawn in through the anus. This ability allows the Fitzroy River turtle to remain submerged for up to 3 weeks. However, this is not to be confused with what we call breathing, which is the taking in and expelling of air. The Fitzroy River turtle breaths air in the normal manner when it isn't submerged.

A turtle's cloaca is normally used for defecation, urination and the laying of eggs. There is not known to be any other animal that uses cloacal breathing.

Increased sedimentation of its river habitat hampers the Fitzroy River turtle's ability to breath through its cloaca and has resulted in it being classified as "vulnerable" in conservation terms, one step down from "endangered".

What became of Mota Fuel – water transformed into fuel using a "gasoline pill"?

Mota Fuel was a petty fraud that has passed into urban legend as a conspiracy by the oil industry to prevent the world from having cheap fuel.

Guido Franch, a factory worker from Illinois, claimed to have developed a chemical that turned water into fuel for motor vehicles. To bolster his claims, he created a fake German scientist by the name of Dr Alexander Kraft, who was supposed to have been the original inventor of Mota (it's atom in reverse).

Franch took money from small investors who had read about his fuel pill in the newspapers. He said he had to keep the recipe for Mota secret, lest the oil industry sabotage him. When challenged to produce a sample he supplied a small quantity of green food dye.

Franch was first prosecuted for fraud in 1954, but convinced a jury that his fuel pill might work. Other trials followed. He was eventually convicted in 1979.

Franch was not the only "inventor" to suggest that water could be turned into gasoline. In 1904 Louis Enricht, another American, made a similar claim. He was convicted on an unrelated fraud charge.

In 1996 Ramar Pillal, an Indian, claimed to be able to convert water to gasoline by the use of a herbal mixture obtained from a specific type of bush. He fraudulently obtained 20 acres of land on which to grow the bush, but it turned out he was using sleight of hand to substitute kerosene for water in his samples.

In 1983 Wang Hongcheng received funding from the Chinese government for his "Magic Liquid", a few drops of which turned water into fuel. Hongcheng was imprisoned for 10 years once the fraud was discovered.

Between 1995 and 2007 an Australian businessman, Tim Johnson, defrauded investors, mainly in Australia and New Zeeland, of A$100 million by claiming to have invented a "magic pill" that cut exhaust emissions and made fuel last longer. Many governments, including that of Britain, were persuaded of the efficacy of his product. Johnson's company, Firepower Holdings Group Ltd, was registered in the British Virgin Islands and when it collapsed no assets were recovered and no evidence was found of the "magic pill". Johnson was banned from managing a company for 20 years.

The idea of a "magic pill" or similar formulation to convert water to fuel is a physical impossibility due to the amount of carbon required to achieve it. Gasoline is a mixture of hydrogen and carbon, while water is a mix of hydrogen and oxygen. For every 9 molecules of water it would be necessary to add 8 atoms of carbon to achieve the conversion. Essentially it would require 8 kilos of carbon to convert 9 litres of water. No pill or magic liquid could achieve that and the cost of doing it on an industrial scale rules it out as a substitute for fossil fuels because of the need to find the huge quantities of pure carbon involved.

As carbon is a non-renewable resource, it would run out just as quickly as fossil fuels are destined to do.

24th August 2017

Does anyone know the story of World War II pilot Stanley Streeter, whose likeness Bernard Arnold used to create a painting of St George?

On 1st/2nd April 1943 a De Haviland Mosquito aircraft (DD742) from 85 Sqn, RAF Hunsdon, Hertfordshire, was taking part in an offensive Ranger patrol over France. This particular patrol was over the Le Bouget/St Dizier area, about 10km from the centre of Paris.

The aircraft was piloted by Sqn Ldr Kenwyn Roland Sutton DFC of the Royal New Zeeland Airforce. His navigator was Fg Off Stanley Robert Streeter DFM, aged 22.

The aircraft was returning to its base when it was hit by "friendly fire" from an anti-aircraft gun situated near Hove, Sussex. The pilot struggled to try to land the aircraft, but was unable to do so. At very low level, probably no more than 500 ft, he bailed out, losing his left arm and foot in injuries caused in the attempt. Fg Off Streeter had been badly injured by the anti-aircraft fire and was unable to bail out and he died. The aircraft crashed close to the Shoreham to Hove railway line.

Stanley Streeter was the youngest of 3 brothers, born in Kings Heath, Birmingham and he attended Moseley Grammar School. He left school at 16 and went to work at the same textile company as his father, before moving to Birmingham Small Arms Company Ltd (BSA) as an engineering apprentice.

Stanley was already training with the RAF as an Observer (navigator) when WW2 broke out and he first flew as a Sergeant Observer. He served with 144 Sqn at RAF Hemswell (Lincolnshire) where he had been forced to bail out of Hampden bomber P2079 on 9th November 1940. He also served with 23 Sqn at RAF Ford (Sussex) before joining 85 Sqn. His DFM was awarded to him on 19th May 1942 by King George VI.

As a Navigator Stanley flew under the command of both Peter Townsend and Johnnie "Cats Eyes" Cunningham and he was a pallbearer at the funeral of HRH The Duke Of Kent on 29th August 1942. Given this prominent roll, Fg Off Streeter must have been commissioned sometime between the award of his DFM and his participation in the Duke's funeral.

FG Off Streeter is buried at Brandwood End cemetery, Birmingham. His epitaph reads "Tell England We Died For Her And We Rest Here Content."

The painting by Bernard Arnold was commissioned by Stanley Streeter's parents and was presented to St Jude's Church, Yardley Wood, where Stanley and his brothers had been altar servers.

Sqn Ldr Sutton survived his bale out and continued to fly with the aid of a prosthetic arm. He passed away at Kapiti, New Zeeland, on 6th July 2003.

Which jobs or professions use algebra?

We all use algebra, but we don't always realise that we are using it. Anyone who has ever planned a journey and tried to work out how long it will take, has used the algebraic formula t=d/s (time = distance ÷ speed). So the first job that can be named as users of algebra is navigators. However, some professions are more dependent on it than others.

Algebra is simply the representation of numbers and the relationships between them by the use of letters and symbols; you replace $1 + 1 = 2$ with $a + a = b$. Because so many mathematical relationships are complex, it is easier to work with letters and symbols, especially when so many of the actual numbers are unknown and have to be derived from the relationships between other numbers. Once you have used algebra to reduce the complexity down to the simplest relationship(s), you plug the numbers in to replace the letters and "solve" the equation.

Mathematics is the underpinning for science. You can't understand the universe and all that is in it without using algebra to do the maths for you. Engineering is the application of science to practical tasks and, again, is underpinned by mathematics. If you want to build a bridge you're going to use a lot of algebraic formulae to work out how strong it's going to be and, of course, the same applies to constructing tall buildings, so add architecture to the list. As an electronics technician in the RAF I used a number of algebraic formulae in my work, including Ohms law: V=IR (voltage = current x resistance). Doctors use algebra to calculate doses of medication, as well as your BMI (body mass index) and computer scientists uses it to design and programme computers. The computer games that people play are basically the products of algebra presented in graphic form.

Statistical analysis would not be possible without the use of algebra, neither would economics, where algebra is used to model whole economies. Geography uses it to model population shifts and meteorologists use it to model weather systems. Basically, if it's got an "ology" on the end it probably uses algebra somewhere along the line to create models of the world and the people in it.

However, more day to day jobs use algebra than we might think. A painter and decorator, working out how much paint to buy, is using the formula $a \div c = q$ (area $\div$ coverage = quantity). They will then use the formula $(q \times p) + L = b$ ((quantity x price) + labour = bill), before working out how much VAT to add, which also uses an algebraic formula based on percentages. It may not appear to the painter that he or she is doing that, but they are. Farmers will use a similar formula to work out how much fertilizer to buy for their fields, how much feed to buy for the animals etc and to predict how much revenue they will receive from a crop.

An easier question to answer might be "which professions don't use algebra?" because so many do without even realising it.

30th August 2017

Did the Isle of Wight once have a King?

Prior to the arrival of the Romans in Britain, in 42AD, the Isle of Wight had been part of the lands of the Atribates, who ruled in modern day Wiltshire and Hampshire. King Verica of the Atribates was exiled following the invasion of his lands by Caraticus, King of the Catuvilauni and the principle defender of Britain against the Romans. It is thought that Verica was reinstated as a client king following the Roman conquest of southern Britain in 43 AD.

Following the collapse of Roman rule, around 410 AD, the Isle of Wight was invade by the Jutes, who came from southern Denmark (now known as Jutland) and were close relations of the Saxons. They established the Kingdom of Whitwara (literally "Men of Whit"). Its capital was at Whitwarasburgh, close to modern day Carisbrooke. The Kingdom was supposedly named after Whitgar who, with his brother Stuf, were the first two Jutish kings of the island. However, this may have been more of a legend than a fact, to provide an origin for the name of the island.

There were, however, real Jutish Kings of the Isle of Wight, the last of whom was Arwald. In 661, Wulfhere of Mercia conquered Wessex and the Isle of Wight along with it. The Kingship was handed to Aethelwalth of Sussex, Wulfhere's godson, who converted the islanders to Christianity. After Wulfhere's departure the island returned to paganism. Arwald was reputedly killed in 686, fighting against Caedwalla of Wessex, who tried to wipe out the islanders and replace them with his own followers.

Arwald had a sister (name unknown) who married Egbert of Kent, another Jutish Kingdom, and through her lineage was an ancestor of Alfred the Great.

After the Norman Conquest, the island was granted to the Redvers family in 1101, who were known as the Lords of the Isle of Wight. Edward I claimed that the island was sold to him by Isabella de Fortisbus, last survivor of the Redvers family, before her death in 1293, making it a Crown property.

In 1444 Henry IV named the Duke of Warwick, Henry Beauchamp, "King of the Isle of Wight", though this was probably a nickname. Beauchamp died shortly afterwards and the title was never used again.

22nd September 2017

A former SAS soldier I knew would never talk about his service, but would say: 'The ethos of the SAS is enshrined in the story of Lalaba and Mirbat'. What did he mean by this?

The Lalaba part of this quote refers to Staff Sergeant (SSgt) Talaiasi Labalaba, of 22 Regt SAS, who died at the Battle of Mirbat on 19th July 1972.

In 1963 a civil war broke out in Oman, with the Popular Front for the Liberation of the Occupied Arabian Gulf (PFLOAG, also referred to as the Adoo) resisting the rule of the Sultan of Oman in the province of Dhofar. The war continued until 1976 when the rebels were defeated.

Britain agreed to provide military support to the Sultan of Oman between 1970 and 1976. The SAS and other military elements of this were known as the British Army Training Team (BATT).

Early on the morning of 19th July 1972 a force of approximately 200 – 300 Adoo attacked a building outside the port city of Mirbat, which housed 9 SAS soldiers. Also in the building were some Omani Intelligence Service operatives, some Pakistani soldiers (also on loan to the Oman government) and some British Military Intelligence personnel. The rebels knew that to reach the city they would first have to defeat the soldiers in the house, who were guarding the approach.

At first the CO, Captain Mike Kealy, ordered his troops not to fire, thinking that the attackers were in fact the "night picket", a force of loyal Omanis, returning from their observation post forward of his position. Not realising that the night picket had all been killed, he allowed the Adoo to get dangerously close before they were engaged.

While the Adoo were still out of range of the SAS's 7.62 mm rifles, SSgt Labalaba made a run for the unit's 25 pounder artillery piece, located outside a small fort 800 metres from the SAS's building and manned by soldiers of the Omani Special Forces, who remained inside the fort.

Operating the weapon was normally a 6 man job, but SSgt Labalaba managed it by himself, keeping up a rate of fire of about one round per minute. His action diverted attention away from the BATT house, but resulted in SSgt Labalaba being seriously wounded in the ensuing fight.

Trooper Sekonaia Takavesi went to Labalaba's aid and ran from the BATT house to help him, while under intense fire. The Omani soldiers inside the fort engaged the Adoo with small arms fire while Labalaba and Takavesi continued to fire the 25 pounder, sometimes at point blank range, despite both now being wounded.

Captain Kealy and Trooper Tobin also went to help Labalaba and Takavesi. Tobin was wounded by gunfire, later dying in hospital from an infection. 3 BAC Strikemaster aircraft (modified Jet Provosts) of the Sultan of Oman's Airforce (SOAF) arrived to provide air support until more SAS from G Squadron arrived to drive off the remaining rebels. The battle ended at about 12.30. Around 80 of the Adoo had been killed and an unknown number wounded.

SSgt Labalaba, a Fijian serving in the British Army, was finally killed crawling across open ground in an attempt to reach a 60mm mortar position and was awarded a posthumous Mention In Dispatches, the 3rd highest award for bravery after the VC and GC. There is an ongoing campaign for his bravery to be recognised by the award of a Victoria Cross.

The other SAS soldiers who fought at Mirbat that day were Sgt Bob Bennet, Cpl Roger Cole, Cpl J Taylor, LCpl P Warne and Trooper Austin 'Fizz' Hussey. Capt Kealy was awarded a Distinguished Service Order, Trooper Takavesi the Distinguished Service Medal and Sgt Bennet the Military Medal,

Capt Kealy died on 1st February 1979 during an endurance training exercise in the Brecon Beacons. The 25 pounder gun used at Mirbat is now housed in the Firepower Museum, at the former Woolwich Arsenal.

In 1972, as a young airman stationed at RAF Masirah, an island off the coast of Oman, regular visitors to our base were the Shorts SC.7 'Skyvans' of SOAF, bringing in British dead for repatriation to the UK. The wounded were flown by Hercules aircraft direct from RAF Salalah (now a civilian airport) to RAF Akrotiri, Cyprus (a 7 hour flight away), which was the nearest British military hospital.

No newspaper or TV reports of any of the British operations in Dhofar were made at the time, and officially there was no British involvement in Oman's civil war. Officially our military personnel were in Oman purely for 'training' purposes. In 1991 a fictional account of The Battle of Mirbat, entitled The Feather Men, was published by Sir Ranulph Feinnes.

It remains a strong tradition in the SAS that former members don't discuss their experiences. Given the sorts of operations in which they engage, this is as much a matter of personal safety as one of national security.

5th October 2017

Is 'Craic' a fake Irish word?

The word 'craic' appears to have entered the Irish language during the 1970s, probably from the English word "crack", meaning to have a laugh and a gossip.

The origin of "crack" goes back to Middle English, with the word crak, meaning loud conversation or bragging talk. This sense was carried forward into the question "what's the crack?" ie 'what's the news?' or 'what's the gossip?' which was widely used in northern England and Scotland. In Scotland it came to be associated with having a good time and from there probably migrated to Northern Ireland first, where many Scots from the Clyde shipyards went on holiday during the 1950s and 60s. It first appears in its Irish form in the 1970s.

In military circles the word crack is used as a verb, as in 'to crack on' ie to get on with a task or mission.

At the start of the Dubliners song "MacAlpine's Fusiliers", singer Ronnie Drew introduces it with the spoken lines:

The crack was good in Cricklewood,
And they wouldn't leave the town.
There were glasses flying and biddies crying,
Sure Paddy was going to town.

Oh Mother Dear, I'm over here,
I never will come back,
What keeps me here is a rake of beer,
The ladies, and the crack.

It can't be certain if Drew uses the word 'craic' or 'crack' in his introduction because of the similarity in pronunciation. There is no clear origin for these lines as they don't appear to form part of the original lyrics and it's possible that Ronnie Drew composed them himself.

The song was written by Irish writer Dominic Behan, who is thought to have composed it with the Dubliners in mind. He was very involved in the development of the Dubliners performances during their early years. The song was first performed in the 1960s, which may have widened the popularity of the word "crack" in Ireland and prompted its translation to its Irish form.

The 'borrowing' of words between languages isn't uncommon. The French have borrowed 'le weekend', and Welsh is littered with English words given a Welsh flavour, for example ffrind (friend), nerfus (nervous) and nyrs (nurse) amongst many others. Many words accepted as being English were originally borrowed from other languages. Many were introduced into Britain by soldiers and civil servants returning from abroad. Both 'bungalow' and 'pyjamas' are Indian and there are hundreds more from the same source, brought back during the days of Empire.

It is difficult to say that any word in popular use is "fake" as such. As many as 1700 words in the English language, including 'assassination', 'madcap' and 'swagger', have been attributed to Shakespeare, but in reality, may have been borrowed from foreign, dialect or slang words and popularised in his plays. Shakespeare may just have been the first to write them down in the form they are used.

In truth, all words are 'fake', as language itself is only an assembly of sounds for which there is a general agreement as to their meaning. However beautiful our language may be today, it started out as the grunting and croaking of our distant ancestors and comes down to us via the Celts, Romans, Saxons, Danes and Normans.

16th October 2017

Why do we 'sally' forth?

Like many military terms, this one has its origins in the French language. Most were brought to English through the Normans or, later, during the Hundred Years War (1337 – 1453) which was fought on French soil by generations of English and Welsh soldiers.

In this sense 'sally' originates in the French word 'salier', meaning 'to jump'. In practical terms it was a sudden rush made by soldiers, intended to swamp the enemy's defences. The term is also found in 'sally port' which was a small door or gate in a castle wall, often hidden from view, through which a covert attack (two more military words with French origins) could be mounted. 'Port' is the French word for 'door'.

An excellent example of a sally port can be seen in Edinburgh. High up, above the rock at the western end of Edinburgh Castle, a small door can be seen, which allows access to a very narrow path leading around the rock. The area of the city directly below this door is known as the West Port, and has nothing to do with the sea.

This meaning of port can also be found in another French word, portcullis, a heavy grating that can be lowered down to block a gateway.

Whole English paragraphs can be written using French military terms that have been incorporated into our language. Here is a short list: Commander, conquer, defence, castle, armour, enemy, battle and billet. There are hundreds more and it's hard to find any English military terminology that doesn't have French origins. Even soldiers going to work have to march, from the French 'marcher', to walk.

25th October 2017

Flying over central Spain last week, I saw a large number of round fields. Different sizes, different colours, some brown but all perfectly circular. What is the reason for them?

In 1940, American farmer Frank Zybach invented a system for irrigating crops which rotated around a central pivot which, in turn, created 'circular fields'. He used the system to irrigate his cotton fields during periods of drought. The system is called 'centre pivot irrigation', but is sometimes also known as 'waterwheel' or 'circle' irrigation.

Long tubular metal structures, supported along their length by wheels, are connected to a central pivot to provide a rotating sprinkler system. The radius of the circle created can vary from a single span of a few feet, to multi-spans with radii of up to 1600 ft (500 metres). That is a field diameter of one kilometre, which is why they can be seen from high flying aircraft. Seen when the water is turned off, the spans appear like a series of lattice bridges connected end to end.

To prevent the spans from breaking apart, modern systems have stress detectors fitted so that the speed of rotation can be adjusted along the whole length to prevent the spans twisting out of line.

The nozzle sizes set along the length of the spans are smaller near the middle than at the ends, as the area to be irrigated is greater on the outside of the circle than at the centre. The number of nozzles and their spacing can also be adjusted to take into account the amount of ground to be covered.

If it is preferred that the crop is watered at its base rather than from above, hoses can be suspended from the spans to release the water at ground level.

To prevent scarce water being extracted from rivers or reservoirs, the systems often use water pumped up from underground through bore holes. Once the water in the bore hole is exhausted, time must be allowed for it to be replenished by the rain, often over several years. To allow this the fields are left fallow and the whole contraption is moved to a new field. This creates the brown fields that can be observed, where crops aren't being grown but the imprint of the field can still be seen from the air. At ground level they would be almost undetectable.

The type of crop varies. It can be anything from grain crops to potatoes and root vegetables, but used in areas of low summer rainfall they can produce two and sometimes three crops a year, making them well worth the investment.

10th November 2017

What is the origin of Mel Gibson's middle name, Colmcille?

Colmcille is a place in Co Donegal, Ireland, which in turn is named after Saint Columba. Colmcille is the Irish rendition of his name.

St Columba is one of Ireland's three patron saints, the others being St Brigit and, of course, St Patrick. He is also the patron of the city of Derry, which he is said to have founded. In Irish the city's name is Doire Colmcille. The Catholic church in the city is also dedicated to him.

Columba is given the remarkably accurate birth date (for the period) of 7th December 521, in Gartan, Co Donegal. At the age of 20 he entered the priesthood at Clonard Abbey, Co Meath, and then travelled northern and western Ireland converting the pagan Irish to Christianity. He is credited with founding 30 monasteries in just 10 years, including one at Killmacrennan in his native county.

However, Columba was something of a trouble maker and was accused of starting factional wars between the Irish clans. As a punishment he was exiled by the High King of Ireland. With 12 companions he went to Scotland where he established the first Scottish Christian community on the island of Iona, from where he is credited with converting the Scots to Christianity.

Amongst Columba's feats and miracles he is supposed to have encountered the Loch Ness monster while trying to cross the loch. At the sound of the saint's voice the monster is said to have fled. This is thought to be the first historical reference to the monster. Columba died on Iona in 597 and is buried there.

Most of what is 'known' about St Columba is to be found in the Vita Columbae, a three part life history written by Adomnàn, the 9th Abbot of Iona, more than a hundred years after the saint's death.

Adomnàn was born in Raphoe, Co Donegal and is also known as St Eunan. The cathedral in Letterkenny, Co Donegal, is dedicated to him.

In Donegal, Glen Colmcille is a beautiful valley containing Lough Gartan. A local spring, close to the small church at the side of the lough, dispenses water which is said to have healing powers.

Pieces of white clay, found close to the saint's birthplace in Gartan, are said to protect travellers from harm. This has caused problems for some Irish travellers, as the clay pieces resemble a certain banned drug and have raised suspicious eyebrows amongst customs officials abroad.

In 2012 Mrs Sheila Sweeney of Letterkenny, Co Donegal, was arrested by customs officials when entering Australia because of Gartan clay found in her luggage. It was a present for her sons who were working there. She was released two days later with an apology and a hamper full of Australian memorabilia. The incident was revealed on the TV show "Nothing To Declare – Australia".

13th November 2017

Where does the word snorkel come from? When was it invented?

The formal use of the word snorkel comes from the German Navy, meaning an airshaft for submarines, or U-Boats as they called them. The installation of a snorkel on U-Boats allowed them to remain almost completely submerged while at the same time using their diesel engines to power the boat and charge its batteries.

The air needed to aspirate the engine would be sucked in through one tube while the exhaust would be expelled through another. With the snorkel having such a small profile it made the boat difficult to detect using radar. If it was detected at all it was because of the tell-tale black exhaust given off by the engines, which wouldn't be visible at all at night, when most 'snorkelling' was done.

Its origins is in German Naval slang, schnorchel, meaning nose or snout. Its root is in Schnarchen, to snore.

Although the Germans used the snorkel, they didn't invent it. Shipping engineer James Richardson came up with the first designs in 1916 and they were trialled by the Scotts Shipbuilding and Engineering Company of Greenock. Although a patent was granted, the Royal Navy weren't interested in the development and it was never used by them.

The Italian Navy carried out similar successful tests on a submarine in 1926, but these again came to nothing. From 1938 onwards the Dutch Navy had been carrying out trials on their submarines with a system designed by Dutchman Jan Jacob Wichers. It was called a snauver (sniffer) and when the Germans invaded the Netherlands in 1940 the designs fell into their hands. The Germans originally used the snorkel only as a method of taking fresh air into the boat while it was submerged, but the increasing use of radar on allied ships from 1943 onwards drove them to adapt its use for the operation of the engines.

The word first appears in its German form in 1944. It's first English spelling appears in 1949. It's current definition, a "curved tube used by a swimmer to breathe under water" first appears in 1951.

13th November 2017

Is Ken Dodd's Happiness an old country music song?

The song Happiness was written by country music writer Bill Anderson, who also recorded it.

Born James William Anderson on 1st November 1937 in Columbia, South Carolina, he worked as a radio DJ while still at college, before turning to writing and performing country music. He is responsible for 7 number 1 hits in the American country music charts as well as 51 albums, of which only "I Love You Drops" made it to No 1 in the charts, in 1966.

Anderson never released Happiness as a single. It appears on his second album, Still, released in 1963, which reached number 10 in the US country charts.

Anderson is still alive and released his last album, Life, in 2013.

In an interview with The Big Issue, Ken Dodd recalls singing Happiness for the first time at The Grenada, Shrewsbury. He released his recording of Happiness in July 1964, giving it a far more upbeat flavour than the original. Despite being so well known it only reached number 31 in the UK charts. Its resonance comes more from it being used in Ken Dodd's TV, radio and theatre performances.

17th November 2017

At how many miles per second do e-mails travel?

The simple answer to this question is that, as an electrical signal, an e-mail travels at the speed of light, which is about 186,000 miles per second. However, for that speed to be achieved the transmitting device would have to be connected directly to the receiving device, which it isn't.

An e-mail is analogous to a physical letter, in that once it is 'posted' it goes through a number of processes and distribution channels in order to get to its destination, eg a letter goes from the post box to the mailcentre, where it goes through several sortation processes, is then transported to a distribution centre, from there to another mailcentre, to a delivery office and finally to the front door. In addition, at each stage there will be some waiting time when it isn't actually being handled, processed or transported.

Similarly the e-mail goes from the sender's 'outbox' to the e-mail service provider, where its address information is read and interpreted. It is then sent on to the receiver's e-mail service provider, where it will be transferred to the recipient's 'inbox' which allows the recipient to read it when the text is sent to the recipient's computer or phone. However, that is not a straight line journey. It will go through a variety of 'servers' which route it from one place to another, much as a physical letter may travel on several different vehicles while completing its journey. A server is just a device where files can be stored temporarily, while they are waiting for a gap to open up in the electronic traffic on their designated route.

As the e-mail arrives at each server it will be held in a queue while it waits its turn to be sent on the next stage of its journey. All the address reading and interpretation also takes a finite amount of time, slowing the e-mail from its potential speed of light transmission to something much slower.

To speed up the process 'packet switching' is used, whereby the e-mail will be broken down into smaller packets of information which may be sent over different routes and is then recombined at the destination. In simple terms, one 'packet' from an e-mail sent in London may be routed via Birmingham and Manchester to get to Glasgow, while another may be routed via Leicester, Leeds and Newcastle.

Having said all that, an e-mail travelling from the UK to Australia will arrive approximately 0.2 seconds after the 'send' key is pressed. By comparison, a blink of an eye takes approximately 0.35 seconds.

That makes an effective speed of approximately 85,000 miles per second, or slightly less than half the speed of light. That multiplies up to 5.1 million miles per minute or 306 million miles per hour.

Delays between the sender pressing the key and the recipient seeing it on their 'inbox' are usually accounted for by the processing speed of the sending and receiving computers and the broadband speed available to the sender and recipient. Businesses in cities tend to use fibre optic cables for transmission, which offer much faster broadband speeds than copper wire and country dwellers can expect much slower speeds of transmission and delivery than city dwellers as they are more dependent on copper telephone lines.

What is the origin of the word Troika and why does it have political overtones?

In common with many words beginning with the letters tr, such as triangle, triplets and tripod, troika indicates a connection to the number three.

Specifically, a troika is a type of sled originating in Russia, which is pulled by three horses. The word translates from Russian as 'triplet' or 'trio'. The troika was a very speedy form of transport used by the wealthy, travelling at up to 30 mph over snow. The origins of the troika date back to the 17th century.

Another form of troika is a Russian folk dance, in which a man dances with two women.

In political terms, the word troika dates back as far as 1918 and means a group of three administrators. The very first troika was Felix Dzerzhinsky, Yakov Peters, and V. Aleksandrovich. They were empowered to pass down sentences against people charged with counter-revolutionary offences against the newly founded Soviet Union. Later it came to denote groups of 3 NKVD officers who served a similar purpose during the purges carried out by Joseph Stalin.

Felix Dzerzhinsky, nicknamed Iron Felix, was a Polish born soviet revolutionary, remembered mainly for establishing Russia's post-revolutionary secret police, the Cheka. The square in Moscow where the secret police services, under their various names, had their headquarters was named Dzerzhinsky Square between 1926 and 1990 and is now named Lubyanka Square. This square is still home to the FSB, the present day Russian intelligence service.

Yakov Peters was Latvian born and played a less well known part in the establishment of the Cheka. Alexandrovich seems to have faded from history, possibly an early victim of the Cheka.

From those origins the term has now come to mean any alliance or grouping of three politicians or political groups. Because of its earlier origins, the use of the word troika to describe these alliances is not a compliment.

A current Troika that is talked about a lot in countries such as Greece, Cyprus, Ireland, Portugal and Spain is that of the European Commission, The European Central Bank and the International Monetary Fund. This troika is heavily involved in the decision making around the financial bailouts of these and other EU member countries.

19th December 2017

Enjoying a tinned pie, I began to wonder where the name "Fray Bentos" came from.

Fray Bentos is a city in the Rio Negro Department (province) of Uruguay. It is so well known in this country because it gave its name to the corned beef that was processed there.

As a town it was founded by government decree on 16th April 1859 and became a city on 16th July 1900. Its name loosely translates as "Friar Benedict", who was a reclusive Polish friar of the 13th century who travelled to the Mongol empire as part of a mission from Pope Innocent IV.

The Vestey Group purchased the Leibig Extract of Meat Company in 1924, operating under the name Figorifico Anglo de Uruguay (The Anglo, or English, Refrigeration Company) and began the manufacture of corned beef to be sold in the UK under the Fray Bentos brand. They later branched out into soups, meat balls and other food products for the British market. Later they focused more on pies and puddings.

The Fray Bentos brand was sold to the Campbells Soup company and is now owned by Premier Foods, which owns the Baxters soup brand and, since 1990, has concentrated production in Scotland

The original plant in Uruguay is now owned by a Brazilian company, the Marfrig Group.

An area within the city made up of single story houses, built along the River Negro, is still known as the Barrio Anglo, where the workers at the Anglo plant lived. The city is now home to about 25,000 Fray Bentinos (as the population is known).

1st January 2018

What is the origin of the expression cock-a-hoop?

The origins of this term's meaning of "being in a state of elation or boastful high spirits" comes to us from the 16th century. However, in the 16th century this phrase meant "to drink without restraint; to celebrate drunkenly." It is easy to see how the migration might have occurred from drunkenness to simple happiness.

How this term came to exist at all is more of a mystery. The Oxford English Dictionary suggests that the more people tried to find the origin of the term, the more muddied the waters became.

The "cock" part of the saying may originate with the 15th century term used for a spigot on a barrel, linking it to the references to drunkenness. The extension to this explanation is that the spigot might be removed from the barrel and be placed on top, on one of the barrel's hoops, allowing revellers to drink directly from the barrel without restraint.

This version comes from the Glossographia, a dictionary compiled in 1670 by Thomas Blount. However, he doesn't cite any sources for this assertion. It may be based on a line from the "THE COMEDYE OF ACOLASTUS", translated from Latin in 1540 by John Palsgrave "Let us sette the cocke on the hope and make good chere within doors." However, this translation doesn't indicate the meaning of either "cocke" or "hope", which had several at this time.

Another explanation is that a cock standing on the hoops of a barrel might have been used as a pub sign as early as the 14th century. Records dating back to 1335 show a number of pubs with names such as The Hen on the Hoop and The Cock on the Hoop. There are records of a pub in Hanbury Street, Mile End, London, called the Cock A Hoop from as early as 1825 until 1923. It has since been demolished.

Just as plausible an explanation is that cock-a-hoop is a translation from the French "coq a huppe", which means a cockerel raising its crest (huppe), ie, putting on a display.

4th January 2018

Has anyone any information on RAF Spitfire Squadrons operating in Russia during World War II?

151 Wing, RAF, was formed in 1941 and served briefly in Russia. It was equipped with Hawker Hurricanes, however, not Spitfires.

When Germany commenced Operation Barbarossa, the invasion of Russia, the Russian air force was considerably weaker than that of the Germans. While superior in aircraft numbers, the technology and tactics they were using were out of date. When Finland allied itself with Germany to attack Russia, Britain formed 151 Wing, combining reinforced elements of 81 and 131 Sqns using the code name "Force Benedict", under the command of Wing Commander H N G Ramsbottom-Isherwood. They were dispatched to the Kola Peninsula and based at Vaenga airfield, close to Murmansk.

The objectives of the force were threefold: 1. To introduce the Russians to modern technology, 2. To introduce them to modern fighter tactics and 3. To demonstrate to the Finns that Russia was now supported by the Western Allies. In achieving their objectives, the RAF pilots flew combat patrols in the Murmansk area as well as providing training for Russian pilots. Most of the RAF sorties were as escorts to Russian bombers targeting the Finns who were trying to sever the Murmansk railway.

The Wing was deployed between 7th September and 22nd October 1941, carrying out 365 individual sorties and claiming 11 Messerschmitts and 3 Ju88 bombers shot down, without loss. Wg Cdr Ramsbottom-Isherwood was awarded the Order of Lenin for his leadership of the operation and 81 Sqn were awarded the battle honour "Russia 1941". RAF air operations ceased on 7th October and the air and ground crews returned to the UK by sea later that month, having handed over their aircraft to the Russians.

In July 1942 there was a plan to send 153 Wing, made up of 4 squadrons of Spitfires and 2 of Hurricanes, to Russia, again to Vaenga airfield, but this operation was cancelled because of operational needs at home.

Air operations from Murmansk continued intermittently throughout the war years, mainly using bombers and maritime patrol aircraft to protect the Arctic convoys. Following the destruction of convoy PQ17 (July 1942), in September 1942 11 Handley Page Hampden bombers from 114 and 455 squadrons, Royal Australian Air Force, were lost en-route to Russia to protect convoy PQ18, some from engine failure, some succumbed to the Arctic weather and some were brought down by anti-aircraft fire. The convoy didn't come under attack from surface shipping and the squadron personnel returned home by sea, once again leaving their remaining aircraft for use by the Russians. Both squadrons then re-equipped with Bristol Beaufighters.

In addition to the direct assistance of the RAF, the British government also supplied the Russians with 3,000 Hawker Hurricanes and 1,500 Spitfires. Problems with the unpaved Russian runways and difficulties in aircraft recognition, as a consequence of changes to the wing configuration, resulted in the Spitfires being withdrawn from the front line, though the Hurricanes with their stronger undercarriage were better able to cope. The Spitfires remained in service, but in the quieter Southern areas of the country.

11th January 2018

When and where did cotton farming originate?

Precisely when cotton farming started isn't known, but it was almost certainly in what is now known as Mexico. Traces of both cotton bolls and cotton cloth dating back 7,000 years have been found in caves there.

However, the cotton plant wasn't exclusive to the New World. Evidence exists that cotton was being used to make cloth along the Indus Valley in modern day Pakistan up to 3,000 years BC. At about the same time it is known that the Ancient Egyptians were wearing clothes made from cotton, though whether they were growing the cotton or importing it isn't clear.

Arab merchants brought cotton to Europe around 800 AD, however, it was only one of the clothes used for making clothing. Wool and linen had been the staples of cloth manufacture since the Bronze Age and they remained the most popular fibres, probably because they were cheaper than imported cotton. England grew very wealthy on the export of wool to Europe during the Middle Ages. As a symbol of this the Lord Chancellor, the equivalent in the House of Lords of the Speaker, still takes his seat on a "wool sack", a cushion stiffed with wool, a tradition that dates back to the reign of Edward III (1312 – 1377)

When Christopher Columbus arrived in the Bahamas in 1492 he found cotton plants growing and by 1500 it was known about throughout the world.

The first cotton seeds in North America are believed to have been planted in Florida in 1556 and in Virginia in 1607, starting the cotton growing industry that was one of the foundations of the wealth of the Southern States of America.

One of the problems of manufacturing using cotton was the difficulty in spinning it into a useable fibre. This was overcome by the invention of the Spinning Jenny in 1764, by James Hargreaves, of Oswaldtwistle in Lancashire. This predates the development of an American cotton gin (short for engine), patented by Massachusetts native Eli Whitney in 1793.

The first cotton mills to be established in the UK were in 1730, providing the basis of an industry that was to dominate the North West of England from the start of the industrial revolution, right up to the middle of the 20th century. The cotton was imported from the

USA. To get the raw material into the Manchester area as quickly as possible, and to avoid the hefty tariffs charged by the port authorities in Liverpool and by the railway companies, the Manchester Ship Canal was built in 1887.

The development of manmade fibres has reduced the demand for cotton, pushing down the global price. To reduce the cost of manufacture the industry has moved to areas where labour costs are cheapest. The Indian sub-continent and the Far East now dominates the world cotton market, exporting it as woven fabric.

12th January 2018

Was James Doohan, Scotty in the original Star Trek, a war hero?

James Montgomery Doohan was born in Vancouver, British Columbia, on 3rd March 1920. Whether he would regard himself as a war hero is questionable, but he certainly saw military service during World War II, first as an artillery officer and then as a pilot.

At the outbreak of World War II James Doohan volunteered for the army and was commissioned into the Royal Canadian Artillery with the rank of Second Lieutenant, joining the 14th Field Artillery Regiment of the 2nd Canadian Infantry Division. In 1940 he travelled to Britain for training.

On D-Day, 6th June 1944, Doohan went ashore on Juno Beach, one of the three beaches allocated to British and Commonwealth forces. Juno was the objective for the 3rd Canadian Infantry Division, to which the 14th Field Artillery Regt had now been assigned.

Doohan, by now a Captain, and his comrades had to cross a beach sewn with anti-tank mines. Fortunately the soldiers weren't heavy enough to detonate the mines and they passed through safely. At 11.30 that night James Doohan fell victim to German machinegun fire, being hit six times.

One bullet took off the middle finger of his right hand, four more hit him in the leg and one hit a silver cigarette case in the pocket of his jacket before lodging in his chest. Had the bullet hit him with full force it would certainly have killed him. The cigarette case had been given to him by his brother.

As well as being an artillery officer, Doohan also qualified as a military pilot. In 1945 it earned him the title of "The craziest pilot in the Royal Canadian Airforce", though he wasn't actually a member of the air force as the squadron on which he served was an army unit, flying as airborne artillery spotters in support of 1st Army Group. To earn that title Doohan slalomed his aircraft between two telegraph poles on Salisbury Plain "to prove it could be done". The incident earned him a reprimand.

James Doohan was made a Lieutenant of the Royal Victorian Order (LVO) in recognition of his war service. This is an award instituted in 1896 by Queen Victoria and granted at the discretion of the monarch.

After leaving the army James Doohan undertook a course of technical studies, but soon turned to acting. He won a two year scholarship at the Neighbourhood Playhouse in New York, where he was classmates with Leslie Neilson, Tony Randall and Pat Boone. In 1946 he worked on radio plays before moving on to theatre, TV and films. He became Montgomery "Scotty" Scott in Star Trek in 1966 for the second pilot of the show. The part of Scotty was almost cut on the orders of Gene Rodenberry, who thought that the series didn't need an engineer. The idea to make the character Scottish was Doohan's own, because he considered that Scotland produced the best engineers.

During his acting life, James Doohan always did his best to disguise his missing middle finger, though it can occasionally be observed in episodes of Star Trek. When asked in an interview about his D Day experiences, Doohan just said "The sea was rough, we were more scared of drowning than of the Germans".

James Doohan boldy went on 20th July 2005. Famously, 7 grams of his ashes were launched into space on 28th August 2007 along with the ashes of 308 others, completing a 4 minute sub orbital flight before being returned to Earth by parachute. They were then launched again on 3rd August 2008, but the rocket motor failed two minutes after launch and the rocket crashed, losing the ashes in the desert. The remainder of James Doohan's ashes were scattered onto Puget Sound, Washington State.

13th January 2018

Did Scotland have a 16th century tax called 'buttock mall'?

This wasn't a tax, it was a fine for acts of fornication outside of marriage. It has strong connection with acts of prostitution and the running of brothels, such as a buttock – a harlot, buttock-ball – a dance frequented by prostitutes, buttock-banqueting – to associate with harlots and buttock-broker – a procurer of prostitutes.

The 'mall' part comes from an earlier Scottish practice of marking a person on their body for acts such as insulting a person of higher social status. The positioning of the mark and the degree of injury it caused was dependent on the severity and nature of the insult.

13th January 2018

Why do most zips have YKK printed on them?

YKK is the trademark of the largest zip fastener manufacturer in the world, *Yoshida Kōgyō Kabushiki geisha,* or Yoshida Manufacturing Corporation. As well as manufacturing zips, it also makes other types of fasteners, architectural products, plastic hardware and industrial machinery. It has 109 companies located in 71 countries around the world.

The company was founded in 1934 as San-es Shokai, changing its name in 1938. The YKK trademark was registered in January 1946 and the company has come to dominate the zip-fastener market around the world.

The first fastener that might be regarded as a zipper was patented in 1851 by Elias Howe, an American inventor and pioneer of the sewing machine, calling it an "automatic, continuous clothing closure". In 1893 Whitcomb Judson, another American, marketed a 'clasp locker' and exhibited it at the Chicago World's Fair that same year, however, it was never a commercial success.

The name of zipper, or zip-fastener in the UK, comes from the B F Goodrich company, who sold boots with an inbuilt zip-fastener from 1923 onwards.

The primary innovation that allowed the Japanese company to dominate the world of zip-fasteners seems to be their manufacturer in plastic, which was cheaper than the metal that had been used up to that point.

16th January 2018

What are the earliest examples of Trench warfare?

Trench warfare started as an extension of siege craft, the besieging of cities or fortresses in order to overcome their defences. There was no tradition of using trenches as part of a battle on an open battlefield right up until the American Civil War.

As the use of firearms became more common, especially artillery, it was necessary for troops attacking fortresses or fortified towns to be able to fight from safety in order to prevent unnecessary casualties. This was achieved in two ways, the building of redoubts, small fortresses with earth walls where artillery could be mounted, or by the digging of trenches. Trenches were also used as a method of moving troops forward to within attacking range to exploit the breaches made by artillery in defensive walls. They might even be used to allow engineers to undermine walls and bring about their collapse.

The tactical ancestor of modern trench warfare was a Frenchman, Sebastian Le Prestre de Vauban (1633 – 1707), who designed systems for the attack of fortresses in the 17th century. De Vauban was the principally a designer of fortresses, but in designing them he also came up with tactics by which fortresses could be overcome.

De Vouban developed a system of attack using parallel lines of trenches, which was first used at the Siege of Maastricht (1673). It may have been based on methods used by the Turks at the siege of Candia in 1668.

Trenches remained principally a siege tool until increases in the power of both small arms and artillery forced both sides to use trenches during the American Civil War. The trench lines of Petersberg-Richmond, in Virginia, towards the end of the Civil War, were the most extensive of the 19th century and were the forerunner of the trench warfare of World War I.

Trench warfare reached its pinnacle during World War I. With both the Allies and the Germans unable to achieve an early victory through manoeuvring, the opposing sides were forced to dig in to protect themselves against artillery and machinegun fire. In order to circumvent these defences, both sides tried to outflank the other, leading to ever longer trench lines. Only a natural barrier could ultimately prevent outflanking, so there was a race to the Alps on one side and the sea on the other, as both the Allies and the Germans hoped to either outflank the enemy's trenches or to prevent themselves from being outflanked.

The race ended as a dead heat in late 1914 and the two opposing sides had to settle for trying to batter their way through the trench lines for the next 4 years. This objective was never really achieved and victory, when it came, was won more by wearing the Germans down through starvation and casualties than by military victory.

18th January 2018

If the voltage in the U.S. is half that in Britain, does a kettle take twice as long to boil?

If the kettle is one designed to work on the American voltage of 110 volts, then no. If it were a British kettle then it would be yes. An

American kettle transported to Britain, however, would be a dangerous item and would run the risk starting fires if plugged in.

The power used by a kettle is a function of the voltage applied and the current drawn. Power = voltage x current.

The average British kettle consumes about 1,800 watts of power. From this it is possible to calculate that the amount of current drawn is about 8 amps. This current, however, is dependent on the resistance built into the heating element. Using ohms law this can be calculated as approximately 27 ohms. It is the flow of current through this resistance that converts electrical energy into heat energy. All electrical appliances convert a certain amount of energy into heat, often as a waste product.

If the British kettle is transported to America, the reduced voltage and the kettle's fixed resistance will mean that it can only draw about 4 amps of current. This halves the heating capability of the element, roughly doubling the time it will take to boil.

However, an American kettle will have been designed to work on the lower voltage and its heating element will have a resistance of about half that of its British counterpart, roughly 14 ohms, which allows it to boil in the same amount of time.

If the American kettle were to be used in Britain, its lower resistance would allow it to draw roughly 16 amps of current. The plugs of British domestic electrical equipment are fitted with a 13 amp safety fuse which would burn out under these conditions, but the plugs of American domestic equipment aren't, so the mains cable, between the plug and the kettle, could overheat and catch fire. The heating element can't catch fire as it is immersed in water. However, the heating elements of an American toaster could catch fire, as could an American fridge or a TV.

Many Americans moving to Europe and not understanding this have destroyed their domestic electrical appliances by plugging them into the European power supply. American diplomats and forces personnel posted to Europe are told to bring portable transformers with them to change the voltage and power their American appliances.

All domestic electrical appliances sold in Britain and Europe, regardless of country of manufacture, are designed to work on the European mains voltages of between 200 and 250 volts. Small appliances, such as phone and computer chargers, draw very small amounts of electrical current and have been specifically designed to work on dual American/European voltages.

25th January 2017

Why is the shiny brown belt worn by Army officers called a Sam Browne?

General Sir Samuel Browne VC GCB KCSI was a cavalry officer in the Indian Army. He was born on 4th October 1824 and died on 14th March 1901. He served with distinction, especially during the Indian Mutiny and the Second Afghan War, but his name is now largely known for the diagonal brown belt he designed for his uniform.

On 31st August 1858, whilst a Captain, Sam Browne took part in an action in Utar Pradesh that earned him the Victoria Cross and cost him his left arm. It was as a result of this injury that he developed the belt that bears his name.

After recovering from his wound, Captain Browne discovered that with only one arm he had difficulty drawing his sword, an essential capability for a cavalry officer of the day. His right hand was able to grip the hilt, but without his left hand to hold the sword's scabbard he was unable to complete the task in a single fluid movement. He designed the diagonal belt that bears his name to hold the sword's scabbard in position and allow him to draw his sword one handed.

The idea was copied by other officers and soon became quite fashionable. Later, when soldiers began carrying revolvers, the belt was found to support the weight of the heavy weapons better. Carrying the gun holstered, with the butt pointing forward, it could be drawn right handed, across the body. It gained even wider approval during the Boer War and eventually became a standard part of the uniform for officers.

Although it was invented by a British officer, use of the Sam Browne spread to several armies, and it can still be seen in the uniforms of Finland and Poland. In the USA it was introduced by General Pershing, the commander of US Forces during World War I, but it is no longer worn there. Both Mussolini and Hitler wore Sam Browne belts with some of their uniforms.

In the British military the Sam Browne was traditionally only worn by officers and Warrant Officers who carried swords, but later spread to all officers. Later it was worn by soldiers whose duties included the bearing of side arms, such as the military police, though there it was usually blancoed white and it was worn over the left shoulder, as they carry their side arms on the right.

The Sam Browne was also used by civilian police officers for a while, especially in Commonwealth countries. However, the ability of a felon to grab the belt and use it to strangle the wearer earned it the nickname of 'the suicide belt' and it became obsolete on safety grounds. It is still part of the dress uniform of the Royal Canadian Mounted Police.

The Sam Browne belt is still worn as part of an officer's No 2 dress uniform and, in certain regiments, the No 1 ceremonial uniform. From World War II onwards it has been replaced in day to day use by standard webbing which is used to carry far more than just a revolver.

2nd February 2018

Where does the term 'last ditch attempt' come from?

This saying has its origins in a speech by William of Orange, later William III, who exhorted the people to "fight and die in the last ditch". In the context that the phrase was used, the 'last ditch' refers to the innermost defensive ditch around a besieged position.

Some claim that the speech was made after William became joint monarch of England with his wife Mary, in exhortation to the English to save their own country, but it is generally recognised as originating during the Anglo-Dutch wars.

In early July 1672 William of Orange, commander of the Dutch army, blocked the advance of a French army, who were allied to England. He achieved this by flooding large parts of Holland between Amsterdam and Dordrecht. It is from this action that the quote originates. Charles II had previously tried to bribe William by offering to make him the Stadholder (leader) of the Dutch nations in return for his surrender. William refused the offer, but was awarded the title on 17th July by the Dutch, following his victory.

There are two citations for the first written use of the saying. The first is from a Daniel Defoe poem of 1706 entitled *The True Born Englishman*. The poem was a satire on English nationalism which would not seem out of place today. The second is from *Bishop Burnett's History Of His Own Time*. Its date isn't known, but was written some time before 1715.

William of Orange became joint monarch of England in 1689 as a result of the Glorious Revolution, when the British Parliament invited his wife Mary to take the throne in place of James II, Mary's own father. A Protestant Dutch King was preferable, in Parliament's view, to an English Catholic. After the death of Mary in 1694, William continued to reign as sole monarch until his death in 1702.

5th February 2018

What technology is used in speed cameras and how accurate is it?

There are at least 14 different types of speed camera in use on UK roads. They can be broken down into two different types: those that calculate speed at the instant the car passes in front of them and those that calculate speed over a fixed distance.

The majority of fixed speed cameras use radar technology to calculate the speed of the vehicle, in the same way as military radars are used.

A radar pulse is transmitted outwards. When it hits a solid object the pulse will be reflected back to its source. The time taken for the pulse to make the round trip is calculated, usually in microseconds, and that allows the distance from the source to be calculated. The next pulse repeats this procedure, but because the target has moved in between pulses, the time taken for the pulse to return will be either shorter or longer depending on whether the target is approaching or retreating. By calculating the time difference between the two returns, the speed of the target can be calculated.

The Gatso camera always produces two photographs so that there can be no doubt about how fast a car was going. As well as using the radar calculation, a series of painted white lines on the road in front of the camera also indicates speed. Every white line crossed between the first picture and the second picture represents a speed difference of 5 mph. For example, in a 30 mph speed limit the camera will be set to trigger if a car passes at a speed of 31 mph or more. It will then take two pictures, indicated by a double flash of the camera's light. However, if the car is travelling at less than 35 mph it will not cross a white line between the taking of the first picture and the second. If it is travelling at 35 mph or more it will cross at least one of the white lines. The images are subjected to physical checking to confirm this. For this reason drivers are rarely prosecuted for travelling at speeds between 31 and 35 mph, even though they have exceeded the speed limit.

Gatso cameras always photograph the rear of the car, so that the camera's flash doesn't dazzle the driver.

Mobile speed cameras and some types of fixed speed camera use another form of radar technology to calculate speed. This is the doppler frequency shift system. When a radar beam makes contact with its target its frequency is either fractionally increased or fractionally decreased by compression or expansion, depending on whether the target is approaching or retreating. This is known as the doppler effect. By comparing the amount of frequency shift against fixed reference levels, it is possible to calculate the speed of the target. This type of fixed speed camera utilises infra-red imaging to capture the car's number plate, so the driver may be unaware that they have triggered the camera until they receive a summons.

If you have ever been at a railway station when a speeding train has passed through, the sound of the train approaching will have been at a higher pitch than the sound of it after it has passed. The same affect can be heard when listening to cars and lorries while standing on a bridge over a motorway. This phenomenon demonstrates the doppler effect on the audible frequency range.

The Specs system, often used within the speed restricted areas of road works, uses 2 cameras, one to take an image of a car's number plate as it enters the zone and another to capture it as it leaves. The cameras are linked together to allow the system to calculate the time taken for the car to pass between the two points, which is then used to calculate the average speed of the vehicle. Automatic number plate recognition (ANPR) is used to identify individual cars. Specs cameras may be no closer together than 200 metres so that a representative average speed can be calculated, disregarding any deceleration or acceleration as the car enters or leaves the restricted area.

Because all of the camera types use electronic means of calculations, measuring small fractions of time, distance or frequency shift, they are very accurate, certainly to within 1 mph.

6th February 2018

In cricket, players often throw the ball into the air instantly after making a catch. How long does the ball have to be held for it to be deemed a catch?

Law 33.3 of cricket states that "The act of making a catch shall start from the time when the ball first comes into contact with a fielder's person and shall end when a fielder obtains complete control over both the ball and his/her own movement."

It is a matter for the umpire to decide if the catch was fairly made within that law and that the throwing of the ball into the air was an act of celebration, or if the catch was 'dropped'. A player diving for a catch who then threw it into the air before he hit the ground might not be regarded as having complete control over their own movement and the catch might be disallowed.

Having made contact with the ball and it going into the air, if the catcher retrieves it without it touching the ground or going over the boundary rope, there would be no issue and the decision would stand. However, if the ball were to touch the ground or go over the boundary rope, the batsman would be entitled to challenge the catch if he thought that the catch didn't comply with the law.

The fact that so few catches are appealed is an indication that batsmen generally know if a catch was fairly made or not. The catches that are usually appealed are those taken close to the ground, where there is some doubt about whether the ball carried to the fielder's hands, or whether the fielder wasn't in control of the ball and spilled it.

12th February 2018

Why is a picture that expresses an idea online called a 'meme'?

There are two definitions of the word meme and from the first it can be seen how the second emerged. The first definition is "an element of a culture or system of behaviour passed from one individual to another by imitation or other non-genetic means." While the second is "an image, video, piece of text, etc., typically humorous in nature, that is copied and spread rapidly by internet users, often with slight variations."

The posting of an image on social media doesn't make it a meme. It is the copying and spreading of the image from one person to another that earns it the title.

The origins of the word pre-dates the internet by some years. In 1976, in his book "The Selfish Gene", Professor Richard Dawkins coined the term to explain the way cultural information is spread. The modern-day internet meme is just a subset of that information using a specific channel. Although it isn't clear why he chose the term, given the title of the book it is quite possible that he was expressing the idea of 'me, me'.

While Professor Dawkins may have coined the word, the concept is as old as time. Innovations such as agriculture and the wheel were cultural information that spread from its source to the rest of the world. With the spread of the information came a desire to know how it worked and to replicate it.

In popular culture, ideas about fashion were spread as memes long before the invention of the camera. For example, the ruffed collar that first appeared at the court of Elizabeth I went on to spread throughout Europe. Initially it was copied by courtiers, then the idea spread when people wore the ruff on their travels, described it or saw it in paintings.

Modern memes, however, are not just a passive passing of information. They also influence behaviour. The most benign are those such as the 'ice bucket challenge' where people pledged a sum of money to charity in exchange for having a bucket of ice water tipped over them. Part of the challenge was for the victim to have the act videoed and placed on social media, at the same time extending the challenge to a friend, which further spread the meme.

More sinister, however, are those memes that encourage more dangerous activities. One such activity was known as planking. This involved individuals being photographed lying flat, face down in a public space, with the photo being shared via social media. The places people chose to have their photo taken became more bizarre and more dangerous, which encouraged even more dangerous behaviour. Locations included busy roads, railway lines and the jet intake of an aircraft.

There was at least one known death as a consequence of planking. In 2011, 20 year old Acton Beale plunged to his death from a 7th floor balcony in Brisbane, Australia, after attempting to 'plank' on the balcony railing. His death encouraged the makers of the U.S. cartoon series 'South Park' to dedicate an episode to demonstrating how dangerous copying memes could be. Fans of the show can guess what happened to Kenny.

15th February 2018

What is the origin of the American slang term "cracker"?

The origin of the American slang term 'cracker' goes back as far as 1783. The descendants of convicts sent to America from England were given this nickname. Nowadays it is used to describe mainly poor white people from the southern states of the USA.

Benjamin Franklin provides the first written citation for the term in the USA, in his Memoirs written in 1790, where he describes 'a race of runnagates and crackers, equally wild and savage as the Indians' who inhabited the woods and mountains.

The origins of this word in the English language, however, are much earlier. It may share its roots with the modern Irish term craic. The Middle English word crac, craic or crack originally meant the sound of a whip's crack, but it then came to mean loud, bragging talk. It appears in Shakespeare's King John, written in 1590, in the line "What cracker is this same that deafs our ears with this abundance of superfluous breath?"

In a letter to the Earl of Dartmouth, Shakespeare explains the term as being a description of 'great boasters; they are a lawless set of rascalls (sic) on the frontiers of Virginia, Maryland, the Carolinas, and Georgia, who often change their places of abode.'

From this source the term extended to become 'corn crackers', derived from the cracked corn that was a staple diet for poor white people in states such as Georgia. This is also the derivation for the type of dry biscuit on which cheese is served.

One darker derivation of the term may be a return to its Middle English roots to describe the way white slave masters used to 'crack the whip' over the backs of slaves.

As is often the case with English, one word can have several meanings and equally as many sources.

27th February 2018

The gap under bridges for big lorries, especially loaded car transporters, looks very small from a car. What is the clearance that the loaders of these lorries work to?

The Road Vehicles (Construction and Use) Regulations (1986), known as the C&U regulations, lays down the rules for the manufacture of all vehicles used on British Roads. These regulations don't just cover lorries, they cover all vehicles, including cars and agricultural tractors. Principle amongst those regulations are those for maximum length, width, height and weight.

There are numerous caveats to these regulations for the transportation of abnormal loads, the number of axles the vehicle has, etc, but in broad terms the maximum dimensions for a road vehicle licenced for use in the UK are: length 18 metres, width 2.5 metres (2.58 for refrigerated vehicles), height 4.57 metres and maximum laden weight 44 tonnes. These dimensions cover not just the vehicle, but also any load it is carrying, so they apply to car transporters.

Interestingly oversized vehicles, like the giant dumper trucks used on construction sites, may not be driven on the road, but may be transported on the back of lorries under the caveats governing abnormal loads.

These rules are common throughout Europe, though several countries have their own maximum weights. For example, in the

Netherlands the maximum weight is 50 tonnes but in many other EU countries it is only 40 tonnes.

The maximum permitted height for vehicles is governed by the minimum height of bridges across motorways and their equivalents across Europe. In Britain the minimum clearance for a bridge across a motorway is 5 metres. So a vehicle of maximum height passing under a bridge with a minimum clearance will have a 43 cm gap above it. That is approximately 17 inches.

Bridge strikes on roads other than motorways are not uncommon because many bridges in the UK were built before the current C&U regulations were introduced and, of course, many railway and canal bridges were built long before the advent of motor transport. Lorry drivers have been known to deflate their tyres so they could pass under a bridge when no other route was available.

Companies operating lorries are required to display signs in the cab advising drivers of the height of their vehicle and its load, in an effort to reduce bridge strikes. There are special satnav devices designed for the motor transport industry which will plan routes for lorries which avoid bridges with too low a clearance for the vehicle height. These devices also take into account width and weight restrictions.

In 2016 the M20 in Kent was closed for several days because a lorry carrying a mechanical digger hit a pedestrian bridge because the articulated arm of the digger hadn't been lowered enough when it was loaded. The lorry driver was found guilty of causing serious injury by dangerous driving, because the driver is responsible for the safety of his vehicle and its load.

28th February 2018

What did Nazi propagandist Joseph Goebbels predict the world would look like in his article The Year 2000?

The Second World War was nearing its end when, on 25th February 1945, Joseph Goebbels, Minister for Public Enlightenment and

Propaganda and Reich Plenipotentiary for Total War, published his predictions entitled The Year 2000 (Das Jahr 2000) in the newspaper Das Reich. The article was a rallying cry to the German people, aimed at rekindling the idea that Germany could still be the intellectual leaders of Europe, but only if the Germans stood fast and defeated the Allies.

In the opening paragraph, Goebbels states that the Allied leaders, Churchill, Stalin and Roosevelt, had already decided the fate of Germany, which was true, and his predictions apply mainly to the German people and to Europe, rather than to the world as a whole.

The first prediction is that the population of England (the term commonly used at that time to describe the whole of the UK) would decline to 20 million inhabitants. The UK currently has a population of just under 66 million. Why this decline would happen isn't clear, but is probably based on the idea that Britons would migrate to other countries rather than remain in an insignificant off-shore state in a Soviet dominated Europe.

It was Goebbels who used the term 'Iron Curtain', later used by Churchill, to describe the Soviet takeover of eastern Europe. He didn't, however, originate the term as it dates from the 19th century. This prediction is one of only two that were in any way accurate. However, he didn't foresee the collapse of the Warsaw Pact in 1989.

Goebbels did foresee a united Europe, but under the yoke of Soviet Russia, not under the governance of the EU.

Not foreseeing the death of Roosevelt, Goebbels predicted that Roosevelt would be defeated in the first post-war election and America would elect a Republican President who would be more isolationist and withdraw American troops from Europe. This would lead to a Third World War which would be won by Russia because western Europe would be too weak to withstand the Soviet block.

Instead, Democrat Harry S Truman succeeded Roosevelt, won the 1948 election and remained in office until 1953. NATO was born to counter the Soviet threat (1949), the Treaty of Rome (1957) was signed to encourage political and economic unity through the

Common Market (now the EU) and there has been no Third World War (yet).

The second prediction that Goebbels made that was correct was that Germany would not be an occupied nation in the year 2000, though his prophesy was based on Nazi Germany winning the war, not on NATO winning the peace.

The whole of the article is focused on the political map of Europe and makes no mention of social or economic conditions in a post war era.

1st March 2018

Did Britain's lighthouses remain operational in World War II?

During World War II some Trinity House lighthouses were kept fully lit, some had their lights dimmed and some were turned off completely.

The organisation worked with the Admiralty to decide which lights should be kept working, on a case by case basis. The Admiralty then notified the Royal Navy and the merchant and fishing fleets of their decisions in the daily 'Notes to Mariners', which were sent as encoded radio transmissions.

Where a light might be used by the enemy to navigate into a harbour to lay mines, they would usually be dimmed or turned off completely. Where lights warned of significant danger, such as rocks or sand banks close to navigation channels, they were usually kept lit, as to turn them off might do as much harm to our own shipping as it would to aid the enemy.

Where lights were dimmed or turned off completely, Trinity House pilots were used to guide vessels through danger as an alternative. Many Trinity House pilots lost their lives doing this work and their sacrifice is remembered on a war memorial in Trinity Square, close to the Tower of London.

In addition, many lighthouses were painted in camouflage colourings to reduce the ability of enemy sailors to use them as navigation markers during daylight hours.

3rd March 2018

Why is the principle of gun ownership so important in the US?

To understand this issue, it is first necessary to understand the climate and culture that grew up as the United States of America established itself as a nation.

The Second Amendment to the Constitution of the United States of America granted the right of the people to bear arms. This was passed in 1791 as a consequence of the need to defend the fledgling USA against future attempts to re-colonise, not just by Britain but by any of the major European powers.

There was a perceived need to maintain a citizen-militia capable of responding speedily to any threats, which meant that the citizens had to have firearms available to them. This threat is epitomised by the Battle of the Alamo (1836), where a small force of Texan civilians stood against an invading Mexican army intent on keeping Texas part of Mexico.

Firearms were also seen as a defence against tyranny; it is more difficult for a government to tyrannise the people if the people are armed and capable of fighting back.

As the country started to expand westwards there was also a need for settlers to be able to defend themselves. The indigenous population weren't too happy with the steady advance of the European migrants. Criminals also roamed freely around the frontier lands. Farms were often far from any form of law enforcement. Firearms were seen as a means of survival as much as anything.

Of course, hunting was another reason for having firearms. Much of the food eaten by the advancing settlers had to be killed, because there was no way of keeping meat fresh while on the move. In times of drought, when food was hard to grow, if you couldn't hunt you starved.

Right up until the 20th century, access to law enforcement in rural areas was limited. There was no telephone to summon the sheriff and even if he could be summoned, he was many miles away and travelled by horse. The ability for rural folk to defend themselves in a society where the law enforcement was slow to respond was seen as essential.

While the advances of the 20th century may have done away with many of the arguments for gun ownership that applied in earlier times, the Americans saw it as their right, under the Second Amendment, to keep their guns and their politicians have always been reluctant to challenge that, despite the regular atrocities that have occurred as a consequence of easy access to firearms.

As late as the 1940s, the Japanese government saw gun ownership in America as a deterrent against them invading the American mainland. They argued that they wouldn't just be facing the American military, but also every man, woman and child with access to a gun.

In America today it is still legal to shoot an intruder, even if he isn't armed. In Britain it is not, as Tony Martin discovered in 1999 when he shot two intruders at his Norfolk farm and found himself imprisoned for life for murder, reduced on appeal to five years for manslaughter. In America he would have been found not guilty on grounds of self-defence.

In the USA a culture of gun ownership has grown up over a period of 250 years. In Britain there never was a such a culture. Here, gun ownership is seen as something for a small minority of enthusiasts who own their weapons under very tight legal restraints.

6th March 2018

What's the origin of the Japanese shogun? How did they become more powerful than the Emperor?

The Shogun was the foremost military commander within the Japanese Empire.

The term Shogun was first applied to military leaders during the 8th and 9th centuries in the wars against the Ezo tribes of northern Japan. Sakanoue Tamuamaru was the first to be named seii taishogun – literally 'barbarian quelling generalissimo' - later shortened to Shogun. The Shogun of this period gradually gathered power to themselves and away from the Emperor's court until they were able to persuade the Emperor to make their position both official and permanent.

From 1192 to 1897 the title of Shogun was applied to hereditary military dictators. While legally the Shogun ruled under the authority of the Emperor, this was often more of a symbolic gesture. The feudal nature of Japanese politics during that period meant that the Shogun exercised almost total control over the country. Landlords more or less owned the people, in a form that we know as serfdom. The landlords, from the aristocratic families, in their turn got their authority from the Shogun and owed their allegiance more to him than to the Emperor.

Not all Shogun were equally powerful and weaker ones were replaced, creating new Shogun dynasties. The third and final dynasty was the Tokugawa, who ruled from 1603 to 1867. It was this dynasty that built a new capital, away from the Imperial city of Kyoto, calling it Edo. We now know it as Tokyo, which means 'Eastern Capital' (kyo means 'capital').

This dynasty is noted for its isolationist policies which cut Japan off politically and economically and earned the country the reputation of being a backward nation in an increasingly modernising world.

In 1897 the 15th Tokugawa Shogun, Yoshinobu, was forced to return power to the Emperor's court. The seat of Imperial government was moved to Tokyo and the old feudal practices were swept away and replaced with a form of parliamentary rule. Even then the military remained highly influential, as can be seen from the governments between the two world wars. Six of the Prime

Ministers in power between 1922 and 1945 came from either the Navy or the Army.

What is the history of the three bridges built one on top of the other at Pontarfynach in Wales?

The Devil's Bridge, as it is named, has existed since at least medieval times. The first bridge built there, around the 12th century, was a wooden structure, and was mentioned by chronicler Giraldus Cambrensis (Gerald of Wales).

The first stone bridge is the subject of the legend that gives the bridge its name. Supposedly an old woman was dismayed to see her cow had wandered across the steep ravine and had no way of crossing to get it back. The Devil appeared to her and offered to build her a bridge, but would claim the soul of the first living thing to cross it. The old woman agreed to the terms and in an instant, the bridge was built. However, the old woman had tricked the Devil. Instead of crossing the bridge herself, she threw a bit of bread which her dog ran across the bridge to collect, thus becoming the first living thing to cross.

This bridge dates from medieval times though its precise date of construction isn't known.

The second bridge was built in around 1753, reducing the slopes into the ravine needed to cross the original bridge. That bridge was left in place to reinforce the ravine walls below the new bridge. The final bridge was built in 1901, removing the slopes into the ravine completely. It was renovated later in the 20th century, though the caste iron railings were retained.

The name Pontarfynach means Bridge over the Mynach (Mynach is Welsh for Monk) and in the 16th century was recorded as Pont ar Vynach. The river may have been named after a hermit or because it marked the border of monastery lands. The bridges cross the ravine at a point where the river drops 90 metres, through a series of stepped waterfalls and cascades.

12th March 2018

If intelligent life on a planet in Alpha Centauri's solar system viewed Earth through a powerful telescope, what part of our history would they be observing?

Visual images travel at the speed of light, which gives rise to the measurement of the speed in light years – the distance a single photon of light can travel in one year. As Alpha Centauri is only 4.37 light years from the Sun, the occupants of the star system would be viewing events from approximately November 2013.

What the observers might see and which would give them reservations about visiting us, would be suicide and other terrorist bombings. On 8th November alone there were 3 separate bombings, killing 34 people in Damascus, Baghdad and Mogadishu. At the same time, Typhoon Hayain killed 6,000 people in the Philippines. There were further terrorist and crime related deaths on other days of the month.

Other than that, the most significant event that month was Sebastian Vettel winning his 8th F1 championship.

Alpha Centauri is a star system made up of 3 stars. Two of them, Alpha Centauri A and B, make up a binary system called Alpha Centauri AB. The two stars are too close together to be separated by the naked eye when viewed from Earth. The third star is a red dwarf called Alpha Centauri C which isn't visible to the naked eye. There are no planets in the star system so it must be concluded that anyone making observations of Earth from there would have to be in some sort of space craft and would have travelled there from another star system.

The 53 nearest stars to Earth would all be viewing history within the 21st century. Number 53 in the list is DEN 0255-4700, which is 16.2 light years away. The first star where you could view the 20th century is Sigma Draconis, which is 18.81 light years away and you would be able to see events taking place around May 1999.

The further back you wish to view history, the greater number of stars there are from where it could be witnessed. By the time you get to stars from where you could view the 19th century, the numbers go into the thousands. Our galaxy is approximately 100,000 light years across and scientists estimate that there are between 100 billion and 400 billion stars in it. If Earth was in the middle of the galaxy (it isn't) you would be able to view the last third of the last ice age if you were in a star system on the outer edge of the galaxy.

Only about 2,500 stars are visible with the naked eye from Earth and they are the largest and closest.

15th March 2018

Nancy Mitford coined the term U and non-U to describe certain words. What words are on the list?

The concept of U and non-U stems from a line in a Kipling poem, "We and They" published in 1926 and goes "All the people like us are we, and everyone else is they." The "people like us" (PLU) part was adopted by some as an indicator that they belonged to a self-identified elite, the upper class, whereas 'they' were from a lower order. U and non-U differentiates the sort of words that PLU would use compared to those who weren't like them.

However, it wasn't Nancy Mitford who coined the term. The debate was started in 1954 by linguist Alan S C Ross, from the University of Birmingham, who wrote a paper for a Finnish linguistics journal. Nancy Mitford took up the idea in an essay entitled "The English Aristocracy", published in the magazine *Encounter* in the same year. This, in turn, sparked something of a national debate about class and snobbery.

There is no definitive list of U and non-U words. PLU don't need telling what words to use. Mitford only used 31 words as examples of U words, but there are another 3 that are non-U because they don't have equivalents. For example, it is non-U to ask for the cruet, because U people would ask for condiments individually ie, "Please pass the salt and pepper". Condiments as a word may even be non-U.

In alphabetical order some of the U words are: coat, false teeth, jam, knave (the playing card), lavatory (or loo), looking-glass, pudding, scent, spectacles, sofa and what?

Their non-U counterparts are: jacket, dentures, preserves, jack, toilet, mirror, dessert, perfume, glasses, settee (or couch) and pardon?

George Bernard Shaw was another who understood how words can be used to differentiate people. In Pygmalion, first performed in 1913, Professor Higgins says "It is impossible for an Englishman to open his mouth without making some other Englishman despise him." Though, of course, Shaw was referring to accents as much as vocabulary.

3rd April 2018

The association of colours with moods and emotions goes back at least as far as the Ancient Greeks.

The Greeks thought of the world as being made up of 4 elements: Earth, Fire, Water and Air. Each element was allocated a colour: black, red, yellow and white. The Greeks believed that all things, including humans, were made up of these 4 elements and therefore their moods (referred to as humors) could be represented by a mixture of those colours.

Not surprisingly, anger has a strong element of 'heat' to it, so it would be represented by fire and coloured red. We still refer to people who are easily angered as being 'hot headed'.

This idea was prevalent until the Age of Enlightenment began to discover more about our universe and presented new theories about the make-up of our world. However, the 4 elements philosophy was certainly still in use in Tudor times.

The idea of green becoming the colour of jealousy or envy seems to come from Shakespeare. By that I don't mean that he created the idea, only that he was the first to write it down. It may have existed as a concept long before that.

In this case the citation is from Othello, Act III, Scene 3, when Iago warns Othello "O, beware, my lord, of JEALOUSY; it is the GREEN-eyed monster which doth mock the meat it feeds on."

While envy and jealousy are not the same, they are often interchanged, with jealousy being seen as a more extreme form of envy.

25th April 2018

What is the bird on the RAF badge? I have seen it referred to as an eagle and an albatross.

According to the College of Arms, who authorise all military badges and crests, the bird is an "eagle volant and affronté head lowered and to the sinister". In plain English that is an eagle with its wings spread for flight, viewed from the front, looking downward and to the left.

However, in heraldry, the naming of animals is confusing. The lions on the England football badge are actually called leopards in heraldry, because historically the two animals were considered to be the same. In this case the original design, thought to be by Gieves Ltd of Savile Row, may have been intended as an albatross but was named an eagle by the College of Arms because an albatross doesn't appear in the list of birds normally depicted in heraldry.

There has always been some debate within the RAF as to whether or not the bird was an eagle or an albatross and it has certainly been referred to as the latter on many occasions. I remember as an apprentice in the RAF in the 1960s referring to the bird, incorrectly, as an albatross and its depiction does appear to have more in common with that species than with an eagle. To remove confusion the Air Ministry issued order number A.666/49 on 15th September 1949, stating that the bird was an eagle.

Only officers' cap badges contain the eagle symbol. Other ranks wear an eagle badge, made of cloth, on the upper sleeve of each arm of their No 1 Home Dress uniform, the one on the right arm facing forward and one on the left facing backwards "to watch your 6 o'clock". Sergeant and Flight Sergeant aircrew also wear a gilt metal eagle on each arm above their stripes.

Author's note: This answer was published and there was a response from another correspondent (who hadn't served in the RAF) who maintained that both eagles on an airman's uniform faced forward, based on something that had appeared on an obscure website. I managed to find an old photograph which showed two airmen side by side, their left and right sleeves both visible as they faced inwards. This showed that I was correct and that one eagle faced rewards, but this definitive correction wasn't published by the newspaper.

27th April 2018

What is the difference between tea, afternoon tea and high tea?

Taxes on tea, introduced by Charles II in 1676, were high and at one time reached 119%, which encouraged large scale tea smuggling. Coffee was the more common drink and the introduction of the tea tax was to protect the coffee trade. The tea tax wasn't reduced to a more modest 12.5% until 1785, but tea smuggling remained common, as was the adulteration of tea with other products. It was the high price of tea that influenced the way it was consumed.

The tax on tea sparked the Boston Tea Party (1771) as the importation of tea to the British colonies in America was also taxed, but the revenue went to London, sparking the revolutionary maxim of 'no taxation without representation'.

Tea is a beverage taken as a form of refreshment at any time. Its use in this way gives rise to the expression 'tea break'. This form of tea drinking only came about when the plant started to be grown on an industrial scale in India from the 1820s onward, using seeds smuggled out of China, which had held a monopoly on growing the plant.

The price of tea was further reduced, bringing it within reach of the working classes, when tea clippers, fast sailing ships like the Cutty Sark, were introduced for the large-scale transportation of tea to the British market. The monopoly on tea sales in Britain was held by the East India Company who not only grew the tea, but also owned the clipper ships.

Afternoon tea is the creation of wealthy ladies of the 17th, 18th and 19th century who used to visit each other in the afternoons. To demonstrate their wealth, they would serve their guests tea, accompanied by delicacies. As the price of tea dropped, the middle classes also adopted afternoon tea as a social activity and it also started to appear alongside other leisure activities, such as cricket, tennis and croquet. This evolved into the tea, sandwiches, scones and small cakes that are served today. Afternoon tea for the wealthy also served to bridge the gap between lunch and dinner, which wouldn't be served until about 8 in the evening.

Even in the 19th century the expense of tea made it a luxury for the working classes and it couldn't be squandered on anything as frivolous as an afternoon refreshment. They would only drink tea as part of their main evening meal, which is the origin of 'high tea'. This would be served when the bread winner returned home from work and was usually a family meal. When the idea of holidays for the working classes started to become popular, seaside restaurants and cafes offered 'high tea' to the tourists coming from the cities. This term was still in use in some cafes when I was a child, though its use in this question is the first time I have heard it since then.

1st May 2018

In 1613 the future Charles I's sister, went to Germany to marry. Whom did she marry, what became of her and are any descendants still alive?

Elizabeth Stuart, daughter of James I of England and VI of Scotland and sister to Charles, went to Germany to marry Frederick V, King of Bohemia and Elector of Palatine (ruler of a part of the Holy Roman Empire on the River Rhein). Not only are many of her descendants still alive a new one, Louis Arthur Charles, was born on Monday 23rd April 2018.

Elizabeth is the link by which our current Queen can trace her lineage back to the first Stuart King of England. She is our present Queen's 8 times great grandmother.

From Elizabeth's marriage to Frederick came a daughter, Sophie. She married Ernst Augustus, Elector of Hanover and their son, George, became King George I in 1714, because William III and Mary II and then Mary's sister Ann, died childless. The alternative was to maintain the direct Stuart lineage through James Frances Stuart (the Old Pretender), son of James II.

Elizabeth was known as the Winter Queen as her husband, Frederick, served only one short term as the elected King of Bohemia before being forced from the throne by Ferdinand II, the Holy Roman Emperor. This sent Frederick and Elizabeth into exile in the Hague.

Sophie was the 12th of 13 children born to Elizabeth, so it is plausible for several other candidates to have been chosen to take the English throne. However, the Act of Settlement of 1701 had defined the lineage should William and Mary and then Ann die childless. Sophie's family, as Protestants, would be the next in line to the throne. George was the first of 8 children borne by Sophie.

The claim to the throne of the Old Pretender and his son Bonnie Prince Charlie, the Young Pretender, were the cause of the Jacobite rebellions against George I and George II that were ended at the battle of Culloden in 1746.

As James Stuart (the Old Pretender) was a Catholic he was barred from the line of succession by the Act of Settlement, which determined that only Protestants could ascend to the throne of England. This law was only changed in 2013 when a new Act of

Succession replaced The Act of Settlement. The same new law also permits a female to take precedence over a male in the line of succession if she is older than her brother. This means that Princess Charlotte now takes precedence over Prince Louis.

The line of descent to our present Queen then runs through the Hanoverian family to Queen Victoria, who was a niece of both George IV and William IV, both of whom died childless and from her directly to our present Queen and then on to the new Royal baby.

One of Elizabeth Stuart's other children was Prince Rupert, famed for his exploits with the cavalry of Charles I during the English Civil War.

15th May 2018

In a TV series about gold hunters in Australia, the precious metal is obtained from tons of soil by a machine, turned into a liquid and stored in tanks to be reconstituted into solid gold. How is this possible?

A system of treating ores (not just gold) to separate them into their constituent elements, was developed by British scientist William Crookes.

The mined ore, still mixed with the soil around it, is milled to reduce it to a 'sand' before being mixed with water to create a slurry. This slurry is then fed into large settling tanks.

The lighter elements in the slurry are allowed to overflow and are fed away to waste tanks while the heavier elements, such as gold, sink to the bottom of the tanks and are extracted through pipes. About 70% of the waste mixture, known as tailings, is removed in this way, then the remainder is fed into another tank where the process is repeated, removing another 70% of the waste and so on, until all that is left is gold in fine granules.

It is an industrial version of 'panning for gold', seen in films about the gold rush in California, which is the washing of the gravel found in rivers to separate the metal from the tailings.

The tailings are also allowed to sit in 'leaching tanks' where a 0.25 to 0.3 % mixture of cyanide of potassium is used as a catalyst in the process, to leach gold out of the finer sands, which is why the waste from goldmines is considered toxic. In the leaching tanks the gold forms into a gold 'slime' at the bottom of the tanks which requires another process to solidify it before it can be used. Leaching is a process similar to that used by coffee percolators to extract the flavour molecules of coffee from the grounds.

The average gold processing plant will use 16 separating tanks and 16 leaching tanks, operating in series, to extract the maximum amount of gold from the ore. About 150 tons of cyanide/water solution are used for each 100 tons of ore sands. Depending on how rich the original sands were. This will produce between 5 and 50 grams of gold per ton of sand.

The gold granules are then melted in crucibles to turn it into ingots before being shipped out to manufacturers or banks.

This process was first used in the gold fields of South Africa before being used in Australia. Gold was first discovered on that continent as early as 1820 in New South Wales but the first major finds weren't until 1851, sparking a gold rush. They continued predominantly in new South Wales and Victoria until the early 20th century, though there were finds in all of the Australian states.

William Crookes (1832-1919) was an eminent British scientist who is best known for his work on developing vacuum tubes for use in electronics. However, he was interested in a wide range of scientific fields, including the devising of the process by which gold could be recovered from ore on an industrial scale. He was preeminent in his field for his ability to turn scientific principals into money making ventures.

18th May 2018

Is it true that hundreds of soldiers were killed in a rehearsal for the D-Day landings?

Deaths during military training exercises are not unusual, though great efforts are made to prevent them. However, in the case of the deaths at Slapton Sands, Devon, there was a combination of events which led to the deaths of hundreds of American soldiers on a single night.

Slapton Sands was selected as a training area because it bore a similarity to Utah Beach in Normandy, one of the two beaches where American troops would land. A series of training exercises, given the name Exercise Tiger, were staged there.

Poor communications resulted in several deaths by 'friendly fire' as soldiers came ashore during these exercises, but it was an attack on a naval convoy by German E Boats that caused the greatest loss of life – 551 soldiers and 128 sailors. This was more than would die on Utah beach on D-Day itself.

In 1943 Slapton Sands was identified as a potential training area. Several villages were evacuated to prevent civilians being injured, and to reduce the risk of gossip leaking out about what was happening. Some the of the 3,000 inhabitants had never before left their villages. The first training exercises started in December 1943, leading up to larger scale rehearsals, Exercise Tiger, which were scheduled for April and May 1944.

On 27th April 1944 a friendly fire incident involving a naval bombardment caused the deaths of an unknown number of soldiers who were trying to land on the beach. It is thought as many as 500 were killed. This was caused by a change in timing for the assault which wasn't communicated to all those involved.

On 28th April, a flotilla of German E Boats, similar to British Motor Torpedo Boats, were alerted to the shipping activity off the Devon coast by the high volume of radio traffic in the area. Investigating, they found a 3 mile long convoy of tank landing ships, waiting to start the beach assault.

One of two Royal Navy ships that were supposed to be protecting the ships had been ordered into Plymouth for repairs after a collision with one of the landing ships, leaving the rear of the convoy undefended. The E Boats attacked the rear of the convoy first. Three ships were hit by torpedoes and two were sunk, while another was hit by friendly fire as the remaining craft tried to defend themselves. Casualties were exacerbated by the troops wearing their life jackets incorrectly and the freezing cold of the water, which killed many by hypothermia.

Because of the potential effect on morale, so close to D-Day, the tragedy was covered up by both the American and British authorities and didn't come to light until after the war. The relatives of the victims were never told the real story of how their loved ones died until the 1980s.

A local resident and diver, Mr Ken Small, recovered a Sherman tank from one of the landing ships and mounted it as a memorial to the disaster. He received a letter of thanks from President Ronald Regan and the memorial has been officially recognised by Congress. Mr Small also wrote a book about the disaster, called "The Forgotten Dead". Author Leslie Thomas also wrote a fictionalised account of the tragedy, called "The Magic Army".

25th May 2018

For D-Day in 1944, the Allies had a pipeline called Pluto towed across the Channel to supply petrol from England to Normandy. What became of it?

Operation PLUTO (pipeline under the ocean) was one of the major successes of World War II. From the outset of planning for the invasion of France it was recognised that the supply of fuel for tanks and other vehicles would be a limiting factor on operations if a suitable re-supply system wasn't in place. Later this demand would be increased when airfields were captured and the allied air forces started to use facilities in France.

One of the solutions available was to ferry fuel ashore from tankers until a port was captured to allow the direct discharging of fuel ashore. However, ships were vulnerable to air attack and so this option, although used in the early days, was not considered to be the final solution.

As early as 1942 work was started to build pipelines to connect ports on the British side of the English Channel to the major oil refining plants at Bristol and Liverpool. These would be extended as far as Shanklin on the isle of Wight and Dungeness in Kent, with above ground facilities cleverly disguised as bungalows and other innocuous looking buildings, including an ice cream parlour. These pipelines would, eventually, feed the underwater pipeline across the English Channel to France.

Special pipe laying ships were designed to lay the pipe as existing ships, which had mainly been used for cable laying, couldn't do the job quickly enough.

The pipeline was manufactured in long sections and was sealed at both ends, because it had to be pressurised to prevent it becoming distorted. The lengths of pipe were coiled around giant drums and fed out in lengths. Each length of pipe was then connected to the next while still sealed, but when fuel was pumped through it under pressure the seals burst, allowing the fuel to flow. Each pipe was made of lead and had an internal diameter of 3 inches and an external diameter of 4.5 inches, the difference being made up of protecting layers of steel tape and wire armour. Each mile of pipe used 24 tons of lead, 7.5 tons of steel tape and 15 tons of steel armour wire.

The first fuel supply operations following D-Day were conducted using tankers anchored offshore, pumping their fuel ashore through pipes of the same design as PLUTO. When Port en Bessin, between Omaha and Sword beaches, was captured the tankers were brought into port to discharge their fuel through pipes to holding tanks, constructed for the purpose.

The laying of the pipeline from the Isle of Wight took just 10 hours and it came ashore at the port of Cherbourg, which was captured on 29th June after a lengthy battle. A second pipeline was laid later, between Dungeness and Ambleteuse (Boulogne). At peak operations the pipelines were capable of delivering 46,000 gallons

(200,000 litres) of fuel per hour. Nearly 500 miles of pipeline were also laid across France to keep the fuel flowing right up to the front line. Average laying time was around 5 hours for a 30 mile stretch.

By the end of the war there were 21 pipelines crossing the English Channel, to Cherbourg and Ambleteuse but by 1947 PLUTO was redundant and operations started to salvage the pipework, both on land and sea. It is probably one of the largest salvage operations ever mounted and was carried out by Marine Contractors Ltd.

The ships that were used for the sea recovery were former Royal Navy vessels and were re-named Empire Tigress (formerly a landing craft), Empire Taw and Empire Ridley (two of the original pipelaying ships), and Redeemer (a motor fishing vessel which had been pressed into wartime service). The pipeline recovery was conducted during the summer, while winter was used to recover the materials for recycling. By late 1949 778 miles of pipeline had been recovered, out of approximately 800 miles laid. Remnants of the pipelines can still be seen at Port en Besson and at Shanklin Chine on the Isle of Wight.

30th May 2018

Where does the expression 'throw your hat in the ring' come from?

This term originates in the world of prize fighting and, later, boxing and dates back to at least 1805.

In the days of prize fighting, boxing rings were circular, made up of a 'ring' of people who had come to watch, rather than the squared, roped off areas of today. Prize fighters would often turn up in a town or village and offer to take on anyone for a modest prize purse put up by the promoter, who was usually the fighter's manager. The promotor made his money from people foolish enough to bet against his fighter. Any local champion who fancied his chances would throw his hat into the ring. This was presumably more reliable than trying to shout over the hubbub of the crowd.

The earliest citation of the use of this saying comes from "THE SPORTING MAGAZINE (OR MONTHLY CALENDAR OF THE TRANSACTIONS OF THE TURF, THE CHACE, AND EVERY OTHER DIVERSION INTERESTING TO THE MAN OF PLEASURE, ENTERPRISE AND SPIRIT)", *PUBLISHED IN 1805.*

NOWADAYS THE TERM MEANS BEING WILLING TO PARTICIPATE IN ANY CONTEST AND HAS OFTEN BEEN USED IN POLITICS, MEANING TO STAND FOR ELECTION.

ALSO STEMMING FROM THE ERA OF PRIZE FIGHTS ARE THE TERMS "TO STEP UP TO THE MARK" AND "UP TO SCRATCH".

STEPPING UP TO THE MARK MEANT STANDING AT A LINE SCRATCHED INTO THE GROUND IN THE CENTRE OF THE RING, INDICATING THAT YOU WERE READY FOR THE FIGHT. THE USE OF THE WORD 'MARK' IN THE SENSE OF A LINE OF THE GROUND DATES TO AT LEAST 900 AD, BUT ITS USE IN BOXING DATES FROM THE 18TH CENTURY. THIS HAS TRANSLATED INTO THE WORLD OF BASEBALL AS STEPPING UP TO THE PLATE AND NOW GENERALLY MEANS TO TAKE RESPONSIBILITY FOR SOMETHING.

BEING UP TO SCRATCH MEANT BEING FIT TO CONTINUE A FIGHT. THE LINE WAS SCRATCHED ONTO THE GROUND AND THE BOXER HAD TO GET UP TO IT TO CONTINUE. BEING 'NOT UP TO SCRATCH' HAS THE REVERSE MEANING, YOU AREN'T IN GOOD ENOUGH CONDITION TO CONTINUE THE FIGHT. THE TERM DATES TO 1778.

11th June 2018

Do we still need radar?

In the commercial aviation environment, it is possible to use global positioning systems (GPS) to plot an aircraft's position and to combine that with speed, course and height information which can be relayed to a computer to produce a real time 3 dimensional display for use by air traffic control. However, an electrical failure on board an aircraft would result in the communications systems being unable to broadcast the vital information which would render the aircraft invisible, so radar would remain a sensible back-up.

While this technology is feasible, it doesn't yet exist in practice, so radar remains the solution for commercial air traffic control for the time being.

Radar is the basic technology behind collision avoidance systems in aircraft, warning of the proximity of other aircraft that may have gone unnoticed by air traffic control. This could be replaced with infra-red systems, but that is just radar operating at higher frequency ranges.

GPS based systems could also be used to track maritime traffic and provide early warning of collision risks, but it would rely on all ships to installing and using it. Two ships not fitted with the system, but each thinking that the other was, would present a sizeable risk to safety.

In terms of national defence, however, radar is destined to remain in use for many years to come. It is unlikely that an enemy aircraft or ship would be considerate enough to leave its GPS and communications systems in operation, allowing the aircraft or ship to be tracked. All nations will, therefore, continue to use radar as their primary means of airborne and maritime threat detection.

In the event of a major global conflict it would be possible to use 'hunter killer' satellites to destroy GPS and communications satellites, which would increase reliance on radar both for air traffic control and military purposes.

In the world of meteorology, satellite imagery can map and track weather systems, but radar is used to measure the water content of cloud formations and therefore, in conjunction with other information, predict whether or not the clouds will produce rain. At present there is no alternative method of doing that.

Finally, radar is the basis for many speed camera systems, especially hand held types. Whether or not we 'need' those, however, is a matter of opinion.

13th June 2018

What is the Pareto principle?

The Pareto principle is a form of statistical analysis carried out as part of quality improvement projects. Basically, the Pareto Principle states that 80% of all quality failures in a system stem from just 20% of possible causes. The nickname for this is "the vital few, not the trivial many".

For example, in an examination paper, 80% of the incorrect answers are likely to come from just 20% of the questions. Identify those 20% of questions and the causes of the incorrect answers can then be used to improve teaching, or the way examination questions are written, or whatever else is identified as the cause(s) of wrong answers.

When this is applied to quality management the Pareto principle becomes an important tool with which to analyse quality failures in order to identify the 20% of a process or system that is behind 80% of quality failures.

This would be followed up by root cause analysis to identify the underlying cause of the failures. It may be something wrong with the process design or the machinery, but equally it might be something wrong with the raw materials, the training or even the way staff are recruited, managed or paid.

If root cause analysis isn't carried out then the tendency is to treat symptoms rather than causes. This would be like putting a sticking plaster on a child's cut finger, without asking how the child managed to get hold of a knife in the first place. If the root cause is not addressed, the problems are likely to re-occur, as many managers have found in the past.

After addressing the first set of 80/20 issues the process is then repeated, meaning that the number of quality failures is potentially decreased by 80% on each repetition, until the number of quality failures is so small that they defy analysis.

Joseph Moses Duran (24/12/1904 – 28/2/2008) was a Romanian born American engineer and champion for the cause of quality management. In 1941 he discovered the work of Italian statistician Vilfredo Pareto (1848-1923), who had first noted the 80/20 relationship, which occurs in many structures and organisations.

Duran devised a new nickname for the analysis, the vital few and the useful many, just to remind people not to ignore the 20% of quality issues in the 80% of the process that hadn't yet been addressed.

13th June 2018

Did Channel 4 recruit for a show called Lapdance Island?

In 2003 Channel 4 advertised for "10 hot blooded males to battle it out as 40 lap dancers do everything in their power to make it hard for them". 20,000 men applied, and some were auditioned – but it was a hoax.

Channel 4 really did place the advert, but it was for a show called "The Pilot Show" which would run on their E4 channel, in which people would be filmed doing silly things for the amusement of the audience. In the audition for "Lapdance Island" the men were filmed trying to complete tasks while girls in bikinis tried to distract them.

The presenters were Marc Wooton and Sharon Horgan. Just as in a real lap dancing club, the men weren't allowed to touch the girls. One of the questions the applicants had to answer was "What is it about a tropical island inhabited by lapdancers (sic) that appeals to you?"

As well as this stunt, they also filmed Eastenders star Dean Gaffney in a fake audition for a show called "Soul Searching", which was supposed to be a show about celebrities searching for American TV actor and singer David Soul, who would be hiding.

The Pilot Show ran on E4 in 2004. In 2005 it was remade for American TV as "BSTV" and ran for 16 episodes.

17th June 2018

Did the Germans concentration camp military personnel use captive doctors and specialist consultants to treat themselves and their resident families?

The term 'concentration camp' has come to have a catch all meaning, whereas the Nazis actually had three levels of camp that they used.

The lowest level were the labour camps. These were mainly used for native Germans who were political prisoners or in some way 'delinquent'. There was an understanding that these prisoners were capable of being 'rehabilitated' back into German society, consequently they suffered considerably less than the occupants of the other two types of camps. It was above the gates of these camps that the slogan "Arbeit Macht Frei' (labour makes freedom) was first displayed.

The second type of camp was the concentration camp. This was used primarily for people from population groups that the Germans despised, such as Poles, Slavs and Russians from the territories occupied by the Germans. Also sent there were native Germans considered to be beyond rehabilitation, such as the mentally and physically weak, homosexuals, gypsies and habitual criminals. The normal fate of the populations of these camps was to die from any number of causes, such as cold, overwork, starvation, disease and casual beatings.

Finally there were the extermination camps, which were the final destination for the Jews of occupied Europe. These were camps such as Auschwitz-Birkenau and Treblinka. Auschwitz itself was actually made up of 3 camps. Originally it was a concentration camp, but the inmates were used to build Auschwitz-Birkenau, the extermination camp.

People who were shipped to Auschwitz-Birkenau could calculate their lifespan in hours, not days, had they known why they were there. No effort was made to establish skills. There was a selection process for work, but it was based on physical appearance, not skills or qualifications. Women, children, the old and the infirm were sent straight to the gas chambers, as were the majority of the men. The remainder were given a short reprieve to carry out work within the camp, until they died of neglect or were sent to the gas chambers themselves.

In the labour and concentration camps, however, skills were identified and used or, more accurately, exploited. Inmates were hired out as slave labour to a wide range of enterprises. They would also be required to use their skills and knowledge within the camps. Medically trained staff were used to provide medical services to the other inmates. However, as some of the doctors were highly skilled, they would also treat their captors when ordered to do so.

The guards at these camps were not military personnel. They were part of the Nazi security apparatus, specifically the SS-Totenkopfverbände (Deathshead units). Many of the guards weren't German, but Lithuanians, Latvians, Estonians, Poles and Romanians who had volunteered to serve the Germans.

30ᵗʰ June 2018

What is the origin of 'the road to hell is paved with good intentions'?

This phrase is often attributed to Samuel Johnson (1709 - 1784) and he did say something similar. His biographer, James Boswell, records him saying "Sir, Hell is paved with good intentions." However, the key part of the phrase that is missing is the 'the road to Hell'.

The inference of the phrase is that there is no use just having good intentions. Those intentions must be acted upon to achieve good. Ultimately the person having the good intentions may find themselves in Hell for not acting upon them.

The origins of the phrase may be traced back to the Bible. The book of ECCLESIASTICUS CH 21 V 10 SAYS 'The way of sinners is made plain with stones, but at the end thereof is the pit of hell.' This seems to have been adapted over time until we receive our modern version.

The earliest version that approximates to our modern usage is from St Bernard of Clairvaux (1090 – 1153), after whom the St Bernard dog is named, who said *'l'enfer est plein de bonnes volontés ou désirs'* which translates as 'hell is full of good intentions and wishes'. There is then a 500 year gap until the phrase reappears in St Francis de Sales' CORRESPONDENCE: LETTRES D'AMITIÉ SPIRITUELLE

PUBLISHED IN 1640. IT IS LIKELY THAT IT IS THIS VERSION THAT JOHNSON PARAPHRASES.

As an aside, the St Bernard dog, though used for rescuing stranded travellers in the Alps, never wore a barrel around its neck. This was an invention of the artist Sir Edwin Landseer in his 1820 painting ALPINE MASTIFFS REANIMATING A DISTRESSED TRAVELLER. *IT IS THAT IMAGE THAT HAS ENTERED POPULAR CULTURE.*

3rd July 2018

In the TV series The Last Ship, on more than one occasion the captain orders a full stop by reversing the engines. Everyone is then thrown forward as though in a car making and emergency stop. Would this happen in real life?

For the answer to this question we must start with Newton's first law of motion: every object will remain at rest or in uniform motion in a straight line unless compelled to change its state by the action of an external force.

So, if a ship is in forward motion and it is suddenly stopped, then the people on board the ship will continue to move forward. This effect is seen more often in cars and trains, where emergency braking is applied and the passengers lurch forward. In a car this could result in the passengers being thrown through the windscreen if they weren't held in place by seat belts.

However, ships don't suddenly stop. If the thrust of the propellers is reversed to 'apply the brakes', it first takes time for the propellers to stop turning and then more time for them to start turning again in reverse and apply a force sufficient to stop the ship.

The fastest way to stop a ship is to reverse the thrust of the propellers while at the same time changing the direction of the ship by turning it, increasing the resistance of the ship though the water. This is known as a 'crash stop'. However, it will still take several minutes for the ship to come to a stop and the rate at which it decelerates would not be enough to cause the crew to lurch forward.

The only time that would happen is if the ship were to hit a solid object such as a rock, an iceberg or another ship.

It is estimated that a fully laden supertasker takes about 20 minutes to some to a stop from cruising speed. Smaller ship may do this more quickly, but they still require several minutes, not seconds to stop. In practice ships rarely execute emergency stops as they increase the wear on very expensive engines. Instead they slow down gradually over a period of several hours.

Small boats, such as speedboats and cabin cruisers, are able to stop much more quickly, because they don't exert so much inertia - the tendency to keep still or to keep moving in the same direction in accordance with Newton's law. Passengers or crew in those types of boats might be thrown forward if the boat were to undergo an emergency stop.

8th July 2018

Were the Finns Vikings?

Technically speaking there are no such people as Vikings. In Old Norse the word means 'a freebooting voyage or piracy'. The raiders would 'go on a viking'. However, common useage has resulted in the verb also being used as a name for the people who did it.

The Vikings were the Norse, who gave their name to Norway and Normandy, and the Danes. The Norse also populated southern Sweden. 7th century advances in both ship building techniques and navigation allowed the Norse and Danes to raid across the North Sea to Britain and Ireland and to venture as far as Iceland, which they colonised and also, it is believed, to the coast of North America in the area now known as Newfoundland. Norse settlements were established in Britain at York (Jorvick) and in Ireland at cities such as Dublin, Cork and Limerick.

However, the Vikings traded extensively around the Baltic Sea and also inland, using rivers as highways. Evidence of their trading has been found as far south as the Black Sea.

The Finns are largely descended from three main ethnic groups that settled in the country we now call Finland and who also populated the Baltic coast as far south as modern day Estonia. These groups were called the Finns, the Karelians and the Tavastians.

All of the tribes of northern Germany, Scandinavia, Poland, the Baltic states and Finland share a common ancestry, as they all came from Central Asia in the wake of the last Ice Age, following herd animals as they migrated northwards in search of grazing when the ice retreated. Each tribe settled in its newly found land and established its own culture and language, which come down to us in modern times, but there are strong similarities between them.

It is known that Finland was in contact with the Vikings, both through trade and through Viking raids. There is archaeological evidence of this in the form of Arabic coins which could only have arrived through trade with people who travelled as widely as the Vikings. However, there is no evidence that the Vikings ever established settlements in mainland Finland, though they may have set up temporary camps there.

When the Vikings raided they would have taken slaves, which means it is more likely to find a Dane or a Norwegian with Finnish blood than vice versa.

Apart from its neighbours, Sweden and Gotland (an island in the Baltic now part of Sweden) the existence of Finland was largely unknown in the rest of Europe until Christianity arrived. in the form of the Eastern Orthodox Church, in the 11th century.

Between 1397 and 1523 Scandinavia was united under what was known as the Kalmar Union, established by the Danish Queen Margaret (1353-1412). It was set up in order to counter the growing influence of the German states, known as the Hanseatic League. During her reign, which started in 1387, Margaret became Queen not only of Denmark, but also of Norway (1387) and Sweden (1389). Finland became part of this union and remained under Swedish dominance until 1700, when it became a pawn in a series of wars between Russia and Sweden. In 1809 it became part of the Russian empire until 1917, when Russia's internal political problems allowed the Finns to break away and establish their own nation.

9th July 2018

How many raids were carried out on Port Stanley airport by the Avro Vulcan bomber in the Falkland's War?

Operation Black Buck 1 to Black Buck 7 were a series of bomber raids carried out on Port Stanley Airport in the Falkland Islands, between 30th April and 12th June 1982. Five of those missions were completed. Black Buck 3 (13th May) was cancelled before take-off due to weather conditions and Black Buck 4 (28th May) was cancelled 5 hours into its mission due to a fault on one of the Victor tankers that was supposed to refuel it.

The aircraft and crews that carried out the attacks came from 44, 50 and 101 Sqn, who were all based at RAF Waddington in Lincolnshire. These were the last remaining Vulcan aircraft of the V bomber fleet and the squadrons were due to be disbanded on 1st July 1982, to be replaced by the Tornado GR1.

Although the Vulcans were long range bombers, their range of 2,600 miles (4,160 km) meant they didn't have the endurance to complete a round trip journey of 6,600 nautical miles (12,200 km) from Wideawake Airfield in the Ascension Islands without being refuelled in the air, hence the need for the Victor tankers. In fact 11 Victor tankers were used to refuel one pair of Vulcan bombers on each mission, as the Victors also had to refuel each other in order to reach their stations. The Victor tankers were from 55 and 57 Sqns based at RAF Marham, Norfolk.

This allowed for some level of redundancy in case the Argentinians retaliated with fighter attacks, or for mechanical failure in one of the Vulcans. Only one Vulcan from each pair made the actual bombing run. Each Vulcan refuelled seven times on the outward journey, to keep their tanks topped up, but only once on the return leg so that the aircraft wasn't above its maximum weight when it landed. Each raid took 16 hours flying time to complete, a world record for that sort of operation at that time.

There was considerable debate as to whether the raids would be worthwhile. Even with a full load of 21 conventional bombs or 4 Shrike air to ground missiles there was only a 90% probability of one of the weapons putting a crater in the runway at Port Stanley Airport and only a 75% chance of creating two craters. Conversely, there was a high risk of aircraft being brought down by anti-aircraft gunfire or missiles. For this reason the raids were carried out at night and in the poorest possible weather conditions, so as to disrupt ground defences.

Despite these bombing operations the runway at Port Stanley Airport remained in operation throughout the Falkland's War, even though the bombers did hit the target several times. However, the Argentine Airforce did claim that the raids caused the withdrawal of their Mirage III aircraft from the islands in order to provide protection for the mainland, should the British government decide to extend the air war in that direction. This no doubt had some beneficial effects with regards to the Naval and land forces when they arrived at the islands.

On Black Buck 6, aircraft XM597 developed a fault on its refuelling probe on the return leg and had to divert to Rio de Janeiro, where it was intercepted by aircraft of the Brazilian Airforce. Intense diplomatic negotiations were required to secure its release.

It was concluded by the United States Air Force, in their review of the operations, that the main purpose of the raids was for the RAF to claim a more significant role in the conflict.

Author's note: When this answer was published the last two paragraphs were omitted. Whether this was due to lack of space or the because of the political implications of both, isn't known.

12th July 2018

Does the magnetism of a ship affect its compass?

All magnetic compasses are affected by the presence of ferrous (magnetic) metals, such as most types of iron and steel. This can be observed by holding a piece of ferrous metal close to a compass. The compass needle will deflect either towards or away from the metal.

As a modern ship is effectively a large ferrous metal box it will affect the way the compass works, unless counter measures are applied. However, even in the days of sail there was enough metal on board the wooden ships, in the form of cast iron cannon, to affect the compass.

The simplest solution is to place weak magnets in the compass housing (binnacle) to correct for any errors introduced by the metal of the ship. However, this method isn't perfect as the Earth's own magnetic field varies in strength at different points around the globe, thereby introducing 'deviation' as the ship travels.

Another method of preventing the ship from interfering with the compass is to 'degauss' it. Degaussing involves surrounding the ship with an electrical current which neutralises the magnetic properties of the ship. However, this is also not error free.

In July 1940 Operation Ambassador, a commando raid on Guernsey, used 6 RAF air-sea rescue launches to carry the commandos in to shore from two Royal Navy frigates. Due to an error in the degaussing process the compasses on the launches were pointing south instead of north. The error wasn't spotted on 3 of the launches, so they ended up on Sark instead of Guernsey.

The modern solution for error free navigation is the gyro compass. A gyroscope is a fast rotating metal disc mounted on an axis. The disc is kept rotating by the application of an electric motor. One of its properties is that if the gyroscope is mounted in a free moving frame, the axis will always point in the same direction. Because it isn't dependent on magnetism, the direction in which it points isn't affected by the metal of the ship.

It doesn't matter what direction the axis is actually pointing, because it is a constant and the compass 'card', the visible indication of direction, can be adjusted to make it appear to point in a north-south direction.

14th July 2018

What happened to RAF aircrew during World War II when they were charged with having 'low moral fibre'?

During World War II it was normal in Bomber Command for aircrew to serve a complete operational tour before being able to take leave or undertake non-operational duties. The normal length of a tour was 30 missions. Often a full crew would see out their tour together, as they worked better as an established team.

At the end of a tour the aircrew were posted to other duties, such as training, administration or operational planning, depending on their personal skills and knowledge. However, this was only a respite and they could expect to return to operational duties once again, probably after about six months.

There were only three legitimate ways for aircrew to end a tour prematurely. The first was to be medically downgraded, therefore being unfit to fly. The second was to be posted to other duties, a decision taken for operational reasons by the Air Ministry. The third was being shot down and taken prisoner.

However, the level of stress suffered by aircrew was high. Today this might be diagnosed as a medical condition, such as depression or Post Traumatic Stress Disorder. However, these terms weren't used during World War II, so aircrew that asked to be removed from duty on medical grounds were more usually classified as lacking in moral fibre. In other words, they weren't brave enough.

As a means of being removed from operational duties this was something that the Air Ministry wished to discourage, so they made sure that the person making the request was treated in such a fashion that it discouraged others from making the same request.

There were a number of classifications of being medically unfit on 'nervous' grounds and these changed during the course of the war. From 1941 onwards medical officers could diagnose aircrew as being medically unfit even though they had no physical ailments, in recognition of their mental state. There were no sanctions taken against these airmen, at least not officially. From 1943 onwards aircrew on second or subsequent tours couldn't be categorised as lacking moral fibre, however, this provision wasn't publicised.

Squadron commanders could also remove aircrew from their duties if they considered that they weren't performing adequately or had become a liability to their crew. This could be an arbitrary decision based on a lack of confidence in the airman and required little in the form of evidence. There was no right of redress.

The sanctions available varied considerably. Officers had their commissions revoked and their flying badges removed to prevent them obtaining flying posts in civilian life. Generally they were dismissed from the service, but many were subsequently conscripted to work in the coal mines and other industries that required hard physical labour. Non-commissioned aircrew, who made up the majority, were reduced to the rank of Aircraftsman Second Class, the lowest rank in the RAF at that time and assigned to menial duties, such as cleaning latrines, for a period of at least three months.

Even after that they were unlikely to be assigned duties that had any sort of job satisfaction. Guard duties and kitchen fatigues were the norm. Inevitably, the reason for their employment got out and it wasn't unusual for these airmen to be ostracised by their colleagues. Their service records were stamped with a large W for waverer, which prevented them from getting any promotion.

18th July 2018

During the world wars, were battlefield ambulances and medics respected by all of the combatants?

The first Geneva Convention, 'for the amelioration of the Condition of Wounded and Sick in the Armed Forces in the Field' was created in 1864 by Henry Dunant, a Swiss businessman, after witnessing the

Battle of Solferino (24th June 1859), between the French-Piedemontese and Austrian armies in Northern Italy. This battle left around 40,000 wounded soldiers on both sides, who suffered greatly through lack of medical attention caused by the intensity of the battle.

Returning to Switzerland, Dunant wrote about what he had witnessed and started to campaign for the better treatment of wounded on the battlefield which resulted in the publication of the first convention. There were three other conventions created over the years. The second dealt with the treatment of the wounded at sea and the third and fourth dealt with the treatment of prisoners of war and civilians in wartime, respectively.

The convention covers a wide range of provisions for the wounded, from humane treatment through to the protection of buildings where the wounded are being treated. It also covers the protection of civilians providing aid to wounded soldiers. Amongst the requirements of the First Geneva Convention was respect for the Red Cross symbol in the treatment of the wounded, which included medical staff, ambulances, hospitals and, after the signing of the second convention, hospital ships.

Only those countries who had signed the Geneva Convention consider themselves to be bound by it, though some countries voluntarily treated the convention as guidelines. Only 12 countries signed the original convention on 22nd August 1864, though Britain and Sweden signed in December that year. Today 196 countries, all of those recognised by the United Nations, have signed the Geneva Conventions.

By and large all sides during World War I observed the contents of the Geneva Convention. In France truces were arranged to allow for the collection and treatment of the wounded in 'No Man's Land'. Similar truces were also arranged during World War II. Medical orderlies weren't deliberately targeted, though many died in battle as a result of shelling and machine gun fire.

The Nazis did breach the conventions on a number of occasions, especially with regards to the treatment of Russian wounded and prisoners. The Fuhrer Order, issued on 18th October 1942, which ordered that all captured special forces personnel (mainly commandos) were to be summarily executed was a direct contravention of the Geneva Convention on the treatment of both the wounded and of prisoners. Three wounded members of the SAS were executed under this order, as were many other allied prisoners of war.

Stories of German U Boats machine-gunning lifeboats, in contravention of the Geneva Convention, seem to be largely propaganda and have no basis in fact. No eye witnesses who survived alleged attacks ever reported seeing any U Boat do it. However, U 156, which torpedoed the British troopship Laconia on 12th September 1942, was bombed by an allied aircraft while carrying rescued sailors on her decks and displaying red cross banners. The captain of the U Boat also made an open radio broadcast signalling his intent to rescue the survivors. Several rescued sailors were killed. A second U Boat, U 506, was forced to abandon rescue attempts when it, too, came under air attack. From then on U Boat commanders were ordered not to attempt any rescues, which no doubt cost the lives of many allied sailors.

The Soviets breached the convention regarding the treatment of prisoners and civilians when they executed 22,000 Polish military officers, police and the intelligentsia, following the Russian invasion of Poland in 1939. Many of the dead were buried in mass graves in the Katyn Forest.

The Japanese never signed the first or subsequent Geneva Conventions until after World War II. Their bad treatment of both the wounded and prisoners of war is the stuff of legend.

Breaches of the Geneva Conventions are considered to be war crimes. There are two categories of breach, minor and grave. The term 'grave', however, wasn't introduced into the conventions until 1949. A grave action is one that is carried out deliberately and wilfully, rather than through neglect.

26th July 2018

Why are soap operas so called? Which is considered to be the first?

The origins of this phrase go back to 1920s and 30s America. Radio was expanding rapidly as the main form of entertainment in the home. To pay for the programming, radio stations invited companies to sponsor shows.

Anxious to get the best return on their investment, potential sponsors would try to match their product with the audience for the show. This is still normal practice, as can be seen by the different types of TV sponsorship of different types of show. Sponsorship of televised sports is often by beer companies, for example.

Popular shows in the afternoons were drama serials. The largest audience for these was housewives, so they became the target for soap powder manufacturers, such as Proctor and Gamble and Lever Brothers. The connection between the products and the programme content was soon well established and so the dramas became known as soap operas, a label that has continued to this day. This also spawned a slightly derogatory spin off label, the horse opera, to describe TV and film westerns.

In the world of TV and radio awards, however, these drama shows are known as 'continuing dramas', to signify that they aren't broken down into series with a set number of episodes.

The oldest identifiable soap opera was Painted Dreams. It premiered on radio station WGN in Chicago on 20th October 1930. It was created by Irna Phillips specifically for the radio station. The show followed the relationship between an Irish-American widow, Sue Moynihan and her unmarried daughter Irene. It continued to be broadcast until 1943.

As there was no radio advertising on the BBC and commercial radio didn't come in until 8th October 1973, with the founding of LBC, the first true soap opera in Britain was on TV; Coronation Street, which first aired on 9th December 1960. However, if we disregard the lack of advertising, the acclaim would go to The Archers, which was first broadcast on BBC radio in May 1950. It is now the longest running soap opera in the world.

14th August 2018

How many Scottish clans fought with the Duke of Cumberland's army against the Jacobite army?

The Jacobite cause was primarily supported by the highland clans, who were more loyal to the Stewart dynasty. As supporters of James II the highland clans had opposed the installation of William of Orange as King and defeated his army at the Battle of Killiekrankie in 1689.

The lowland Scots were more prosperous, more closely involved in English trade and politics and more protestant in their religion, which led them to be more pro-English.

However, the rebellion wasn't, as is often depicted, a war between the highlanders and the lowlanders, or the catholics and the protestants. It was more a war of Scottish nationalism over English hegemony.

The majority of clans to support the '45 rebellion were in the north west of Scotland. Chief amongst these were the Camerons, political rivals of their pro-English neighbours, the Campbells, led by the powerful Duke of Argyle. It was something of a surprise, therefore, that Charles Stewart (the Young Pretender) arrived in Scotland in Campbell country and raised his banner at Glenfinnan, just west of Fort William.

The first shots of the rebellion were fired at nearby Spean Bridge when a small Jacobite force chased off a company from the Royal Scots (as they would become; they are now part of The Royal Regiment of Scotland). The Jacobites were from Clan MacDonald of Keppoch and Clan McDonnell of Glengarry.

Later in the war, the Campbells provided 4 companies of the Argyle Militia for Cumberland's army at the Battle of Culloden (16th April 1746).

The picture is far from simple, however. The Gordon clan, who were from the area now encompassed by the Cairngorm National Park, fought on both sides during the rebellion, as did some other clans.

Many of the highland clans actually remained neutral throughout the rebellion, which resulted in them receiving preferential treatment when the war was over. The regiment that became known as the Black Watch was formed after the war from loyal highlanders from the Campbells, Frasers, Grants and Munros, and set to watch over their more rebellious neighbours. With the exception of the Campbells, these clans were all from land north of the Great Glen (Loch Ness).

In lowland Scotland the clan structure had already started to erode as farming and business interests created a more mobile population, with cities like Edinburgh and Glasgow drawing people in from the countryside. The Clyde shipbuilding industry was in its infancy at this time, but had already started to draw craftsmen and their families from inland. Politically the lowlanders had opposed James II and backed the cause of William of Orange, who would take the throne of England with his wife Mary. Later they threw their weight behind the Hanoverian dynasty of George I and George II.

It is difficult to identify specific clans fighting for the Duke of Cumberland's army. As an organised army the troops were formed into regiments, at that time known by the name of their Colonels. A regiment would march from town to town to recruit its soldiers, crossing the invisible boundaries of historic clan territories. In many cases the clan chieftain, or Laird, would remain neutral, but wouldn't object to his clansmen joining the English army or, for that matter, the Jacobites. Some clans were even pro-English but pretended to be pro-Jacobite and vice versa. Such was the complexity of Scottish politics.

The Jacobite army was not the rabble of clansmen that is often depicted. Like their opponents they were organised into regiments, combining members of several smaller clans and were trained in the military tactics of the day. Most of them had modern weapons, purchased from France and Spain. They had advanced as far south as Derby before divisions in the ranks forced them to withdraw back into Scotland. Even then they defeated Cumberland's troops at the Battle of Falkirk Muir on 17th January 1746. That battle, however, served only to delay Cumberland's pursuit of the Jacobites, which culminated at the Battle of Culloden.

The defeat of the Jacobite army at Culloden was caused, in part, by a rift between Charles Stewart and his military commander, Lord George Murray. Charles dismissed Murray and chose a battle site that favoured the Duke of Cumberland's army. The Jacobite soldiers were cut to ribbons by the English artillery before being able to initiate a mass charge, the tactic that they had used successfully on other occasions. The English cavalry was then able to finish the job.

17th August 2018

How did ferry pilots like Mary Ellis return home after delivering their aircraft?

The answer to this question is rather mundane; Mary Ellis would have taken the train.

On the authority of the Air Ministry she would either have been issued with a rail warrant before departure, or she would have reported to the adjutant (the military term for administrator) of the airfield where she had delivered the aircraft to be issued with one. This would entitle her to a free rail ticket to her destination. The railway company reclaimed the cost of the ticket from the Air Ministry.

When I joined the RAF in 1968 we were entitled to a set number of rail warrants per year for leave travel and the use of rail warrants was a normal method of obtaining rail tickets for travel on duty.

Nowadays military personnel, like their civilian counterparts, tend to pay their own way and then claim the cost back afterwards.

The adjutant would also organise road transport for Mary to the nearest railway station, probably alongside airmen going on leave or being posted to other units. Depending on what time she arrived at the airfield, she might have to stay the night, in which case she would have been lodged in the Officers' Mess.

If ferry pilots were required to bring aircraft in from Canada or the USA they would travel across the Atlantic in one of the many ships that crossed the ocean in the wartime convoys or, perhaps, on the fast passenger liners like the Queen Mary and Queen Elizabeth, that crossed the Atlantic independently.

If there happened to be a transport aircraft, usually American, making the journey the ferry pilots might be able to hitch a lift, but only if there was space available. As World War II aircraft couldn't make the journey in a single hop, they flew via Iceland, Greenland and Newfoundland, with the aircraft to be ferried returning along the reverse route. Because of weather constraints, however, a sea crossing was often faster than going by air. Small aircraft, such as fighters, weren't flown across the Atlantic, they were crated up and shipped as freight.

The Air Transport Auxiliary employed a total of 1,320 pilots, of whom 168 were women. They also employed 170 flight engineers and radio operators. From 1943 female ATA pilots were one of the first groups of women to earn the same wage as their male counterparts. Fifteen women lost their lives while ferrying aircraft, including noted airwoman Amy Johnson.

21st August 2018

A World War II documentary stated that during the Battle of the Bulge, 6,000 American soldiers were captured by the Germans. What happened to them?

Once a member of the armed forces is taken prisoner he comes under the protection of the Geneva Convention on the treatment of prisoners of war (POW), one of the four Geneva Conventions, providing his captors have signed the convention.

The prisoner is entitled to be protected from further harm and must be provided with food, clothing and accommodation and the prisoner must be treated humanely. POWs may not be forced to work for their captors, but they may undertake work on a voluntary basis to alleviate boredom or to improve their own circumstances, such as growing vegetables to supplement their diet.

In general the American soldiers captured during the Battle of the Bulge (16th Dec 1944 – 25th Jan 1945) were treated no differently from any other prisoners captured by the Germans in battle.

In the first instance the prisoners would have been removed from the battlefield and taken to a temporary prison camp out of artillery range. Here they would have been interrogated to see what military intelligence they might give up. Prisoners were not, generally speaking, tortured to force them to give information. The Geneva Convention only requires a prisoner to give his service number, his name and his rank, so that his relatives may be notified of his capture, via the Red Cross. After that they would have been sent by road and rail to a regular prisoner of war (POW) camp. These were mainly in Germany, Austria and Poland.

The films "The Great Escape", "The Wooden Horse" and "Albert RN" provide a reasonable depiction of life inside POW camps, though conditions varied according to the temperament of the Camp Commandant and the availability of supplies to feed the prisoners. Some camps were undoubtedly harsher than others.

As the Russians advanced into Poland from the east and Britain and the Americans into Germany from the west, they liberated POW camps, so the prisoners were often marched away from the combat area to POW camps further away. This was to prevent them being liberated and returning to combat. Thousands of POWs were marched across Poland and Germany, enduring extreme hardship along the way, with many dying on route. The POWs were eventually liberated when Germany surrendered and they were then repatriated.

Some American soldiers were executed by the SS during the Battle of the Bulge. At Malmedy 84 American prisoners were shot by their captors, under the command of SS Sturmbannführer Joachim Peiper. Peiper would later be tried as a war criminal along with a number of others. 40 death sentences were passed, but Peiper only served 10 years in prison. There was also a massacre of 11 black soldiers of the US 333rd Field Artillery Battalion, an all African-American unit, at Wereth, a hamlet in Belgium. No one has ever stood trial for that atrocity.

In retaliation for the Malmedy massacre, American troops killed 80 Wehrmacht soldiers in Chenogne, Belgium. The deaths were covered up and only recently became public knowledge.

The Battle of the Bulge was not just an American battle. The British 2nd Army were also involved and suffered 1,400 casualties, of which over 200 were killed.

23rd August 2018

How did the Black Watch get their name?

There are two parts to this answer, relating to the two parts of the regiment's name.

The 'Black' part of the name comes from the tartan worn by the regiment, which contains very dark blues and greens.

The "Watch" part of the name comes from the purpose for which the regiment was first raised.

In 1725, General Wade established a new 'watch' of six independent companies of soldiers whose purpose was to disarm the highlanders, hinder rebels and bring criminals to justice. The watch were stationed in small groups around the highland towns and villages. As was the practice of the day, each company took the name of its commanding officer, so the company led by Lord Lovat were called Lovat's Company of the Watch.

The companies were drawn from several clans loyal to the English crown and were led by their own clan officers. However, it was decided that all 6 companies should wear a tartan that was as similar in colour as possible. It was unthinkable that members of one clan could wear the tartan of another, so what we now know as the Black Watch tartan was chosen for them. The dark coloured tartan became synonymous with the regiment's name, though this wouldn't become the regiment's official title for another 150 years.

In 1739 an additional four companies were raised and all ten companies were formed into a single regiment, the 42nd Regiment of Foot, under the command of The Earl of Crawford.

The regiment was abroad during the '45 Rebellion, so didn't take part. They were fighting in the War of The Austrian Succession and took part in the Battle of Fontenoy in April of 1745. Although the British lost this battle, the Black Watch earned their first battle honour there.

In 1795, at Royston in Hertfordshire, the regiment was awarded a red hackle, or plume of vulture feathers, to wear on their bonnets. The reason for this isn't known with certainty, but is thought to relate to the recapture of two artillery pieces captured by the French at Guildermalson in 1794. Other Highland regiments started to copy the fashion, before an Army Order of 1822 reserved the right of the red hackle to the 42nd Regiment of Foot alone.

In 1881 the 42nd Regiment of Foot were merged with the 73rd, another Scottish regiment, to become the 1st and 2nd Battalions, The Black Watch (Royal Highlanders). They retained this title until 2006 when they merged with the five other Scottish infantry regiments to form the Royal Regiment of Scotland. They are now designated 3

Scots, The Black Watch, 3rd Battalion the Royal Regiment of Scotland.

31st August 2018

What is the origin of the saying "No good deed goes unpunished"?

This phrase has a slightly different meaning than one might at first expect. It suggests that the person doing the good deed will suffer some sort of retribution. However, this isn't what it means.

The actual inference is that the good deed may not achieve the recognition that it deserves, or that the person who is the recipient of the good deed feels that they deserve more. This could lead the person doing the good deed to suffer inconvenience as they endeavour to bridge the gap between what was done and what was expected. Any lack of recognition or inconvenience is the punishment for the good deed.

The phrase has also been rendered as "Every good deed brings its own punishment".

The saying is attributed to several writers, including Walter Winchell, Oscar Wilde, Marie Belloc Lowndes and Claire Boothe Luce.

However, the very first citation of the phrase, goes back to the 12th century. Courtier Walter Map wrote "De Nugis Curialium" (Courtiers Trifles), which was written in medieval Latin and translated in 1923 by an Oxford University scholar, M R James.

From this translation the key phrase appears: "He spared none of his band who inclined to spare any, *left no good deed unpunished, no bad one unrewarded*; and when he could find no rival and no rebel on earth, like Capaneus, he challenged opposition from heaven."

The first appearance after the publication of the 1923 translation is in an article in "The Windsor Magazine" entitled "A Breaker of Hearts". It was written by Marie Belloc Lowndes and was published in 1927. Walter Winchell didn't use the phrase until 1942, in the Philadelphia Inquirer.

The most common attribution for the phrase is to Claire Boothe Luce, but she didn't use it until 1949, in an article published in The Cumberland News (Maryland, USA) and also in the Miami Daily News.

The attribution to Oscar Wilde is retrospective and was first suggested by columnist Ernest Cuneo in the El Dorado Times in 1972 (Arkansas, USA), quoting something that Wilde was supposed to have said, but with no written citation to support the claim.

3rd September 2018

What is the origin of the word "shambles"?

This little word has had a fascinating journey from its original meaning of a stool, to its modern usage of describing a chaotic situation.

The Oxford English Dictionary traces the word back to the Old English sceamel, meaning a stool and that, in turn, may have its origins in the Latin scamnum, meaning a bench or stool. In Old English sc was pronounced as sh, while the b in shambles may have come from a 'non sound', or 'epenthetic', that some people put into words. A similar example is the way that some people pronounce hamster as hamp-ster.

Shambles made its first transition to come to mean a bench or table on which goods were placed for sale and this then became reserved for the sale of meat. The next transition was from noun to verb, still related to butchers, where it was used to describe the killing and butchering of animals. From there the word shambles was used to describe the area in which this sort of work was done.

Any area where butchery was carried out would probably have been known as The Shambles, such as Smithfield in London, but it seems that only in York has the name been retained to describe a whole area of the city. However, there are streets called The

Shambles in other towns and cities including Chesterfield, Guildford, Swansea, Manchester and Armagh.

As large-scale medieval butchery was a messy business, it is fairly easy to identify the final transition of the word to mean any sort of mess or chaos. As the butchering of animals was moved into abattoirs the use of shambles in that sense declined, but the other meaning survived to the present day.

In a 2012 episode of "The Thick Of It" the word appeared in a brand new form, as character Malcolm Tucker came out with "omnishambles", to mean a situation that has been comprehensively mismanaged, leading to a series of blunders. It became the Oxford Dictionaries' word of the year.

14th September 2018

Why are certain artillery weapons called "recoilless rifles", when they are not rifles at all?

Rifling refers to the helical grooves engraved on the interior surface of gun barrels which impart spin on the projectile, which gives greater accuracy. Accordingly, any weapon that has a rifled barrel can, correctly, be referred to as a rifle, regardless of size. In everyday use the term rifle has come to mean a shoulder fired weapon with a rifled barrel, carried by a soldier. This distinguished the weapon from the smooth bore muskets.

Archers first realised that adding a twist to the feathered flights of their arrows allowed them to spin as they flew, increasing accuracy. The earliest experiments with rifling in firearms date as far back as the 15th century.

The earliest practical rifles were to be found in the American state of Kentucky in the 18th century, where they were used by hunters. The earliest known rifles of this type were manufactured in 1750 by Jacob Dickert, a German immigrant. Their first military application was during the American War of Independence, when George Washington authorised the formation of ten companies of riflemen, who were able to engage the enemy at far greater distance and accuracy than the soldiers equipped with smooth bore muskets.

It is likely that Lieutenant General Sir John Moore, father of the British Light Infantry, saw these weapons in use when he was a young Lieutenant serving in America and adopted them for use in his new units. For this reason a soldier in the Light Infantry regiment is given the rank of Rifleman, not Private. The ones first used by the British were the Baker rifle, produced from 1800 in Whitechapel, London.

The development of the elongated bullet for use in rifled weapons came in the 1840s, replacing the round musket ball.

Although the rifling of artillery barrels can be traced back to Augsburg in 1498, it didn't feature heavily in artillery weapons until the 1850s, when Armstrong-Whitworth breach loading guns started to be introduced into the Royal Navy.

The recoilless rifle is a rifled artillery weapon which ejects some of its propellant gas rearwards, reducing the amount of recoil produced by the weapon, which allows it to be mounted on lightweight carriages or vehicles. There are even man portable versions. However, the redirection of the propellant gases reduces the range of the weapon. They are usually deployed with infantry units rather than artillery units.

The L6 Wombat recoilless rifle used by the British army and Royal Marines has been in service since 1964. It has a calibre of 120 mm, an effective range of 1,000 yards and is served by a crew of 3.

17th September 2018

How does an airliner know if it has a head or tailwind?

Before take-off pilots have to file a flight plan which describes the route that they will take to their destination, including estimated timings at certain points along the route. These routes normally follow pre-set air 'corridors' which are designed to prevent aircraft on different routes conflicting with each other, but pilots sometimes have a choice of which corridor they will take.

Flight plans originated as a flight safety process, so air traffic controllers would know if an aircraft was overdue and might have gone missing, but it now serves to help air traffic controllers to know when to expect aircraft in their air space and to allocate 'slots' in air corridors to keep aircraft apart.

As part of the flight planning process the pilots will study a weather forecast, so that they can identify any problem they might encounter on route. This forecast will include details of wind speed and direction at different heights, as well as any adverse weather conditions that might be encountered, such as storms or fog.

At one time every airport had its own meteorological department who provided the weather forecast, with airports exchanging weather information with each other to help with flight planning. With the advent of the internet, pilots now have access to a wide variety of meteorological information. This allows the pilot to choose routes that will help them.

Flying across the Atlantic Ocean from west to east the pilot will usually try to take advantage of the Jetstream, which will speed them on their way and save them fuel, but flying in the opposite direction they will try to fly either north or south of it, because the Jetstream will slow them down.

As they fly along their routes pilots are able to get updated weather information over the radio, but they are also able to calculate the effect that the wind has on their aircraft. They can compare their airspeed, as shown on their airspeed indicator, with their ground speed, which is measured by calculating the travelling time between fixed points on the ground. Nowadays this is calculated electronically from bearings taken from radio beacons. The difference between the two measured speeds will show if the aircraft is being aided or hindered by the wind.

26th September 2018

Were any of the mid-west or western states involved in the American Civil War?

In 1861 there were 34 states within the USA, of which 7 broke away to form the Confederacy. The majority of these states lay between the Atlantic Ocean and the banks of the Missouri and Mississippi rivers. However, 3 Union states lay to the west of that: Kansas, California and Oregon. There was also 1 Confederate state, Texas, to the west.

Although the major reason for the split was the issue of slavery, there were other issues, such as the rights of states to make their own decisions. 4 other states, known as the border states, later joined the Confederacy, leaving 23 northern and western states in the Union.

The status of states was by no means clear. The "border states" permitted slavery but didn't immediately join the Confederacy. They tried to remain neutral, but were eventually coerced into fighting. Maryland surrounded the Union capital, Washington DC, and so was invaded by the Union and martial law was declared. Delaware didn't provide any troops for the Confederacy but Virginia and Kentucky did, following what we would call a referendum, Virginia split in two and the state of West Virginia was formed in 1863, which then joined the Union. There were also a number of Union states that permitted slavery, along with 3 "territories".

All the recognised states made some contribution to war in one way or another.

The main concern of Texas at this time was possible invasion by Mexico, but it did provide some troops for the Confederate Army. The state's main contribution to the war effort was as a supply route, a source for food and horses and an export route for cotton, avoiding the eastern ports that had been blockaded by the Union.

California provided volunteer units to replace Federal troops withdrawn from Oregon and they also protected the New Mexico territory from invasion by Mexico and Confederate incursions from

Texas. California was also the main source of gold for the Union treasury.

Some supporters of slavery crossed the border from Union states to join the Confederate Army. Approximately 1,000 were known to have done that from the state of Kansas, which was isolated from the Union by the Confederate state of Missouri. It was the last state to join the Union prior to the 1861 split and the most westerly before the start of the "territories". The state itself provided approximately 20,000 soldiers for the Union army, 4,000 more than the conscription quota allocated by the Union government.

To the west were what was known as the "territories", to which settlers had started to move but which were not yet states. These were the Washington, Dakota, Nevada, Utah, Nebraska, Colorado, New Mexico and Indian territories. They were considerably larger areas than the states which now bear some of those names. These territories were reduced in size over the years as parts of them became states, but not until after the Civil War ended. Indian Territory would become the state of Oklahoma in 1907, followed by New Mexico and Arizona in 1912.

Settlers living in the territories weren't subject to the conscription imposed by either the Union or Confederate states as, legally, they weren't part of either. Settlers were free to join the army of whichever side they favoured, or to stay neutral if they wished.

The majority of conscripts that fought in the war came from east of the Mississippi River and many of those were poor immigrants, paid to take the place of richer citizens. There were at least 170,000 of these immigrants serving in the Union army alone.

28th September 2018

How did large, heavy sea-going sailing ships leave or enter harbour when the wind was blowing in the wrong direction or was too light to power the ship?

This wasn't actually much of a problem.

If a ship was outside the harbour it could anchor and unload its cargo into oar powered lighters to deliver the cargo to shore. The lightermen had to be paid, which put up the cost of the goods, but it prevented a more costly delay while the ship waited for the wind to change or strengthen.

If the ship was inside the harbour and unable to leave, there were two choices. If the harbour was on a tidal estuary, it could drift out to see on the ebbing tide. If not, then rowed boats could be used to tow the ship out to sea.

The towing of sailing ships was a common practice. If a ship was becalmed while at sea a long boat was often put out with a tow line attached, powered by as many as 20 sailors with oars. The main effort was needed to get the ship moving. Once it was, the rowing became easier. There are contemporary paintings of ships being moved this way.

Access to Bristol harbour, which has existed since the Middle Ages, is along the narrow Avon gorge, where sailing is almost impossible unless the wind is directly behind, so it was common practice for ships to be towed up and down the gorge between the harbour and the Bristol Channel.

9th October 2018

Does anyone know the circumstances around the sinking of the submarine HMS Affray?

HMS Affray (P421) was a Royal Navy submarine that sank sometime between 21.00 hrs on 16th April 1951 and 08.00 hrs the next day. The last visual reports of her were made by the destroyer HMS Contest. The ship and the submarine exchanged normal naval courtesies as they passed each other and the submarine made a routine report of position, course and speed at 21.00 hrs and indicated that the Captain was preparing to dive.

Affray had been built towards the end of World War II, one of 16 submarines of the Amphion Class, whose names all started with the letter A. She was built at Birkenhead by Cammell-Laird and launched on 12th April 1944. She and her sister ships were intended to serve in the Pacific Ocean against the Japanese, but as the Affray wasn't commissioned until November 1945 she was too late to serve in the war. The Affray was the only one of her class to have sunk and was the last British submarine to be lost at sea.

The boat's mission in April 1951 was essentially a training exercise. Her normal crew was reduced from 61 to 50 to allow a number of junior officers to be taken on board for essential submarine training. Along with a Sergeant, a Corporal and two Royal Marines of the Special Boat Squadron, her compliment when she set sail was 75. She was to undertake training in the English Channel, approaching beaches in South West England to drop the marines ashore, before returning later to recover them, repeating this exercise until 23rd April, when the boat was scheduled to return to port for essential maintenance.

When the boat failed to make its routine report at 08.00 hrs on 13th April, the Admiralty listed the submarine as missing and launched a search for it which would result in the involvement of 24 ships from 4 nations. During the search a morse code signal was heard on Asdic by two ships, presumably made by survivors tapping on the boat's hull, but it didn't help in locating the lost submarine.

After 3 days the search was gradually scaled back, but not abandoned by the Navy, until the Affray was finally located on sonar by HMS Loch Insh on 14th June. It was found to be at the bottom of the Hurd Trench, a deep valley in the sea bed 17 miles from Alderney, closer to France than to England. An examination was carried out using an underwater camera.

Investigations into the wreck revealed that the "snort" mast (its snorkel) had broken off. The possibility of it hitting an object on the surface was discounted after the broken section of the mast was recovered and examined. The snort mast had been fitted during a modification programme in March 1949. The theory for the Affray's sinking is that the mast broke off while in use, allowing water under 10 tonnes of pressure to flood into the hull, however, this theory has never been verified and the official cause for the sinking is unknown. The possibility of a mutiny on board was also considered and discounted. The reason for the snort mast breaking has never been established.

22nd October 2018

What is the origin of the phrase 'clutching at straws'?

This phrase refers to the way a drowning person will clutch at anything in an attempt to save their life, even straws which, although they float, offer no prospect of supporting a person's weight.

When we 'clutch at straws' we are pinning our hopes on a vague possibility of being helped in some way.

The use of the word straw appears in a number of metaphors because it is a waste product of little value. For example, a now obsolete usage is "to not give a straw", which translates into modern usage as "couldn't care less". A "man of straw" was an unworthy opponent and to "condemn someone to straw" was to declare them ready for the insane asylum. In modern business terms, people talk about constructing a "straw man", a metaphor for an idea or proposal that can be challenged until it falls apart, so that the weaknesses in the idea can be identified.

The first known citation of the phrase "to clutch at straws" in the sense it is now used was made by cleric John Prime in his 1583 book FRUITFUL AND BRIEF DISCOURSE, *IN WHICH HE WRITES* "*We do not as men redie to be drowned, catch at euery straw.*" THIS MAY BE A VARIATION ON AN EARLIER PHRASE USED BY SIR THOMAS MORE IN HIS 1534 BOOK A DIALOGUE OF COMFORT AGAINST TRIBULATION *IN WHICH HE WRITES* "*A man in peril of drowning catchest whatsoever cometh next to hand... be it never so simple a stick.*"

During the World Wars, how were conscientious objectors treated in Germany?

During World War I, British conscription laws provided limited exemptions for war service on religious grounds. Conscientious objectors for religious or pacifist reasons had a right of appeal to a tribunal and if their case was considered legal they were permitted to undertake other work, usually in what was called "the Non-Combatant Corps". In practice many conscientious objectors joined the army as medical orderlies and several were decorated for their bravery. If the tribunal turned down the appeal, as many were, then the conscientious objector could be imprisoned if he still refused to join the military.

Out of approximate 750,000 cases heard by tribunals, only 16,600 British men won their case during World War I. This rose to 60,000 during World War II.

This, however, was not the case in Germany. While some consideration was given to religious groups, allowing them to serve in non-combatant roles, such as medical orderlies and stretcher bearers, there was no blanket exemption and non-combatant roles were not guaranteed.

Conscientious objectors who took an absolutist stance, refusing military service altogether, had no right of appeal. They were either sent to prison or mental asylums on the grounds that a German man refusing to do military service was either mad or a criminal. There are no reliable figures for the number of men treated this way.

In 1938, as a preparation for war, the Nazi government passed laws which made any form of avoidance of military service a crime. This was known as *Wehrkraftzersetzung,* a term which could be interpreted in a number of ways, such as "subversion of the war effort", "undermining military morale" or "sedition and defeatism". While these laws initially applied only to the military, in 1939 they were extended to the civilian population. The maximum penalty available to the courts was the death sentence.

Conscientious objectors found guilty of *Wehrkraftzersetzung* were normally sentenced to imprisonment in concentration camps. If they recanted they could earn their release providing they took up military service, but refusal to recant amounted almost to a death sentence as so few people survived the camps.

During World War II there were between 14,000 and 30,000 convictions for *Wehrkraftzersetzung*. The figures vary as the offence wasn't always recorded as such. As the war turned against Germany, the number of death sentences passed increased in comparison to custodial sentences.

A number of opponents of the Nazi regime were executed under the *Wehrkraftzersetzung* laws, not just conscientious objectors. These included members of the White Rose group, who advocated non-violent resistance to the Nazis, which included refusal to serve in the German military.

After the war the offence of *Wehrkraftzersetzung* remained in military law until 1998. However, in practice, civilians conscripted into the military were permitted to undertake humanitarian work instead of military service if they were conscientious objectors, however, their pay was restricted to that which could be earned by a conscripted soldier. In 2011 conscription into the German military was suspended indefinitely.

30ᵗʰ October 2018

How did the check-mate system of ship identification work during World War II?

The check-mate system was based on knowledge of the location of ships, coupled with a challenge and response to confirm identity. The phrase emanates from 'check he's your mate' rather than from the chess term.

Allied aircraft and ships hunting for German surface raiders, disguised as merchant ships, would be provided with information on friendly shipping in their patrol area that they might be expected to encounter. This information was updated by the Admiralty on a daily basis. When a ship was encountered it would be challenged using a coded message and was expected to respond using a coded reply. The system could be used with radio, Aldis lamp or flag signals.

In practice only about half of Allied shipping responded with the correct coded reply, making the system unreliable. One German raider, the Atlantis, which was disguising itself at different times as the Norwegian ship MV Tamesis and the Dutch ships Abbekirk and Brastagi, was passed as friendly twice despite having failed to respond correctly.

From June 1943, aircraft and naval vessels were required to carry out two additional actions to bolster the check-mate system. One was to classify the suspect vessel using the Merchant Ship Description Code and the second was to compare the suspect with a silhouette of ships that conformed to that classification.

The Merchant Ship Description Code was a list of characteristics that told mariners what another ship should look like, eg the type of ship (passenger, freighter, tanker, trawler etc), approximate dimensions, the number and position of funnels, the position of the fore, centre and aft castles, the number of decks etc.

If identification of the ship was still doubtful, the patrol ship or aircraft could make a radio call back to shore asking for confirmation of identity or further details. The response would decide whether or not further checks were required, which could include boarding the suspect ship or, in the case of aircraft, shadowing it until a surface vessel arrived.

30ᵗʰ October 2018

If an intermediate missile has a range of 3,000 miles, what qualifies as a long-range missile?

Long range missiles, or inter-continental ballistic missiles (ICBM), to give them their correct name, are a class of weapon that has a range in excess of 3,400 miles (5,500 km). To achieve this they are blasted out of the Earth's atmosphere and travel part way around the Earth while in space, then re-enter the atmosphere closer to their target.

The first ICBMs carried only a single nuclear warhead of up to 1.5 megatons. However, later versions carried multiple independently targetable re-entry vehicles (MIRVs) capable of striking a number of targets within a designated geographic area. The Trident II missile carries between 8 and 14 MIRVs (depending on type) and each has a yield of up to 475 kilotons.

As the missile re-enter's Earth's atmosphere, the payload bay at the top of the missile falls apart to release the MIRVs, which are then directed by their internal guidance systems to their targets.

ICBM development started during World War II with Germany designing the A9/10 missile system, which planned to allow Germany to attack cities on the Eastern Seaboard of the USA. This programme never came to fruition, but did provide the groundwork for later developments by both the USA and Russia.

The first test launch of a Russian R-7 long range missile took place on 15th May 1957. It crashed 250 miles from the launch site and the first successful launch wasn't made until August 1957.

The first US launch didn't take place until 11th June 1957. The flight of the Atlas missile lasted just 24 seconds before it blew up. Its first successful launch wasn't until November 1958.

Both nations explained their tests as prototypes for use in space travel and, indeed, both types of missile were later used to launch satellites. The building of the ICBMs undoubtedly accelerated the civilian space programmes of both nations.

The first American Atlas D ICBM was declared operational in January 1959, but it hadn't been test fired. The first Russian ICBMs were ready for operations by 9th February 1959. By the mid 1970s both nations had the nuclear capability to destroy the other country several times over.

From the 1950s onward, Britain's nuclear deterrent was based around the RAF's V-Bomber fleet (Valiant, Victor and Vulcan bombers). Britain's ICBM programme didn't start until 1963 with the announcement of the building of the first nuclear submarine which would carry the American built Polaris missile. The first submarine, HMS Repulse, was commissioned on 28th September 1968. It was the first of five boats, which were all named after ships in which Lord Louis Mountbatten, the former Chief of Naval Operations, had served.

1st November 2018

Why do modern windmills turn clockwise and traditional windmills turn counter-clockwise?

Traditional windmills are buildings in which people worked, so the direction in which the sails turned was a matter of safety.

The cap at the top of the mill, where the sails are attached to the axle that connects to the mill wheel, is capable of being rotated so that the sails can be repositioned to catch the wind. This means that with the wind in a certain direction, the sails pass in front of the door to the mill. Someone leaving the mill is in danger of being struck by the sail, so it makes sense for the sail to only approach from one direction, so that workers only had to look that way to see if the sail was approaching. By convention this became counter-clockwise. With sails turning in a counter-clockwise direction the employee only had to look right, which is the majority of people's stronger side.

Later innovations, such as sails that could be tilted to catch a change in wind direction, much like the sails of a ship, meant that they no longer had to have their position adjusted so much, but by that time the counter-clockwise convention had been established.

Wind turbines in Britain turn clockwise. There is no reason for this convention and some types of wind turbine do turn counter-clockwise, but the need for standardisation of parts dictates that a common direction of turn is going to be less expensive to manufacture.

2nd November 2018

Is it illegal to serve snakebite, a mixture of half lager and half cider?

It seems to be an urban myth that the serving of snakebite is, or was, illegal. When I was a teenaged apprentice in the RAF in the 1960s it was certainly rumoured to be the case, but in fact we were never refused service when we ordered it in pubs. With the ready availability of local cider in the area of Somerset where we were based, it was a cheaper drink than a pint of beer or lager.

It is alleged that in 2001, in the Old Bell Tavern in Harrogate, Bill Clinton was told that he couldn't have a pint of snakebite as it was illegal to serve it. Former President Clinton had been a Rhodes Scholar at Oxford University, so it is possible that he had developed a taste for the drink while studying there in the late 60s.

During the First World War strict measures were introduced to reduce alcohol consumption amongst factory workers, including limiting the strength of beer. It is possible that banning the sale of snakebite, which is a much stronger mix, may have been introduced at that time as a temporary measure.

In practical terms it would be difficult to ban the sale of snakebite, as it would still be possible for the customer to buy a half pint of cider and a half pint of lager and mix them himself.

Traditional, snake bite is ¾ cider and ¼ lager or bitter, not half and half. In the 1970s some pubs used to add blackcurrant cordial to give it a more appealing colour, especially as some locally brewed cider could be quite cloudy.

It is possible that some pubs ban the sale of snakebite because it is mainly drunk by young people and its greater alcoholic strength can lead quickly to bad behaviour. However, this would be a matter of prejudice, not legality.

5th November 2018

In the TV series Foyle's War, why does a police officer have a military driver?

In the TV series Foyle's War, the character of Samantha Stewart is played by Honeysuckle Weeks. She is a member of the Mechanised Transport Corps (MTC) and, although she wears a military style uniform, she is not actually in the military.

The Motorised Transport Training Corps (MTTC) was founded in 1939 as a volunteer service. It was formally recognised by the Ministry of Transport in 1940 and renamed the MTC. It provided drivers for a variety of government departments and agencies. The drivers were also given some basic mechanical training so that they could carry out running repairs on their vehicles. This is the plot point that allows Samantha Stewart to drive for Inspector Foyle as he carries out his duties.

Before the war an officer of Foyle's rank would have been provided with a male police driver, but with so many men volunteering for army service, he has been provided with Sam instead. However, there is no record of an MTC driver ever having been attached to the police, so we have to allow writer Anthony Horowitz an element of poetic licence.

The Police were a "reserved occupation" until 1942 and so were not liable for conscription and couldn't volunteer for military service, but conscription across the country resulted in shortages of police recruits. For this reason women were allowed to join the police force in greater numbers than they had before the war.

As well as driving Foyle around, members of the MTC drove ambulances in France and also served in Syria, Egypt and Palestine. Several were awarded civilian honours for their work. General Dwight D Eisenhour was driven by an MTC driver, Kay Summersby, while based in Britain, who subsequently claimed she'd had an affair with him.

**Is the word cancer (illness) associated with cancer (star sign)?
When was the disease identified?**

The two meanings of the word are indeed related, but the connection is the word for 'crab'.

This is a Latin word meaning "crab or creeping ulcer", originating in Ancient Greek as karkinos, said to have been used because the swollen veins around certain tumours resembled the limbs of a crab. It seems to have first appeared in writing around 400 BC.

The identification of cancer as a specific disease goes back as far as 1,600 BC to the oldest known victims of bone cancer, mummified remains found in Egypt. The oldest victim of breast cancer was also found in Egypt, dating from about 1,500 BC. As a disease it was known to be incurable and was treated with palliative care. Surface tumours were removed surgically, as they are today. Up until the 17th century the term 'canker' was used to describe the disease we now call cancer, but was then replaced by the word we use today. Canker is still used today in relation to certain animal and plant diseases.

Real understanding of the causes and nature of cancer didn't emerge until the mid twentieth century. Watson and Crick's work on genes and how they might become mutated advised bio-chemists about how body chemistry could change to form cancerous growths. Their work was recognised by the award of a Nobel Prize for Medicine in 1962.

The naming of zodiac signs started around 1,000 BC with Ancient Babylonians, but it is again the Ancient Greeks that seem to have given the name of Cancer, meaning crab, to the astrological sign. They relate it to the story of Heracles. The Goddess Hera sent a crab to snap at Heracles's toes as he fought the Hydra. Heracles killed the crab by stamping on it, but as a reward for its service Hera gave the crab a place amongst the stars.

The star sign of Cancer is the faintest of the 13 astrological signs. Unlike most of the constellations, which are made up of small numbers of stars, connected together by lines like a child's game of join-the-dots, Cancer is made up of 121 unrelated stars, which appear in several clusters. These clusters might be analogous to the appearance of cancerous growths.

13th November 2018

Are there any moles in Ireland?

Of all the mammals native to the British Isle, the only one not found in Ireland is the mole.

When the last Ice Age ended, about 11,700 years ago, warm blooded animals migrated northwards, following the retreating ice as new grass grew. The first to arrive would have been grazing animals; bison, deer and various species of wild sheep and cattle. They were then followed by predators such as bears and wolves. The mole, being a burrowing animal, took longer to migrate.

Firstly, the moles had to wait for their cold-blooded food (earthworms) to move with them and secondly their method of travel, by burrowing, made their northwards progress much slower. Because worms are cold-blooded, they rely on the temperature of the soil to warm them up and provide them with the energy to move. It would have taken several hundred years after the end of the Ice Age for the soil to reach the right temperature throughout the year for worms to survive.

As the ice receded the Irish Sea was formed by the breaking of the land bridge that connected Northern Ireland to Scotland, preventing the migration of any species that wasn't already in Ireland. The low-lying land further south flooded to form the sea itself. At the same time the Isle of Man was also formed from what would have been a mountain range before the flooding.

For the same reason there are also no snakes or lizards in Ireland, as they are cold blooded creatures that rely on the Sun's warmth to give them energy. Like the worms, they also had to wait for temperatures to increase, which warm blooded creatures didn't need. Their thick hides and fur kept them warm.

There are also no moles on the Isle of Man, The isles of Scilly and the Scottish Islands, for the same reasons.

Once the land bridge between England and France was broken, around 6,000 BC, no new animals arrived in the British Isle unless they swam or came in boats. The most common of these is the rabbit, which was introduced in the 12th century when they were bred for their meat. All the wild rabbits that exist are descended from animals that escaped from captivity. Even the hare, which is considered to be a native species, was introduced by the Romans about 2,000 years ago.

When DIY chain B&Q opened its first store in Dublin they stocked mole traps, which attracted some mockery in the Irish press.

16th November 2018

"I disapprove of what you say, but I will defend to the death your right to say it." Is attributed to Voltaire. Is this correct?

Although this quote is usually attributed to Voltaire, it is quite possible that he never actually said it. It is not recorded in any of his works, but is quoted as a verbal utterance.

A book entitled "The Friends of Voltaire" was published in 1906 by S G Tallentyre, which was the pen name of Evelyn Beatrice Hall. In it she uses the quote to describe Voltaire's reaction to the burning of a book by French philosopher, Claude-Adrien Helvétius, entitled "De l'spirit" (On the Mind). The book was written in 1758 and Voltaire didn't have a very high opinion of it but disapproved of its burning by the French authorities.

In 1919 Hall published a collection of Voltaire's letters in which the phrase was included again. She didn't state that the quote was from any of the letters but did declare it to be a "Voltairean Principle". This means that because of Voltaire's belief in free speech it is the sort of thing he might have, could have, would have or even should have said, but may not have actually said. In this later work there was a minor variation of the quote, the inclusion of the word "wholly", as in "I wholly disapprove of what you say," which hadn't appeared in the 1906 book.

With no written citation for Voltaire originating the quote it is possible that it was only attributed to him, on the basis that the concept of free speech was one of Voltaire's major beliefs.

Born Francois-Marie Alouet, Voltaire was his adopted name. He was born on 21st November 1694 in Paris and died on 30th March 1778. His father was a lawyer and his mother was from minor French nobility. He was educated at the College Louis le Grande, a Jesuit run school.

Voltaire was very outspoken on the subject of religion and free speech and advocated the separation of Church and State. He spent a short period imprisoned in the Bastille because of some of his views and it was after his release in 1718 that he adopted his pen name. His best known work was "Candide, ou l'Optimisme" (Candide, or Optimism), a novella in which he concludes that it is up to the people to create a new future. He uses the term "it is up to us to cultivate our garden".

Amongst other well-known quotes attributed to Voltaire is "If God did not exist it would be necessary to invent him." This is more than just a suggestion that religion is manmade rather than divine and would have been considered a considerable blasphemy.

The town of Ferney, where Voltaire lived for the last 20 years of his life, was renamed Ferney-Voltaire in his honour.

28th November 2018

Does the Lake District have only one genuine lake?

In terms of the topographic definition of a lake, all of the large areas of water in the Lake District are lakes. However, in terms of their naming, only one is a lake. Lakes are always filled with fresh water, unlike Scottish lochs which may be salty when connected to the sea, or fresh when landlocked. It is also why the Dead Sea, while appearing to be a large lake because it is landlocked, is technically a sea because it is salty; similarly the Aral and Caspian seas. A lake may be fed or drained by a stream or river, but it doesn't have to be. Many lakes are kept full by rainwater draining from the surrounding hills and are emptied by natural evaporation.

You might think that the single lake in the Lake District is Lake Windermere, which actually uses 'lake' in its title, but it is in fact Bassenthwaite.

There are 16 large areas of water in the Lake District, but the other 15 are either meres (eg. Windermere, Buttermere) or "waters" (eg. Ullswater, Coniston Water).

The difference between a mere and a lake is that in comparison to its length and breadth, a mere's depth is quite shallow. Typically it will have no "thermocline", which is an invisible barrier below which the temperature of the water is significantly cooler than the water above. This means that while the surface of a lake may be warmed by the sun, the deeper levels have a constant, colder temperature. A mere on the other hand, because of its shallowness, may be warmed all the way to the bottom.

There isn't any topographic difference between a lake and a "water" and the naming of the waters in the Lake District is more to do with Anglo Saxon English. They called all lakes "*wasser*", which translates as "water". Interestingly, in Germany, where the Saxons originated, most lakes are called "see" (Wannsee, Bodensee) though they do also use "*meer*".

Thwaite refers to a large area of land cleared for cultivation and is Norse in origin, so in terms of Bassenthwaite the name refers to the larger locality, rather than just the lake itself. Because it hasn't been called a "mere" or a "water" it is a lake by default.

Is it true that Pope Gregory IX hated cats so much that he had thousands of them exterminated?

Pope Gregory IX did seem to have something of a thing about cats and I think it would be true to say that he wasn't a "cat person".

Gregory IX held the papacy from 1227 to 1241. During this time he read the testimonies of many people who had been tortured by Conrad of Marburg, the Papal inquisitor, and there appeared to be a strong connection in their "evidence" between Satan and cats.

On 13th June 1233 Gregory issued the *Vox in Rama*, a Papal proclamation, that declared that Satan appeared to people in the form of a cat and may, at times, be embodied in cats. Based on this the people of 13th century Europe went on a cat killing spree. The small populations of black cats in some countries would suggest that they were particularly associated with Satan and subject to special attention.

This is also the origin of the association between witches and cats that is still a popular image today. In the late 1400s, during the height of witch hunting in Europe, Pope Innocent VIII officially excommunicated the entire species because of their association with witches.

However, it wasn't just in Europe that cats suffered a bad press. At her Coronation, Queen Elizabeth I had an effigy burnt. It was stuffed with cats. Cats were also associated with the Black Death, probably because of their close association with people and it was thought they carried the disease.

In fact, the killing of cats may have contributed to the spread of the Black Death and other plagues, as they should have been predating on the rats that actually carried such diseases.

Even today the Vatican isn't too keen on animals. Pope Frances listed them as the fifth item on which people spend too much money. The first four are food, clothing, medicine and make-up.

3rd December 2018

Was Belgium created to prevent a European War?

Prior to the Napoleonic wars, the area we now know as Belgium had never existed as a nation in its own right, at least not since Roman times. It had been ruled and fought over by its neighbours the French, Dutch and German principalities and even countries further afield. From 1556 to 1714 it had been ruled by Spain and was known as the Spanish Netherlands.

As part of the Congress of Vienna that brought the Napoleonic Wars to an end in 1815, it was decided that the Southern Netherlands should be brought together with the Northern Netherlands to form one nation under the rule of the Dutch King William I.

While William ruled in a relatively benevolent manner, the Catholics of the Southern Netherlands felt they were being side-lined by their protestant neighbours to the north and there was also a strong liberal bourgeoisie growing in and around Brussels that demanded greater freedoms.

In 1828 the underlying resentments bubbled over into open revolution. Brussels was seized and the King's troops, sent to restore order, were evicted. A provisional government was formed and declared independence on 4th October 1830. A National Congress was elected on 3rd November and in February 1831 adopted a constitution that was quite liberal for its day. All this was contrary to the terms of the treaty of the 1815 Congress of Vienna.

On 4th November 1830 a Congress was set up in London to determine the future of the Southern Netherlands, with the British, French, Russians, Austrians and Prussians attending, though not the Belgians themselves. Pragmatism reigned and it was agreed to recognise the new state of Belgium, but under the leadership of a constitutional monarch. Between them France and Britain settled on Leopold I of Saxe-Coburg, widower of Princess Charlotte of Wales, who was endorsed by the other parties.

Officially a state of war existed between Belgium and the Northern Netherlands (Holland) until 1839, but there was no actual fighting. A peace treaty was signed in 1839, which also split off the eastern territory of Luxembourg and assigned it to the Northern Netherlands. Belgium lost the provinces of Limburg, Vlanderen, Zeeuws, French Flanders and Eupen. Luxembourg was split off from the Netherlands as a Grand Duchy in 1890, when William III of the Netherlands and Grand Duke of Luxembourg, died without leaving a male heir. Under the treaty of Vienna his successor, Wilhelmina, couldn't become Grand Duchess, so a distant cousin inherited the title of Grand Duke and established the present day state.

As part of the Congress of London both France and Britain stood as guarantors of Belgian neutrality within Europe. It was this obligation that brought Britain into World War I, when Germany invaded Belgium and Luxembourg in order to bypass the French defences along their own border.

The name of the country derives from the Belgae, a Germanic tribe, who inhabited an area of north west Europe from the River Seine to the River Rhein until the Romans conquered it, starting with Julius Caesar in 53 BC.

6th December 2018

I love the Ian Hunter song Ships that Pass in the Night. What is the origin of this phrase?

This saying implies that people can easily pass each other by without even knowing it, the way sailing ships used to do. It often relates to lovers who come together briefly and then part. It is a more romantic way of saying "short term relationship" or even "one night stand".

In the days of sail the only lighting available aboard ships was candles or oil lanterns. With a lot of tarred rope and sailcloth around to catch fire, this lighting was kept to a minimum. Any lights shining below deck wouldn't be visible, as ships didn't have port holes or windows, except in the Captain's cabin. Above deck, in order to preserve night vision, a single small lantern might be kept lit so that the officer of the watch could see the compass. Even that would be kept screened so that the helmsman's night vision wasn't ruined. With so little light and without a moon, ships were barely visible to each other at night, which was made worse by fog or bad weather.

It was common for ships to pass each other without either knowing that the other was there. Even when the crew of ships did see each other, they often didn't exchange the normal maritime greetings that might have been used during daylight, such as an exchange of names and destinations. This exchange was normal so that if a ship went missing, as they frequently did, there would be some news of where they had last been seen.

The first law that required ships to fit running lights was passed in the USA in 1838 and was aimed at steamboats operating on rivers. This law wasn't extended to sailing vessels until 1849. The first international maritime conference to discuss the subject wasn't convened until 1890 and its decisions weren't universally adopted until 1897.

This required ships to fit a white masthead light, a green light facing forward to indicate the ship's starboard side and a similar red light on the port side. This massively increased visibility and reduced night time collisions.

With the advent of electric generators, deck lighting became common, as did electric lighting below decks. The installation of port holes added to the amount of light that was visible from ships. From World War II onwards ships began to have radar fitted and it is now virtually impossible for ships not to see each other either visually or electronically. Most ships also now use transponders, similar to those fitted to aircraft, which are triggered by radar signals and transmit details of the ship's identity, speed and course. Notwithstanding this, there are still occasional collisions at night, but these are usually caused by the crew not keeping an adequate watch.

8th December 2018

How long would it take space ships from Earth to reach each of the seven stars that make up the Plough constellation?

The fastest space craft ever launched is the Parker Solar Probe, which was sent into space on 11th August 2018. Its mission is to explore the outer reaches of the Sun before burning up. Using its maximum speed of approximately 450,000 mph it is possible to provide a theoretical answer based on current space technology.

The distance from Earth to a star is calculated in terms of light years, the distance a photon of light can travel in one year, which is approximately 6 trillion miles. It would take approximately 13 million years for a spaceship travelling at 450,000 mph to travel one light year.

The 7 stars that make up the Plough (or Big Dipper) are varying distances from the Earth. In order of distance they are Megrez (58 light years), Mizar (78), Mirak (79), Alioth (81), Phecda (84), Alkaid (101) and Dubhe (128).

So, in approximate terms, it would take 754 million years to reach Megrez and 1,664 million years to reach Dubhe, using current space technology. It would take 54.6 million years just to reach our closest star, Proxima Centauri.

Based on Einstein's theory of relativity it is not thought to be possible for a space craft to travel at the speed of light, but assuming that it was possible for one to travel at just less than the speed of light it would still take in excess of 4.2 years to reach Proxima Centauri and over 58 years to reach Megrez. It took 36 years for the Voyager space probe to reach the edge of our solar system, following its launch in 1977.

8th December 2018

Is it true that Colby Landrum was paid compensation by the US Government for injuries received while witnessing a UFO near

Dayton, Texas, on December 29, 1980, when he was seven years old?

This is one of the best known UFO sightings ever recorded, mainly because of the legal action which followed.

On 29th December 1980, Betty Cash, Vickie Landrum and Vickie's 7 year old grandson Colby, were travelling home by car when, at about 9 pm, they allege they saw a bright light above some trees. Shortly afterwards they saw the light much closer and say that it came from a bright, diamond shaped object hovering above the treetops and expelling flame from its base.

Cash, who was driving, stopped the car and they got out to examine the object. Vickie Landrum, a committed Christian, interpreted the object as being the Second Coming of Jesus and told her grandson that the object wouldn't hurt them. However, Colby became scared and returned to the car and Vickie returned with him to provide comfort.

The metal of the car became very hot and Cash said she had to use her coat to prevent her hand being burnt. Vickie Landrum's hand left an imprint on the vinyl of the dashboard which she said had been softened by the heat. Although other witnesses claim the hand print was visible for weeks after the event, no photographs of it were taken. Cash and Landrum then claimed that the bright object was surrounded by 23 helicopters, some of which were identified as twin rotor CH-47 Chinooks. A police officer and his wife later reported seeing a flight of 12 helicopters of the CH-47 type in the area. The object was then reported to have moved higher into the sky and then moved away with the helicopters accompanying it.

After returning home all three witnesses claimed to suffer similar health problems, which included vomiting, nausea, a burning sensation in their eyes and sunburn. They blamed this on their encounter with the object. At one point Cash's symptoms became so bad she had to visit a hospital. A claim was later made in an HBO documentary entitled "UFOs: What's Going On?" that Cash had suffered a cancer caused by the UFO. Their symptoms are consistent with exposure to high levels of radiation, but that level of exposure would also lead to death, which didn't happen in this case. Medical experts concluded that exposure to some sort of chemical, possibly in aerosol form, was more likely.

Following consultation with their state Senators and Air Force officials from nearby Bergstrom Airforce base, Cash and Landrum launched a legal action against the US Government, claiming $20 million for their distress. Military officials testified that the Airforce didn't have any large, diamond shaped aircraft. On 21st August a District Court judge dismissed the case due to a lack of evidence that any of the helicopters that were seen belonged to the US Government.

Betty Cash died in 1998 aged 71 and Vickie Landrum died in 2007, just before her 84th birthday.

14th December 2018

Could Spitfires shoot down V1 rockets in mid-flight?

Theoretically, any fighter aircraft was capable of shooting down a V1 flying bomb, as it was just an unmanned drone propelled by a rocket motor. It was all dependent on the angle of attack. The cruising speed of the V1 flying bombs was only 400 mph. For most aircraft, starting from behind the V1 meant that it was difficult to catch up, but if they approached from the front or side, on an intercept course, then a burst of machine gun or cannon fire could be directed into the rocket.

The Supermarine Spitfires used by the RAF in the Battle of Britain had a top speed of around 370 mph, but later marks could achieve higher speeds. In 1943, during a test programme, test pilot Eric Brown achieved a speed of 606 mph by diving his aircraft at an angle of forty five degrees. Specially tuned Mk XIV Spitfires were introduced for use against the V1.

The first successful intercept of a V1 was carried out on the night of 14/15 June 1944, with a De Havilland Mosquito of 605 Sqn, flown by Flt Lt J G Musgrave.

The record for successful attempts to shoot down a V1 was set by the Hawker Tempest aircraft, though these were only available in limited numbers during the early part of the V1 bombing campaign. However, just 30 aircraft of this type were responsible for bringing down 638 V1s, with 3 Sqn alone bringing down 305 of them.

The Mosquito was the next most successful aircraft against the V1, accounting for 623, Spitfire Mk XIVs accounted for 303 and P-51 Mustangs 232.

One technique for bringing bring down a V1 was to fly a Tempest alongside, then use the increased airflow above its wing to lift the stubby wing of the V1, which would destabilise the navigation gyroscope and send the V1 into a terminal dive. Sixteen flying bombs were brought down this way.

In all, 8,025 V1 flying bombs were launched against the UK. Of those, 4,261 were intercepted and brought down. This was the equivalent to 14,000 tons of bombs, compared to 61,000 tons dropped during the Blitz of 1940. The RAF and its allies launched 44,700 sorties to counter the V1, losing 351 aircraft in the process. Most of these losses were bombers targeting the V1 factories or the sites from where they were launched.

The V1 threat was ended when the Allied advance through France and Belgium meant that they were withdrawn out of range of the UK. The last attack took place on 29th March 1945 when a V1 landed on Datchworth, Hertfordshire. The British Army cross the River Rhein 2 days later.

The V2 rocket, introduced on 8th September 1944, was a ballistic missile which flew in a high arc, reaching an altitude of 55 miles, before descending onto its target almost vertically. There was no airborne countermeasure for this as the approach of the missile couldn't be detected until it was too late. 1,402 V2s were launched against England, the majority of which were aimed at London.

About 1,700 were launched against targets in Europe, the majority being targeted on Antwerp.

The principle method for countering the V2, other than bombing factories and launch sites, was to send messages via a double agent reporting that the rockets were overshooting London by 20 miles. The course corrections that were made resulted in many missiles falling short and landing in Essex, Kent and the Thames estuary. However, even with that counter measure, 1,900 Londoners were killed by V2 rocket strikes.

18th December 2018

Why are more men than women killed by lightning strikes?

This question could be paraphrased as 'why are more farmers than marketing consultants killed by lightning strikes?' As lightning is a purely outdoor phenomenon, it will kill more people who spend most of their time outdoors than those who spend most of their time indoors. Indoor workers have to be very unlucky to be killed by lightning during their brief forays outside.

In terms of employment there is a significant disparity between the number of men who work in outdoor occupations than women. Occupations such as farming, forestry, construction etc are all male dominated. With this sort of gender imbalance it is therefore statistically more likely that a man working outdoors will be struck by lightning because, by comparison, there are so few women.

This statistical likelihood also applies in terms of outdoor sports and leisure activities. While women do participate in these, they are fewer in number than men and therefore less likely to be struck by lightning. In the case of golf, for example, where a number of participants are killed by lightning every year, the gender imbalance is stark. Only 14% of golfers are women, therefore men are, statistically, in far more danger from lightning while on the golf course. In the USA alone about 85 golfers are killed by lightning each year and another 275 injured, of which the vast majority are male.

Lightning strikes the earth somewhere in the world about 100 time per second. About 24,000 people are killed worldwide by lightning each year and another 240,000 are injured. By comparison only 399 people died as a result of aircraft accidents during 2017, making flying statistically far safer than working outdoors on the ground, especially for men.

29th December 2018

Is it true that a U-Boat was sunk by a toilet malfunction?

While it is true to say that a malfunctioning toilet led to a U boat being sunk, it was only the start of a chain of events, not the actual cause of the sinking.

U-1206 was a type VIIC boat and had been launched on 20th December 1943. It became operational in July 1944, entering patrol service with the 11th U Boat Flotilla.

On 11th April 1945 U-1206 left Kristiansand (Norway) to carry out a patrol in the North Sea. On 14th April, while cruising at a depth of 200 ft, 9 miles off the port of Peterhead in Scotland, a leak from a malfunctioning toilet caused large amounts of water to flood into the boat. This water entered the battery compartments, mixed with battery acid and caused a release of poisonous chlorine gas.

Faced with this contamination, the U Boat's commander, Gunter Fritze, ordered the boat to the surface where it was spotted by RAF maritime patrol aircraft and bombed. The damage to U-1206 was sufficient to prevent it from submerging again, so the Captain ordered the boat to be scuttled. One man died in the bombing attack, 3 more drowned in the heavy seas and 46 were taken prisoner.

During survey work in the BP Forties off-shore oil field in the 1970s, the wreck of U-1206 was discovered lying in 230 ft of water. A study of the hull suggested that the boat may have suffered damage from a pre-existing wreck located in the same area, which caused the toilet to malfunction.

23rd January 2019

What is the origin of Tarot cards?

Although it is claimed that Tarot cards arrived in Europe from the East as early as 1375, the first known reference to them is in 1440 when the Duke of Milan ordered several decks of 'triumph' cards for a special occasion.

The claims for the original cards were that they were imported from Islamic countries. This seems unlikely as the Muslim religion has very deep mistrust of fortune telling, associating it with the Devil. It is more likely that the cards are a European creation.

It is probable that the first Tarot cards were created as a game, not dissimilar to those using ordinary playing cards. The game of 'triumph' was similar to what we now call bridge. There were 4 suits and 13 cards in each suit, just as with normal playing cards, but the original tarot cards had an additional 22 picture cards that didn't belong to any suit. In 'triumph', 21 of the additional symbol cards were used as trump cards. By 1530 the game had spread across Europe with people referring to the game as 'tarocchi', the Italian word for Tarot.

There is no evidence of Tarot having any connection to the occult until around 1730, when followers of the occult seem to have discovered the cards. They ascribed more meaning to the symbol cards than just their use as trumps. Since then the cards have moved away from being used as a pastime and have become part of the occult lexicon.

As with most fortune telling, it is the answers to the questions that the fortune teller asks that reveals more than the tool that the fortune teller is using. From the customer's answers the fortune teller is able to establish what the customer wants to know and can tailor their fortune telling accordingly. If the predictions come true, the fortune teller is credited with clairvoyant ability. If they don't come true, the customer usually blames their self for not following the fortune teller's advice – or comes to realise that fortune telling is a lot of nonsense.

Author's note: When this answer was published, the last paragraph was omitted. It may be unconnected, but at that time the *Answers to Correspondent's Questions* feature was on the opposite page to that where the newspaper printed its horoscopes.

25th January 2019

What is the difference between amoral and immoral?

This is the difference between the values a person holds and the behaviour they exhibit.

A person who is amoral does not share the moral values of the society that they live in, therefore they do not adhere to those values in their behaviour. If I don't regard society's moral standards as being valid, I would be seen as being amoral regardless of my actual behaviour.

Someone whose behaviour doesn't conform to the moral standards of their society is considered to be immoral. They may or may not be amoral, but their behaviour shows a lack of regard for morality.

Morality is an artificial construct built upon values that are shared by a society, rather than what is laid down by law. Many of these values are based on the concept of the "seven deadly sins". The behaviour of a lot of people today might be considered immoral compared to what was considered to be moral in the 19th century, which shows that our moral values have shifted over time.

Some of those changes in morality have been reflected in changes to the law, while others were never governed by law in the first place. The decision to become a vegan, for example, is a moral choice, not one enforced by law and the number of people taking that decision shows how our ideas about morality are still changing. As society as a whole does not yet subscribe to veganism, an eater of meat cannot be considered to be amoral, though vegans may think the eating of meat is immoral.

6th February 2019

Has a circle always had 360 degrees?

The short answer to this is yes. It was the ancient Egyptians that first divided a circle into 360 degrees, but they inherited their numerical system from Mesopotamia.

Mesopotamia was the area along the Tigris and Euphrates rivers that makes up a sizeable portion of modern day Iraq. This has always been regarded as the cradle of civilisation. It was where farming began, written languages were first used and mathematics started. The best known ancient civilisation from Mesopotamia is the Babylonians and their first use of mathematics dates from somewhere between the 5th Millennium BC and the 3rd Millennium BC.

The Babylonian system of mathematics is built on a base of 60. We use a base of 10. From this base we get 60 seconds in a minute and 60 minutes in an hour. If we didn't have this base of 60, the design of clock faces would be very different. With a circular clock face of 360 degrees, each minute division equals 6 degrees exactly and it all started with the Babylonians.

The Babylonians had a love of the number 60, perhaps because it can be divided in so many ways: by 1, 2, 3, 4, 5, 6, 10, 12, 15, 20 and 30. That makes it extremely useful when it comes to manipulating it. They passed this love of the number 60 to the Ancient Egyptians, who found that it worked really well when it came to dividing up a circle. Divide a circle into 6 and you end up, effectively, with 6 equilateral triangles, each with 3 internal angles of 60 degrees. A right angle, very important for building pyramids and temples, is a quarter of a circle and is a nice convenient 90 degrees.

360 is a very useful number when it comes to division, because it divides easily by 1, 2, 3, 4, 5, 6, 8, 12 and a few more whole numbers.

The first calendars, also created by the Egyptians, had 360 day years, though this became problematical as the Earth's orbit isn't so accommodating. However, the accuracy was only 5.5 days off, which isn't bad when you haven't actually got any clocks with which to measure time. Even today we find the 360 day calendar useful, as we generally regard 90 days as equalling 3 months or a quarter of a year, even though it is actually 91.375 days.

Following the French Revolution, they invented a metric circle along with their system of metric weights and measures, with 100 degrees representing a right angle. Each degree was called a 'gradion' or 'grad'. It never caught on anywhere other than in France, where their artillery used it.

In engineering, circles are sometimes measured using radians. A radian is an arc of a circle equal in length to its radius, giving a circumference of $2\pi r$, where the r stands for radian rather than radius. However, radians and their fractions are very difficult to work out in your head, which is why most non-engineers use degrees.

7th February 2019

Are certain constellations only visible in the Southern hemisphere and vice-vera?

It is true that many constellations that are visible in the Southern Hemisphere are not visible in the Northern Hemisphere and vice versa. However, in some latitudes closer to the equator, some constellations from the opposite hemisphere can be viewed. It all depends on how far from the equator the observer is standing.

The Pole Star is not visible from the Southern Hemisphere and the Southern Cross is not visible from the Northern Hemisphere, but this would not be true for an observer standing at the equator, who would probably be able to see both, though very low on the horizon.

Constellations that are only visible in the northern or southern hemisphere are called circumpolar, because they circle the relevant polar region of the sky. They also never rise or set, regardless of the season, so are visible all year round in that hemisphere.

Circumpolar constellations in the Northern Hemisphere include: Cassiopeia, Draco and The Plough (or Ursa Major). In the Southern Hemisphere they include Carina, Centaurus and Crux.

The "tilt" of the Earth's axis means that some constellations are visible in both hemispheres at different times of the year. These include Sagittarius and Scorpio which are only visible in the north during the winter. These constellations are said to "rise" and "set" with the seasons.

Constellations that remain visible throughout the year at the equator include Aquarius and Virgo and will be visible from most of the populated areas of both hemispheres, though they get lower on the horizon the further north or south you travel. As you approach the equator from the south, some northern constellations will start to come into view, such as Hercules and Cygnus, while approaching from the other direction you will eventually be able to see Corvus and Pavo.

Constellations are a human construct, an imagining of relationships between stars. In reality the stars have no relationship to each other. In terms of astronomy they only serve as a useful shorthand with which to indicate the position of celestial objects. Most of the names of our northern constellations were given by Middle Eastern astrologers during the pre-Christian era. Most of the names of the southern constellations either use a name applied by the native population or were given by observers from the 16th century or later, when the Europeans first started to venture into southern latitudes.

Who was the first person to use the term 'nuclear winter'?

This is a comparatively new term to enter the English language.

Although scientists had been studying the effects of nuclear explosions on climate for many years, it wasn't until Carl Sagan and four others published the TTAPS study in the magazine "Science" in December 1983 that the term "Nuclear Winter" was first used. This group can be considered the originators of the term, though it is generally attributed, rightly or wrongly, to Carl Sagan alone.

The other four co-authors of the paper were Richard P Turco, Owen Toon, Thomas P Ackerman and James B Pollack. The paper got its informal title from the initials of their surnames.

The paper studied the theoretical atmospheric consequences of a global nuclear war, resulting from the ejection of large quantities of soot, ash, dust and debris into the atmosphere. Similar effects resulting from either volcanic action or a major meteor/asteroid strike are possible explanations for the sudden extinction of the dinosaurs.

The publishing of this study resulted in increased interest in the subject and launched several other studies which used more complex models of the atmosphere and climate. However, there were efforts to discredit the work of the TTAPS group and other researchers, mainly from those who were in favour of strong nuclear defences. A physicist by the name of Edward Teller, who went on to work on Ronald Regan's Strategic Defence Initiative, otherwise known as 'Star Wars'. Both men were called to give evidence before the US Congress.

In 1990 a paper entitled "Climate and Smoke: An Appraisal of Nuclear Winter," also published by the TTAPS group, gave a much more detailed description of the effects that a major nuclear war would have on climate. These included predictions of temperature reductions, light level reductions and rainfall reductions. These predictions were made for the first 3 months after a nuclear exchange and also for 1 to 3 years afterwards.

Perhaps the most damaging long term effect would be the depletion of the ozone layer by up to 70%, which would result in a massive increase in UV radiation. This is known to be responsible for skin cancers, damage to eyes and it depresses the working of the human immune system.

19ᵗʰ March 2019

What are the origins of the Illuminati?

The Illuminati were an historical group of intellectuals and academics whose importance was far less significant than the mythology that surrounds them would suggest. Dan Brown cites them in his books *The Da Vinci Code* and *Angels and Demons*, though he has them founded in the lifetime of Galileo, almost 200 years earlier than their actual founding.

Modern mythology has the Illuminati behaving as Machiavellian conspirators, pulling the strings of power from behind the scenes, or as pan dimensional beings snatching people from imminent death and transporting them to the future to maintain the human population.

The original Illuminati were founded as a secret society on 1ˢᵗ May 1776 in Bavaria, at that time an independent state. Adam Weishaupt (1748-1830) was a lay professor at the mainly Jesuit Ingolstadt University. The Jesuits opposed the appointment of non-clerical teaching staff and campaigned against them. Wishing to spread the ideas of "the Enlightenment", which were abhorrent to the Jesuits, Weishaupt established the Illuminati as a secret opposition to the Jesuit staff at the university. Weishaupt recruited four students into his society and they adopted the Owl of Minerva as their symbol. All members used aliases to disguise their membership.

The group soon expanded outside the confines of the university, establishing a branch in Munich and recruiting more influential members. Ritual formed just as much a part of the organisation as the exchange of academic ideas, as the Illuminati tried to establish itself as a rival to the longer established Freemasons. Eventually the Illuminati was granted a warrant to form its own Masonic Lodge, which was called the Theodore of the Good Council, named after the Elector (ruler) of Bavaria. Most existing Illuminati members joined. The new lodge quickly grew big enough to split from its mother lodge in Frankfurt and was able to start establishing new lodges of its own, under the umbrella of Freemasonry.

Internal dissent and the misbehaviour, both political and social, of members of the Theodores (as they were also known) led to the decline and eventual disbandment of their lodge. The government of Bavaria banned secret societies, which included the Illuminati and they ceased to exist in 1785.

However, rumours persisted that the Illuminati were still in existence, but hidden. Two separate books by 18th century authors John Robison and Augustin Barruell stated that the Illuminati were behind the French Revolution (1789), which would have fitted with the organisation's political ideals. The two books made their way across the Atlantic to the newly founded United States of America and it is likely that these were the folk origins by which the story of the Illuminati was maintained and eventually grew in its present forms.

There are various secret societies that have adopted the Illuminati name in some form, or use it as a 'level' within the organisation to which members can aspire. At its most sinister it might be regarded in the same light as the Freemasons, though because it is much smaller it is far less influential.

20th March 2019

How do stealth planes avoid leaving a tell-tale contrail?

The problem of contrails affecting the visibility of aircraft isn't a new one. During World War 2 the pilots of daytime bombing aircraft took great care to reduce the risk of their aircraft producing contrails, as did the pilots of post war spy planes such as the U2 and SR-71.

At the most basic level, contrails are similar to the steam from a kettle. The steam itself is invisible, but becomes visible when it combines with moisture in the air and condenses into its visible form.

There are some factors which are within the control of the aircraft designers, so they can reduce the likelihood of contrails forming. All aircraft expel some water vapour, which combines with water in the air to form contrails. However, observers will note that while some aircraft are producing a contrail some others, of the same make and model, are not. This is because of differences in environmental factors.

The contrail itself is the condensation of water and other chemicals from the aircraft's exhaust and its formation around particles, such as dust or soot. Without dust in the atmosphere, clouds don't form, so one of the main ways to prevent a contrail forming is to have very clean engines that don't produce particles. There is a limit to this capability, however.

The biggest factor in contrail production is moisture in the air. An aircraft flying through humid air is more likely to produce a contrail. By selecting cruising heights where the air is less humid, it is possible to prevent contrails forming. Not all contrails are persistent. If the air is quite dry, the contrail will be short and quickly disperse. The aircraft also produces water vapour and with improved engine designs this can be reduced to help prevent the formation of contrails.

Finally, contrails only form in air with a temperature of -40° C or lower, which on most days is at a height of around 26,000 ft (8 km). If the aircraft flies through warmer air then a contrail won't form. However, the greater the altitude the less moisture there is in the air and therefore less chance of a contrail being produced.

By paying attention to the design of the aircraft the ability to produce contrails can be reduced, as it is with the stealth bomber and fighter aircraft. By paying attention to the environmental factors for any specific flight, the pilot can further reduce the risk of creating contrails. The pilot can still select a high cruising altitude through air colder than -40° C, providing the air isn't humid.

31ˢᵗ March 2019

Mum told me Dixon of Dock Green star Jack Warner taught French actor Maurice Chevalier to speak English while they were POWs during World War 1. Is this true?

Maurice Chevalier was wounded and taken prisoner during World War I and did learn English while in captivity, from British prisoners of war. However, it wasn't from Jack Warner. The camp in which Chevalier was held housed British prisoners mainly from Yorkshire regiments and Chevalier's English accent was reported as being from Leeds. Jack Warner was famously a Londoner.

Jack Warner served as a driver/mechanic in the Royal Flying Corps during World War 1 and there is no record of him having been taken prisoner.

Maurice Chevalier was born in 1888 and at the outbreak of World War 1 he was already in the army doing his national service. He was wounded by shrapnel during the first weeks of the war and was taken prisoner. In 1916 he was released because of the intervention of King Alphonso XIII of Spain, who was related to the Royal families of both Britain and Germany. Alphonso was a great admirer of the French singer Mistinguett (born Jeanne Florentine Bourgeois), who had been in a romantic relationship with Chevalier.

Chevalier had started his musical career in Music Hall and Cabaret. After the First World War he started to work in films as well as theatre. During the Second World War Chevalier remained in France and continued performing at the Casino de Paris. He was accused of being a collaborator. His death at the hands of the Maquis (French Resistance) was wrongly reported in the US military newspaper The Stars and Stripes. After the war Chevalier was acquitted by a French court, but his alleged collaboration continued to cause him problems and he was refused a British visa for several years after the war.

Chevalier died on New Year's Day 1972 at the age of 83.

Jack Warner was born Horace Waters in Poplar, East London in 1895. He was Grammar school educated and trained as a motor mechanic. His employers, the Sizaire-Berwick motor company, sent him to France in 1913 and he drove completed motor car chassis from Paris to the coast so they could be shipped to England for finishing as complete cars. During his time in France he learnt some of the language and, later, an imitation of Maurice Chevalier became part of his Musical Hall act. This may have been the origin of the story that he had taught Chevalier to speak English.

Warner's war service won him the Meritorious Service Medal in 1918. After the war Warner returned to England and worked in the motor trade until he decided to take up performing in his late 30s. He worked in theatre and radio, mainly doing comedy monologues, before making his first film, The Dummy Talks in 1943. Despite it being his film debut, he was given the leading role.

Warner's most famous role was as PC (later Sgt) George Dixon in Dixon of Dock Green. The role was first created for the 1950 film The Blue Lamp. Considering that PC Dixon had been killed in the film, it was a remarkable resurrection, with the series running on the BBC from 1955 to 1976.

Each episode started and finished with George Dixon standing on the police station steps. His trademark opening was accompanied by a salute and the greeting "Good evening all." The show would open with Dixon telling a homely tale of minor crime and punishment in "the manor" of Dock Green, which would then be acted out through the show. He would then depart, cautioning the audience to "Mind how you go".

Jack Warner died of pneumonia in 1981 at the age of 83.

10th April 2019

How did the church of St Andrew-by-the-Wardrobe in the City of London get its name?

The origin of this lies with the origin of the word "wardrobe". The Old English word 'ward' meant a keeper or protector, so the Wardrobe wasn't a piece of furniture, it was a royal appointment, literally the keeper or protector of the monarch's robes. Over time this came to also mean the place where the robes were kept and through that to the piece of furniture we know today.

It wouldn't be unreasonable to assume that the Wardrobe would be somewhere close to where the monarch lived but was, in fact, another building entirely. Any clothes that were needed would be transported to whichever castle or palace the monarch was occupying at the time.

The monarch saw it as their responsibility to clothe not only themselves, but also their spouse, court officials, ambassadors, companions, servants and retainers. For this reason it was necessary to have a place not only where all the clothes could be kept, but also where they could be made, so all the tailors, dressmakers, seamstresses and embroiderers could work without getting under the Royal feet.

With the Royal clothing being made of the finest materials money could buy and having a lot of gold and gem stones involved in its design and manufacture, the robes also had to be well protected, so the Wardrobe resembled a small castle and was guarded as such. The London Wardrobe was called Baynards Castle and was located between Carter Lane and St Andrew's Church, which is how this church got its name.

Edward III established the first Royal wardrobe at Baynards Castle. Previously the monarch's robes had been kept at the Tower of London, but pressure for space to store weapons meant they had to be moved. During the Commonwealth era the Royal wardrobe was used to house orphans, who were evicted after the Restoration.

The building was destroyed by the Great Fire of London in 1666. The Royal Wardrobe subsequently moved to Buckingham Street and then Great Queen Street.

The author C J Sansom makes reference to Baynards Castle in his book, Lamentation, which is set against a backdrop of intrigue at the Court of Henry VIII.

Today the location of the original Wardrobe is remembered by the naming of Wardrobe Terrace and Wardrobe Place just north of Queen Victoria Street and also by Castle Baynard Street to the south. There is a Baynard House, an office block on Queen Victoria Street and, of course, the church of St Andrews-by-the-Wardrobe. A house built on the site of the original Wardrobe bears a blue plaque to mark the location.

The first mention of the Church of St Andrews is in 1170, though the church itself is older. It too was destroyed by the Great Fire of London and was rebuilt by Sir Christopher Wren, though not on the original site.

11th April 2019

Is it true that church bells weren't rung during the Second World War, but that the bells of St Paul's Cathedral were rung on 1st January 1941?

As the ringing of church bells was to be used to signal an invasion, the Defence of the Realm Act (DORA) was passed in 1914 to prevent the ringing, not just of church bells but also bells on public buildings, such as Big Ben. This was a precaution against false alarms. DORA also imposed restrictions on the use of bonfires and other naked lights that might aid an enemy. During World War II the same measures were enacted, as well as more stringent black out precautions.

The use of church bells to signal an invasion was a practical one. With the exception of very remote areas, such as moors and mountain ranges, most churches are within the sound of each other's bells, so if a telephone call to raise the alarm wasn't received in one parish, the sound of the bells in a neighbouring parish would trigger a chain reaction. The civilian population would therefore be alerted to the danger and volunteer groups, such as the Home Guard, Air Raid Precautions (ARP) Wardens, Auxiliary Fire Service etc could report for duty to assist in the defence of the nation.

St Paul's Cathedral was struck by bombs several times during the Blitz (Sep 1940 – May 1941). During the intense bombing between 29th to 31st December 1940, known as the Second Great Fire of London, St Paul's was hit by at least 29 incendiary bombs, suffering significant damage. Churchill himself gave the order that "St Paul's must be saved".

There is no record of the bells of St Paul's being rung in 1941 and given the existing threat of invasion from across the English Channel, it would be very unlikely that an exception would be made at this stage of the war. The bells of St Paul's Cathedral were rung on 25th August 1944 to celebrate the liberation of Paris and, along with the bells of all the other churches in the nation, they were rung to celebrate the end of the war in Europe on VE Day, 8th May 1945.

29th April 2019

Do sniffer dogs that are trained to detect drugs ever get addicted?

There was an urban myth that sniffer dogs are all addicted to drugs, but there are no known instances of it. Chemical addiction only occurs when some of the chemical substance is injected, ingested or inhaled in significant volumes. The active ingredient acts on the brain and over time the brain becomes dependent on the ingredient, craving more and more of it.

Sniffer dogs don't ingest any of the substance, or inhale it in significant volumes, so chemical addiction cannot occur.

Dogs are trained by using play as a teaching method. Initially the dog will be trained to look for a toy and when they retrieve it they are given a small reward. This is known as positive operand conditioning, first identified by scientists such as Ivan Pavlov (1849 – 1936). Using his basic observations, dog trainers have refined the training techniques over the years.

Once the trainer has taught the dog to search on command, the training toy is replaced by training aids that have been contaminated with a very small quantity of the substance that the dog is being trained to find. The training aid will be offered to the dog to smell, before it is concealed while the dog is outside the search area. To prevent the dog from ingesting the substance, it is usually wrapped in plastic, pierced by pin holes. The sensitivity of the dog's nose means that they can smell the substance through the tiniest holes. A dog's nose is so sensitive that it can even identify contraband that has been contaminated by other strong-smelling substances in order to try to mask the scent.

The dog is trained not to pick up the 'find' but to react in some other way, such as sitting and looking at the discovery. They will often whine or bark as well, but that is the dog asking for its reward, which will then be forthcoming in the form of a dog treat. Dogs are capable of learning to identify multiple substances, which means they could identify a drug smuggler and a currency smuggler in the course of the same period of duty.

Animal welfare is a very great concern for agencies using sniffer dogs and they are limited in the number of hours they can work each day, which are less than those of their human handlers. There are very strict rules governing the dogs' standards of kennelling and welfare.

A dog's sense of smell is between 10,000 and 100,000 times more sensitive than ours, depending on breed. The top five breeds in the smelling stakes are the Coonhound (an American hunting dog), Springer Spaniel, Belgian Malinois, Labrador and German Shepherd. Despite their legendary appearance in detective stories, the Bloodhound ranks only tenth. Fred Basset is ninth.

Competitive scent trailing is a growing leisure activity and there are a number of companies that offer training courses for dogs and their owners.

Author's Note: The inclusion of a paragraph on competitive scent training was a nod to my daughter-in-law's business. She had just started to provide training in this as part of her overall dog walking, boarding and training business.

1ˢᵗ May 2019

Did prisons once have treadmills to prevent idleness?

Treadmills weren't used to give prisoners something to do, they were used as a method of making them productive. It was part of the punishment that was handed down known as "hard labour".

During the 19th century prisoners weren't just sent to prison, they were sentenced to penal servitude, which meant what it said; they had to serve. As well as hard labour, prisoners could also be sent to the colonies as indentured labour; a euphemism for slavery.

The treadmills were long wooden cylinders set between two large metal wheels, about 5ft in diameter, within which several prisoners could work at one time. The diameter of the cylinder meant they couldn't walk upright. As the prisoners walked within the cylinder they rotated a drive shaft. The shaft was then connected to whatever machinery needed power, usually a pump for water or a millstone for milling wheat barley or oats.

The Prison Act of 1865 dictated that every prisoner over the age of 16 sentenced to "hard labour" had to spend at least 3 months of his sentence on "labour of the first class", which meant the treadmill or a device known as a crank machine. This was a device like a small paddle wheel of the type used on steam ships. Turning a handle rotated the paddle in a barrel part filled with gravel, which provided resistance to the turning movement. Unlike the treadmill, it served no practical purpose.

In 1895 there were 39 treadmills and 29 cranks in use in British prisons. In 1902 a new Prison Act did away with both devices.

One of the most famous people ever to work on a prison treadmill was Oscar Wilde, who served a 2 year sentence for "gross indecency" in Reading Gaol between 25th May 1895 and 18th May 1897. One of his quotes was "If this is the way Queen Victoria treats her prisoners, she doesn't deserve to have any."

The design of treadmill that was used was introduced into prisons in 1818 by my namesake, Sir William Cubitt (no relation), who was one of a family of great engineers of the day. Amongst his other claims to fame was the construction of the original Crystal Palace in Hyde Park and the building of the South Eastern Railway in Kent, Surrey and Sussex. As well as being a pioneer of railway construction he also built canals, notably the Oxford canal at Rugby and the Shropshire Union canal.

2nd May 2019

Where does the idea of "getting something off your chest" originate?

The origins of the expression "to get something off your chest" go back to medieval times. Nowadays the expression is used to suggest revealing an opinion or feeling which has been suppressed previously. However, in earlier times it was related to refusing to enter a plea in a trial.

When an accused person "stood mute" as the saying was, they could be "pressed" under weights until they entered a plea. If they failed to do so, more weights were added until they were eventually crushed to death. The accused was laid on the ground and the weights were piled on their chest. It was usually a public spectacle, often forming part of public executions. The process was inherited from the French justice system, where it was known as *Peine forte et dure,* literally forceful and harsh punishment.

Normally people didn't refuse to enter a plea, but it was more common in trials for heresy or blasphemy. If the accused thought that what they had said or done was God's wish, then the question of guilt didn't arise so they might refuse to enter a plea. The legal system refused to recognise the right to remain silent and acted to try and force the victim to enter a plea which could be tested by the evidence.

The accused could end the punishment at any time by entering a plea of guilty or not guilty and then standing trial in the normal manner.

So, to get something off your chest was to enter a plea and have the weights removed from your chest.

The Roman Catholic martyr St Margarette Clitherow was pressed to death on 25th March 1586 rather than enter a plea that might incriminate her children. She was accused of harbouring a Catholic priest, which was a criminal offence under Elizabethan law. As a part of the criminal justice system the punishment remained in use until 1772. Its last known use was in 1741.

An additional saying we get from this form of punishment is to "press someone for an answer". This term is often used during interviews with politicians on TV or radio when the politician wishes to avoid answering a tricky question.

22nd May 2019

What are the origins of the word gallivant?

To Gallivant means "to gad about in a showy fashion".

Its origins appear to be in the early 19th century, with the first written citation being in "Songs For The Exile" published in Literary Panorama in 1809:

Young Lobski said to his ugly wife, "I'm off till to-morrow to fish, my life;" Says Mrs. Lobski, "I'm sure you a'nt", But you brute you are going to gallivant."

Although that is its first citation, it is likely to have been in common use before that.

The term 'gad about' owes its origin to the obsolete German word 'gadling', meaning a vagabond. This in turn suggests someone of a disreputable nature.

The actual origins of 'gallivant' are obscure but may come from the French 'gallant' meaning a dashing man of fashion or one who pays courtly attention to women. That itself comes from the old French word 'galer', to make merry.

22nd May 2019

What is the origin of the expression derring-do?

This comes from Middle English and first appears in writing in 1374. It could also be rendered as "daring do", as in to do something daring.

The Middle English version was dorring don, with dorring coming from the verb dorren, meaning to dare.

Geoffrey Chaucer was the first to use the expression in writing, but in its older form. In his TROYLUS AND CRISEYDE HE WRITES "In durring don that longeth to a knight." In modern translation this phrase would mean daring to do what is proper for a knight.

In 1430 John Lydgate used the phrase in *The Chronical of Troy*, writing it as dorrying do, which was misprinted in later versions as derryinge do, which is the version that has carried down to us today.

Tudor poet Edmund Spencer used the same term in several of his works and is probably responsible for its popularisation. It is used in his most famous work, *The Faerie Queen*, written in 1596.

31st May 2019

What are the origins of the phrase 'Gott mit uns', which is so prominent in German heraldry?

The phrase "Gott mit uns", literally "God is with us", was first incorporated into heraldry in the days of the Prussians, dating from

1701. It was later incorporated into the wider German culture and was painted on the helmets German soldiers during the First World War and engraved on their belt buckles during the Second World War.

Its origins date back as far as the late Roman Empire (250 – 450 AD), with the battle cry "Nobiscum Deus", which has the same meaning. Although Emperor Constantine did not become a Christian himself until he converted on his death bed in 312 AD, he had always followed a policy of tolerance towards Christianity. His mother, *Flavia Iulia Helena,* better known as St Helen, was a Christian. From Constantine's day onwards Christian Roman soldiers appear to have used this battle cry.

The phrase "got mi tuns" was commonly used by the Swedes during the 30 Years War (1618 -1648). The first use of the Germanic version was by knights of the Teutonic Order as a password, or watchword, providing a means of recognition between soldiers on the same side. Its first recorded use was in the army of Gustavus Adolphus, who was King of Sweden from 1611 to 1632.

In 1701 Frederick I of Prussia changed his coat of arms as Elector of Brandenburg and the phrase was incorporated into a scroll beneath the new coat of arms. Subsequently the phrase was engraved on to the reverse side of the Prussian Order of the Crown, one of the lower orders of Prussian chivalry. By the time of the unification of Germany, in 1871, the phrase was in use on the Imperial Standard and also on several coins.

Unlike the Wehrmacht, the SS didn't have the phrase on their belt buckles. They had the phrase *Meine Ehre heißt Treue* meaning "my honour is loyalty". The phrase *Gott mit uns* ceased to be used on the belt buckles of the Bundeswehr (post war German army) in 1962 and was replaced by "*Einigkeit und Recht und Freiheit*", meaning "Unity and Justice and Freedom" which is taken from the third verse of the German national anthem.

Where do the stereotypes 'dumb blonde' and 'blondes have more fun' come from?

Blonde hair has been popular in western culture for over a thousand years, especially when coupled with blue eyes. In both the Anglo-Saxon and the Nordic tribes, blond hair was the most common and no doubt it was generally accepted that if you married within the tribe your partner would be blonde and would produce blonde children. This would make blonde women far more popular than women with other hair colouring whose tribal origins would be more dubious.

Taken to the extreme this produced the idea of the Aryan blonde archetype cultivated by the Nazis in Germany.

In more modern times our literature and film has given us the idea of blondes being more attractive. The idea was first made specific in the Anita Loos novel "Gentlemen Prefer Blondes" published in 1925. It follows that if gentlemen prefer blondes, then blondes are going to have more fun. There was also a 1949 stage musical based loosely on the book, which led to a film in 1953. Marylin Monroe played the eponymous blonde in the film.

However, there has actually been some scientific research done on this subject by no less a man than Charles Darwin. He did some research into hair colour and its influence on finding a mate. By analysing the marital status of women admitted to Bristol Royal Infirmary he discovered that 52% of married women were dark haired and only 15% were blonde. Conversely, among the single women, 29% were dark haired and 22% blonde.

Using modern study techniques this information would be rendered meaningless, as it takes no account of instances of dark and blonde hair in the overall population, which could mean that there were more married women with dark hair simply because more women in the Bristol area had dark hair. Darwin abandoned the research because of such difficulties.

The idea that blonde women might be 'dumb' is based on assumptions about women in general. If a woman is seen to be more attractive because of her blonde hair, she is less likely to have to rely on other talents to make her way in the world as she will always be able to find a man to support her. Therefore, a blonde woman doesn't need to be educated or clever.

The roots of this notion go back as far as 1775 when a French courtesan by the name of Rosalie Duthé was satirised in the play *Les Curiosités de la Foire* when she was portrayed as pausing for a long time before speaking, which made her not only appear slow witted but also, literally, dumb.

Alfred Hitchcock preferred to cast blonde women in his films as he believed that audiences would be less likely to be suspicious of them, thereby sustaining the mystery for longer. The 'blonde bombshell' was always a major character type in films, with such notable actors as Jean Harlow, Marlene Dietrich, Marilyn Monroe et al being cast because of their blonde looks. But being a blonde bombshell didn't imply that the woman was dumb, only that she had a devastating impact on men.

Jokes about blondes being dumb are a variation on the ethnic joke which characterise certain sections of society as being stupid. Most nations have an ethnic or regional group about which such jokes are made and 'blonde' jokes are just a sexist version of this.

Scientific research into intelligence has not produced any evidence that blonde women are any less intelligent than women with any other hair colouring.

15th June 2019

Why might a Victorian have proclaimed 'everything's all Sir Garnet' if all was in order?

Like a lot of popular vernacular, this phrase had its origins in the army.

Sir Garnet Wolseley, later Viscount Wolseley, was a distinguished soldier who served in the Crimean War and the Indian Mutiny as well as several other campaigns across the globe. Although not famed for any big battles, he did distinguish himself in many much smaller wars. He followed his personal maxim that if an officer wanted to do well, he should try hard to get himself killed.

As a general, Sir Garnet gained a reputation for efficiency and good order, which led to the coining of the phrase "All Sir Garnett". The first written record of the phrase is in the Harmsworth magazine of 1901. "They're comin' along," he cried to Mackenzie, as the thud of galloping horses was heard in the rear. "If I can only do the Horatius on the bridge business till they gits 'ere, we shall be all Sir Garnet."

The phrase had particular popularity in the trenches of World War I, but started to decline in use after that, though older people still sometimes use it today.

Sir Garnet Wolseley was born in Dublin on 4th June 1833 of Anglo-Irish parentage. His father had been a distinguished soldier in his own right. When his father died in 1840, the family was too poor for him to follow the traditional public-school route for his education and instead he attended a local school.

Forced to leave school at 14 he started working in a surveyor's office before considering a career in, firstly, the church and secondly in the Army. Unable to find a wealthy sponsor to support him in the church or to purchase a commission in the army, he wrote to the Duke of Wellington for assistance and was eventually commissioned with the rank of Ensign in the 12th Regiment of Foot (The Suffolk Regiment, now the Royal Anglian Regiment).

Later in life Sir Garnett opposed the building of a Channel Tunnel, considering it a likely route for an invading army. So successful was he that the idea was dropped and it wasn't resurrected until after World War II.

Sir Garnett Wolseley died from influenza on 25th March 1913 and is buried in the crypt of St Paul's Cathedral.

Why was the British soldier's pudding basin helmet not changed to a more protective version in World War II?

The Brodie helmet, to give it its original name, was patented by John Leopold Brodie in 1915 and was adopted by the British army the same year. In military terms it became the Helmet, steel, Mk 1 and in the USA the M1917 helmet.

The helmet was introduced as a consequence of the rising numbers of head injuries being suffered in the trenches of the western front. Before the introduction of the helmet, the armies had worn a variety of different head gear, but none of it could stop the deadly shrapnel created by artillery bombardments.

The original issue, made in September 1915, was 50 to each battalion. By the middle of 1916 over a million had been issued. There were some deficiencies in the Brodie design which led to some modifications that resulted in it being renamed the Mk 1 helmet.

The main reason for the helmet remaining in service during the inter-war years and into the start of World War II was the cost of replacing it. By the end of World War I, 7.5 million Mk I helmets had been produced, leaving warehouses full of them when the army was demobilised. It seemed sensible to re-use those rather than manufacture a new type. Some modifications were made to the linings and chin strap, but that was all. In 1940 a Mk 2 helmet was issued, but it was only marginally different from the Mk 1. The main difference in design was a broader rim.

The Americans had issued 1.5 million of the British helmets in World War I, but when they decided to manufacture their own in 1919 they also went for a new design, the M1 helmet familiar from so many World War II and Vietnam War films. Although the Brodie style helmet remained in use with some units until 1942.

The Brodie helmet remained in use with British forces until 1944, when a gradual change was made to the Mk III "turtle" helmet, as it was known. These remained in service until 1982, to be replaced by the Mk 6 and then the Mk6A, which were both more dome shaped and were made of Kevlar armour, making them much lighter. The current helmet is the Mk 7, introduced in 2009 and shaped to fit over the earpieces of a soldier's personal radio. The Mk 7 is now in the process of being replaced by the Revision Military Batlskin Cobra Plus helmet.

15th June 2019

What happened to the British tug Empire Folk, featured on the front of the Daily Mail D-Day pull out dated Saturday, June 10th, 1944?

The Empire Folk was one of 21 tugs built specifically for war work. Although the fleet all carried the same style of name, they were built in different shipyards to different patterns, so they weren't identical to each other.

The Empire Folk was built in 1942 By Richard Dunston Ltd of Thorne and was launched on 5th May. She was a "Maple" class tug of 258 tons. She had a length of 92.5 ft, a beam of 20.5 ft and a draught of 8.5 ft. She was powered by a coal fired steam engine manufactured by McKie and Baxter Ltd. of Paisley.

Empire Folk was initially operated by the Pedder & Mylchreest Ltd of London on behalf of the Ministry of Works and Transport. She was assigned to naval duties and served in a number of locations prior to D-Day. In 1944 she was transferred to C Rowbotham and Sons of London. On 6th June she set sail from Portsmouth and was the first tug to arrive off the Normandy beaches. towing LCT 413 (Landing craft tank), which was carrying ammunition. She remained in service in the English Channel and North Sea until the end of the war.

Following the end of World War II, the Empire Folk was retained in Ministry service until 1947 when she was sold to the government of France and was then re-sold to the Chambers of Commerce in

Dieppe, for general harbour duties. In 1950 she as renamed Jean de Bethancourt. In 1965 she was suspended from service because her surveys for seaworthiness were overdue and she was finally sold for scrap in 1967, which was completed in 1970.

Of all the "Empire" tugs one, the Empire Race, was known to be still in service in 1991 with the Italian Navy, having been renamed the Ustica. None are known to be still in existence.

17th June 2019

Why weren't smoke bombs used to cover the Allied assault on D-Day?

There are a number of reasons for the Allies not using smoke to cover the D Day landings, but the main one was the potential for a smoke screen to be counterproductive.

While a smoke screen would have provided cover for the troops as they came into land, it would also have screened them from the view of the support ships.

One of the features of the landings was the use of naval gunfire to target shore defences ahead of the landing craft. If the gunnery officers on board ship couldn't see their targets, they would be unable to direct the gunfire with any accuracy.

In addition, as the landing craft advanced into the smoke screen, they would have been hidden from those same gunnery officers and therefore ran the risk of being hit by their own bombardment. The only way to prevent that would be to cease firing at a set time. This method of controlling artillery fire had proved to be very risky during the First World War and commanders were anxious to use that lesson to prevent 'friendly fire' casualties on D Day.

Finally, there were many beach defences, so called 'hedgehogs', positioned to prevent landing craft from beaching. Teams of military engineers had gone in ahead of the first wave of landing craft to destroy some of those and provide safe channels through which the landing craft could steer. Using smoke would have obscured the clear channels, meaning more landing craft would have suffered damage and been held further offshore, leaving their troops a long struggle to reach the beach through chest high (or deeper) water while under fire from the enemy.

Rehearsals carried out during the spring of 1944 had revealed some of the complications involved in making large scale beach landings and the complications created by using smoke was one of them.

In addition to the above reasons, the weather also had to be taken into account. It required only relatively light winds for any smoke screen to be blown away. It also meant that the smoke bombs would have to be carefully targeted so that the smoke was blown across the front of the advancing force, rather than away from it. Given the stormy weather of early June 1944, the probability was that the smoke would have been useless even if it had been employed.

Smoke was used on a number of occasions during the Second World War, but mainly to cover infantry or tank advances across open country. One of the occasions it was used during a seaborne landing was Operation Archery, 27th December 1941, which was a commando raid on Vaagso in Norway. Smoke bombs were dropped by Hampden bombers ahead of the commandos' landing craft. One of the aircraft was hit by ground fire and its smoke bomb landed in the middle of my father's landing craft, spattering the occupants with burning phosphorous, killing two men and wounding several others, including my father.

20th June 2019

What is the origin of the saying 'below the salt'?

Since the earliest days of humankind it has been known that salt, in moderate quantities, is an essential part of our diet. A lack of salt can cause health problems and even death.

The converse is also true; ingesting too much salt is bad for our health. The sodium in salt is known to have particularly harmful effects if too much is consumed.

However, because of its essential nature and the difficulty in ancient times of extracting it from natural sources, salt was always a valuable commodity. During the Roman era soldiers were sometimes paid in salt because they would have a ready market to sell it at a profit. It is the origin of our word 'salary', from the Latin *salarium*, the root of which is *sal* meaning salt.

From this origin we get two other salt related sayings: 'salt of the earth' meaning to be a valued member of society and 'worth their salt' meaning an employee who performs well.

Because of the value of salt it had considerable social significance. At banquets, the salt cellar was always placed towards the top of the table, the seats occupied by the nobility. In medieval times, the further away you were from the salt cellar, the lower your position in society.

The word 'salt' also meant the container in which it was held, some of which were made of silver or gold and made in elaborate designs. The value of such objects is indicated by a Will written in 1493 that states *"To John Wymer and Margarete his wife a cup and a salt of silver"*. In the phrase 'below the salt' it is likely that it is the container that is referenced, rather than the condiment itself.

One written reference to the social status of salt appears in Ben Johnson's play 'Cynthia's Revels', first performed in 1600. *"His fashion is not to take knowledg of him that is beneath him in Cloaths. He never drinks below the salt."* In other words, don't judge his status on his appearance, judge him on where he sits at the table. However, a slightly earlier source gives a similar meaning. The Virgidemiarum: Six Bookes; first three bookes (London, 1597) written by the Bishop of Norwich, is the passage *"Second, that he do on no default, ever presume to sit above the salt."* In other words 'know your place'. There are a number of other sources from the early 17th century that convey similar meanings.

Do helicopters have ejector seats?

The provision of ejection seats in aircraft is not standard. In general terms they are only used in military fighters and fighter bombers, to allow the crew to escape if their aircraft has been badly damaged in combat. Their utility for escape in non-combat situations is a bonus, which is why they are also fitted in military training aircraft. Since their first use in 1946, it is known that 7,545 lives have been saved by British built Martin Baker ejections seats. The company provides 53% of all the ejection seats that are fitted.

The inclusion of ejector seats in civilian aircraft is not considered viable because their additional weight would add a permanent penalty in the form of increased fuel costs, which is a high price to pay to mitigate a minor risk. To that must also be added the cost of installation and maintenance. Because the seats incorporate highly explosive rockets, they require frequent expert checking to ensure they are safe.

With helicopters there is an added hazard. With the blades of the helicopter rotating at speed above the cabin, it was considered that the only viable way of escaping using an ejector seat would be to fire the seat out sideways. As it is quite feasible that any incident bad enough to cause the crew to eject might also cause the helicopter to rotate around its vertical axis, the risk was that any crew ejecting sideways might be hit by the tail of their own aircraft as it rotated. This isn't a hazard on fixed wing aircraft.

There are two Russian manufactured helicopters that are fitted with ejectors seats, the Kamov KA 50 and its variant, the KA 52. These work by blowing the main rotors off the central drive shaft before the ejector seats fire, which means that there is no overhead hazard to contend with.

There is a 3 phase firing sequence. Phase 1 fires the explosive bolts retaining the rotor blades, allowing them to fly off under centrifugal force, phase 2 removes the cockpit canopy, just as it does in a fixed wing aircraft and phase 3 extracts the seat. The three events happen in such a rapid sequence that they appear to be almost simultaneous to the naked eye.

Strictly speaking the system used in the KA50/52 isn't an ejector seat as the seat itself isn't fitted with rockets. The rocket is mounted above and behind the seat rather than on the seat itself. The rocket is connected to the seat by a lanyard, which pulls the seat out of the aircraft. The parachute is deployed from the rocket, rather than from the seat as it is with Martin Baker systems.

The KA 50 first flew in 1982. It is a low-level attack helicopter currently in service with the Russian and Egyptian air forces. Its low level operations make it particularly vulnerable to attack by shoulder launched missiles, so the ability to eject is a sensible precaution.

The Boeing V-22 Osprey is also fitted with ejector seats. However, it is not strictly speaking a helicopter, it is a fixed wing aircraft with vertical take off and landing capability which is achieved by rotating the engines into the vertical position. In forward flight the engines are in the horizontal position.

28th June 2019

Did Adolf Hitler have an Irish sister-in-law?

Adolf Hitler did have a relative by marriage who was Irish. She was Brigit Elizabeth Hitler, née Dowling, born 3rd July 1891 in Dublin. She would not have been a full sister-in-law, as she was married to Hitler's half-brother.

In 1850 Alois Hitler, then 36, married Anna Glasl-Hörer a wealthy 50 year old woman in poor health. Because of Anna's age, there were no children from the marriage. In 1880 the two separated because of Alois's frequent affairs and he took up with a former female servant in the household, Franziska "Fanni" Matzelsberger.

As a catholic Alois couldn't divorce or remarry under Austrian law, so all his children were illegitimate. With Fanni he had two children, Alois Jnr born in 1882 and Angela born in 1883. Klara

Pölzi's first child with Alois Hitler, Gustav, was born in 1885, suggesting that the relationship with Fanni was over by then.

Klara Pölzi, Hitler's mother, joined the Hitler household as a maid in 1876. She also became Hitler's mistress. From their union they produced six children, only two of which, Adolf (b 1889) and his younger sister Paula (b 1896) survived to adulthood. Paula lived until 1960.

Alois Jnr married his first wife, Bridget Dowling (b 3rd July 1891) after they eloped to London in 1911. The couple had met at the Dublin Horse Show in April 1910, which Bridget had attended with her father William. Alois had claimed to be a wealthy Dublin hotelier, when in fact he was a penniless kitchen porter. As Bridget was under the age of consent, William Dowling threatened to have Alois charged with kidnapping, but relented when Bridget pleaded with him. For a while the couple lived in the Charing Cross area of London.

The couple later took up residence in rented rooms at 102 Upper Stanhope Street in Liverpool's Toxteth area. In 1891 their only child, William Patrick Hitler, was born. Ironically the house was destroyed in a German bombing raid on 10th January 1942.

When Alois Jnr returned to Germany to try to start a business in 1914, the marriage was effectively over. He had become violent and was beating their child. After World War I Alois Jnr sent word that he was dead and he remarried. The ruse was discovered and he was charged with bigamy in 1924. He escaped jail because of Bridget's intervention, but they soon divorced and Bridget set up home in Highgate, London, taking in lodgers to make ends meet.

William Hitler went to America to lecture on his famous uncle and Bridget joined him there in 1939. They set up home on Long Island, New York, under the assumed name of Stuart-Houston. Bridget appears to have become something of a fantasist, claiming in a book that her uncle Adolf had lived with her in Liverpool, that she had introduced him to astrology and it was she who had persuaded Adolf to clip his moustache into its famous shape.

The existence of Bridget Dowling-Hitler hadn't been known until the British and Irish censuses were digitised and released online. She disappears from the Dowling's Denzille Street address in Dublin for the 1911 census and re-emerges as 'Cissie Hitler', living with husband 'Anton' Hitler and son William in Upper Stanhope Street. Bridget Hitler died in the USA on 18th November 1969.

William Hitler served in the United States Navy during World War II, as a Pharmacists Mate. He formally changed his name to Stuart-Houston after the war. Given his infamous ancestry, he strived for anonymity. With wife Phyllis Jean-Jaques he had four sons the eldest of which, born in 1949, was given the middle name of Adolf. William died on 14th July 1987.

9th July 2019

The 12th Century chronicler Gerald of Wales claimed there was a drowned city under Lough Neagh in Ireland. Is there evidence for this?

In his 12th century "Topographia Hibernia" (Topography of Ireland) Gerald of Wales gives an account of a city that was flooded as a punishment for the population's sinfulness. This is reminiscent of the destruction of the Israelites in the flood from which only Noah and his family were saved. The location for the city is given as that of the present Lough Neagh.

An ancient legend was that if someone drew water from a well or spring and left it uncovered, the water would all flood out and inundate the surrounding land. This is what is supposed to have formed Lough Neagh. Gerald then adds to this legend that local fishermen claimed to be able to see flooded buildings beneath the water.

The most obvious hole in this story is that for the flooding to have taken place and not been recorded, it would have had to have predated the arrival of the clergy to Ireland in the 5th century, when buildings in Ireland were constructed mainly from wood and mud which would not have lasted long once under water.

The story was revived in in 1852 by Thomas Moore who used it in a verse in one of his melodies for Erin Remember "ON LOUGH NEAGH'S BANK AS THE FISHERMAN STRAYS, WHEN THE CLEAR, COLD EVE'S DECLINING, HE SEES THE ROUND TOWERS OF OTHER DAYS IN THE WAVE BENEATH HIM SHINING."

More scientifically, Lough Neagh lies in a depression underpinned by bedrock. Water flows in from the rivers Bann, Blackwater and a few other smaller rivers and flows out through the Lower Bann. It was most likely formed about 10,000 years ago by the retreating ice age which scoured away the looser material above the bedrock, leaving the depression to be filled naturally by melted ice and then by the inflows of the rivers. The loch takes its name from Echaid, the son of a King of Munster. The loch is 19 miles at its longest and 9.1 miles at its widest, covering an area of 151 sq miles. It is quite shallow, with an average depth of only 32 ft and a maximum depth of 82 ft.

Another version of the folk tale says that Echaid fell in love with his step mother Ébliu and they ran away together. He was gifted an enchanted horse and told that it would take the two of them wherever they wanted, so long as Echaid didn't let the animal rest. He did let it rest, while it urinated and this created a natural spring which Eacaid capped to prevent it overflowing. The cap wasn't replaced properly, the spring overflowed and the loch was formed, drowning Eacaid and Ébliu. As the two lovers came to be revered as deities in pre-Christian Ireland, it is unsurprising that the story came to be recorded in an altered form.

Gerald of Wales (Giraldus Cwmbranus) (1146 – 1223 approx) was a Norman/Welsh monk and historian. He travelled extensively in Britain and Ireland, recording folk tales and he visited Rome twice. He was a highly respected author of his time and the majority of his writing survived. He had hoped to become Bishop of St Davids, the highest ecclesiastical rank in Wales, but only succeeded in rising as far as Arch Deacon of Brecon. Most of his writing was done after he retired from this post.

13th July 2019

Who was Betsy Ross? Why is her flag controversial?

It is a popular piece of American folk lore that Betsy Ross, an upholsterer from Philadelphia, sewed the first American flag in June 1776. It consisted of a blue rectangle in the top left quarter of the flag, in which there was a circle of 13 white stars, representing the 13 states that made up the British colony of America. The rest of the flag was made up of alternating red and white stripes, 13 in all, again representing the 13 states. Tourists can visit "Betsy Ross's House" and be told the story.

The reason for the controversy is that there is no factual evidence to back it up.

The story goes that a "committee" appointed by Congress visited Betsy to ask her to sew a flag. This would have been an act of treason against the British government, so Betsy Ross would be seen very much to be a hero if she did make the flag. The first of the three committee members was a wealthy businessman who was financing the colonial army, Robert Morris, who was related to Betsy's late husband. The second was Colonel George Ross, Betsy's uncle and a signatory of the Declaration of Independence. The third was General George Washington.

They supposedly showed Betsy a crude sketch of the flag, which she agreed to make. She also suggested a change to the design, using five pointed stars instead of six pointed.

The design of the flag was legitimised by the first "Flag Act" passed by the US Congress on 14th June 1777.

The reason why this story is shaky is that there is no Congressional record of a committee having been set up to design or produce a flag. Secondly, even if there had been. Washington would not have been a member because he wasn't a Congressman.

The story of Betsy Ross making the flag didn't appear until the late 1800s, when it was told by William Canby, Betsy's grandson. Since then it has been taught as part of American history.

While there is no evidence that Betsy Ross did make the flag, it is equally true that there is no evidence that she didn't.

What is known for definite was that Betsy Ross did make flags. A receipt by the Pennsylvania State Navy Board shows that Betsy Ross was paid the sum of £14 (a considerable amount of money) on 29th May 1777 for the making of "ships colours", a term for flags. That could mean anything from the American flag to more mundane signal flags.

Some historians attribute the design of the US flag to Francis Hopkinson, a congressional delegate from New Jersey who tried to claim a sum of money for the design. The claim was refused, but only on the grounds that he wasn't the only person to work on the design.

13th July 2019

What is the origin of the term 'the thin blue line'?

This term is a variation on the pre-existing term, the thin red line, which originated at the Battle of Balaclava (25th October 1854) during the Crimean War.

On 25th October a column of Russian cavalry approximately, 2,500 strong, was advancing on the port of Balaclava which was the British supply base for the expedition. The only force available to stop them was approximately 200 soldiers of the 93rd Foot (Sutherland Highlanders) and approximately 350 Turkish infantry. A unit of about 400 Russian cavalry broke off to attack the Highlanders.

As the Russians advanced, the 93rd's commanding officer, Colin Cambell (3rd Baron Clyde) told his men there could be no retreat and they must stand where they were. He formed his men into two ranks, "the thin red line" as it came to be called, to face the cavalry charge.

The Turks on the flanks broke and fled, but the Highlanders fired three volleys from their rifles, at 600, 300 and 150 yards, causing the Russians to break off their attack just before the Highlanders could fire again at point blank range.

The Times correspondent William H Russel, who witnessed the attack, said he could see nothing between the Highlanders and the enemy but a "thin red streak tipped with a line of steel." This was condensed by the public into the Thin Red Line. It became a symbol of the ability of British army to stand and face an attack against seemingly insurmountable odds.

The phrase the "thin blue line" first appeared in print in 1911 in a poem of that title by Nels Dickman Anderson, but there it alludes to the United States Army who wore blue uniforms until the end of the 19th century.

Its use to describe the police appears much later, probably in the 1950s when there was a TV show produced by the Los Angeles Police Department in which their commander, Bill Parker, used the phrase. Its first use to describe the British police seems to be in The Sunday Times in 1962, reporting on the policing of an anti-nuclear demonstration. It appears again in 1965 to describe the Massachusetts police.

In 1995 there was a BBC TV series called "The Thin Blue Line" written by Ben Elton and starring Rowan Atkinson which featured the police of Gasforth Police Station. It originated from a sketch on Not The Nine O'Clock News. It ran for two series of 7 episodes each.

15th July 2019

Did Uncle Sam supplant Brother Jonathon as America's mascot?

The term Brother Jonathon was first used as a nickname for the Puritan "Roundheads" of the English Civil War ie the supporters of Parliament and Cromwell. From there it migrated to the fledgling states of New England, where a lot of Puritans had established homes. From this personification he became not just a nickname for New Englanders, but for American colonists in general, especially the northerners.

The origins of the name are probably Biblical, taken from the words of David, describing the death of his brother: "I am distressed for thee, my brother Jonathan" (2 Samuel 1:26). It was first used as a term of abuse for the Roundheads by their opponents, the Cavaliers who supported King Charles.

There are some who claim that it originates with Jonathon Trumbull, a colonist responsible for food supply during the American War of Independence. Washington is supposed to have said the words "Let us confer with Brother Jonathon". However, there is no record of either Washington or Trumbull ever having used the term during their lifetimes.

The term was certainly used by New Englanders between 1783 and 1815, when it was often applied to American sailors, who were called Jonathons in much the same way as soldiers were called GIs during World War II.

The term Uncle Sam appears to have emerged during the War of 1812, when the British attacked the city of Washington, taken from the first two initials in USA. The character of Uncle Sam appeared in American newspapers from 1813 to 1815. His style of dress, including the stars and stripes waistcoat and "Anglesea" hat (wider at the top than the bottom), was borrowed from depictions of Brother Jonathon.

A weekly newspaper called Bother Jonathon was first published 1842 in New York and his name was also taken for a humorous magazine called *Yankee Notions, or Whittlings of Jonathan's Jack-Knife*, first published in 1852.

Brother Jonathon started to slip into obscurity when the epithet "Yankee" was applied to the Unionists of the northern states before and during the American Civil War. Afterwards the federal Government started to become known as "Uncle Sam" and Brother Jonathon started to slip from the public memory. The use of Uncle

Sam still mainly refers to the government, or the nation, rather than the people.

It was General George Wolfe, the British Commander in Canada and victor of Quebec, who is credited with the first recorded use of the word "Yankee" to describe American colonials. He is quoted as saying "I can afford you two companies of Yankees, and the more because they are better for ranging and scouting than either work or vigilance", which dates that term to at least 1758. It's origins, however, are unknown. Sources suggesting it is from some Native American derivation have generally been discounted for lack of evidence. It may have its origins in the Dutch names Jan and Kees which were often combined as a double barrelled first name. The Dutch were the first Europeans to colonise Manhattan Island. But that is mainly speculation.

18th July 2019

From where does the idea of 'keeping up with the Joneses' come?

The term "keeping up with the Joneses" implies a degree of envy of the possessions or lifestyles of friends or neighbours, to the point where it becomes competitive or financially damaging as people try to emulate those lifestyles.

The origin of the term is in a comic strip by American artist Arthur (Pop) Momand entitled "Keeping Up With The Joneses", first published in the New York Globe in 1913. It gained rapid popularity, presumably because people identified with it. The comic strip ran until 1938

There were no actual characters in the comic strip called Jones, but it was a common enough name. The "Joneses" therefore became a synonym for neighbours in general.

There may have been a real Jones family to inspire the name of the comic strip. George Frederick Jones was a 19th century real-estate developer in New York. He and his wealthy neighbours built lavish homes for themselves along the Hudson river valley. Given that wealthy people are often competitive, this may have inspired the idea of "keeping up with the Joneses".

However, the term first appears in the comic strip with no known prior use in the lifetime of the Jones family of the Hudson valley, so that story may not be true. Momand suggested the comic strip was inspired by his experiences growing up in Nassau County in New York State.

25th July 2019

What is the practical purpose of the tricorn hat, as worn by Poldark?

The original bicorne and tricorne hats (in Britain the final e is often omitted, but both spellings are correct) were designed for functionality rather than style.

Their origins were with a large circular brimmed hat worn by Spanish soldiers in the Spanish Netherlands in the 17th century, which were intended to keep rain off the face, neck and shoulders of the wearer.

However, the large brim of the hat was something of an inconvenience as it got in the way when the soldier's bayonet tipped musket was held up at the shoulder, the position known as "shoulder arms" in the British army. This usually resulted in the brim of the hat being torn to shreds. To prevent this, the soldiers folded up one side of the hat and pinned it to the crown to keep it out of the way.

When war between France and the Spanish Netherlands broke out in 1667, this style of hat started to be adopted by French soldiers, from where it found its way back to France as a fashion item. This depiction is familiar, with our images of the French musketeers made famous by Alexander Dumas and in various films. From this basic model the tricorne developed, with three sides being pinned to the crown of the hat rather than just a single side. Its development became more of a fashion than a function, resulting in the folded brim of the hat becoming narrower and no longer having any practical use. Technically the sides could be folded back down to perform the original function of rain protection, but they rarely were.

The bicorne hat was also a development from France. There the wide brimmed hat had a wider brim at the rear than at the front, which meant that the brim couldn't be turned up in three equal portions. This was resolved by pinning it only at the front and the rear. Again this development caught on as a fashion, especially when it was made famous by Napoleon Bonaparte, who wore a bicorne hat in many of the paintings depicting him. The bicorne became very popular from about 1790 onwards, worn by French and American military officers and also by British naval officers.

Depending on the design, bicorne hats could be worn "fore-and-aft" or side to side.

In Britain the front of the brim of the hat was known as the "cock" which is the origin of the term a "cocked hat", meaning a bicorne.

The tricorne fell out of favour at the end of the 18th century, though it was only called by that name retrospectively, first appearing in use in the mid 19th century.

Bicorne hats remained in use in Britain right into the middle of the 20th century, when they were worn as part of the ceremonial uniform of very senior military officers and by the governors of British colonies. These were normally worn in the fore-and-aft style. The tricorne hat remains in use today as part of the uniform of the Chelsea Pensioners and the livery of carriage drivers of the Royal Household. They still sometimes form part of the official robes of Lord Mayors in some towns: the Lord Mayor of London still wears one. They also form part of the regalia of town criers.

20th July 2019

If space is a vacuum, why doesn't it suck in the air from Earth's atmosphere?

The short answer to this is "gravity".

It is said that 'nature abhors a vacuum', meaning that if a vacuum exists, nature will try to fill it. This is only partially true. If you create an artificial vacuum, by pumping the air out of a vessel, for example and you then open the vessel up to the atmosphere, the air outside will enter the vessel and equalise the pressure between the inside and the outside. However, both the vessel and the atmosphere are functioning under the same amount of gravitational pull. This is not the case between the Earth and the vacuum of space.

Unlike gravity, a vacuum is not a force. A vacuum is a defined as a lack of matter. Without matter, no force can exist. The molecules that make up our atmosphere are attracted to a genuine force which has been created by matter, which is gravity.

For a similar reason, there is no atmosphere on the Moon. The Moon's gravity is weak compared to Earth's, so the Earth prevented any atmosphere from forming around it by attracting atmospheric molecules. There is a very thin layer of gases around the Moon, held there by the Moon's own gravity, but they are too thin to be regarded as an atmosphere and they certainly wouldn't sustain human life.

To be totally scientifically accurate, space isn't even a vacuum. It is full of matter. There just happens to be a lot of distance between the individual bits of matter, such as planets, asteroids, meteors etc, which we refer to as "space".

If a large enough source of gravity, such as a much bigger planet, were to pass close to Earth, it could draw our atmosphere away from us and towards itself. However, that might be the least of our problems, as it would also attract the molten rock that forms the core of our planet, causing massive earthquakes, volcanos, floods etc.

30th July 2019

Does eating large amounts of soy cause a dip in testosterone levels?

Soy contains isoflavones, which are a group of molecules known as phytoestrogens which are a plant based substance that mimic oestrogen. Oestrogen is a naturally occurring hormone in women, but men also produce it along with testosterone.

It was thought, for a while, that the photoestrogens in soy increased the amount of oestrogen in men at the cost of testosterone. However, a 2010 study conducted by a group of scientists at the University of Minnesota concluded that there is no evidence to support this view.

If you prefer to get your science from the internet, there are sites that still report soy as reducing testosterone levels, however, the evidence for this is lacking. One German report that is quoted as "evidence" actually says "There have been only singular reports on modified gender-related behavior or feminization in humans in consequence of soy consumption." In other words, there is no significant body of evidence.

A more likely reason for reduced levels of testosterone is obesity and the medical problems that are induced by it.

16th August 2019

Was the two-day weekend a 20th century invention?

Not only was this a 20th century innovation, for most people in the UK it didn't come about until the second half of the century.

Up until 1908, employers had followed the guidance of the Book of Genesis which dictated a 6 day working week. Genesis Ch2 v 2 stated that, after creating the Universe, on the 7th day God rested, setting the pattern for a 6 day working week. This is later reinforced by the Ten Commandments, number 4 of which says "Remember the

Sabbath Day, to keep it Holy." For Christianity this led to a 6 day working week, as it did for most religions, a state of affairs that continued until the start of the 20th century

In 1908 a cotton mill in New England introduced a 5 day working week so that their Jewish workers could observe their Sabbath on a Saturday, while the Christians could have Sunday as their day of religious observance. This coincided with a general movement towards reducing working hours and in 1929 the Amalgamated Clothing Workers Union made it their official policy to secure a 5 day working week for their members, the first American union to do so.

In Britain the 5 day week only started to become an aspiration after the end of the Second World War. The tradition of the Saturday afternoon football match came about from the introduction of half day working on a Saturday which had started earlier in the century. The election of a Labour government in 1945 allowed trades unions to campaign more volubly for a 5 day working week. In the 1960s, when banks started to close their doors on a Saturday, this encouraged more companies to do the same.

The UK was ahead of its European neighbours in this respect. Many European countries retained 6 day working into the 1970s, which is why the French use the English term "*le weekend*" as they see us as the inventors.

Shorter working weeks became the basis of competition in the recruitment and retention of staff. Many companies had to reduce working hours just so they could recruit enough employees, especially in areas of skills shortages. At the same time it was recognised that for many businesses it was actually uneconomical to just open up for Saturday morning. It actually saved money to remain closed for the day, while also allowing more time for maintenance.

When I joined the RAF in 1968, Saturday's were still considered working days, though in practice this day was usually spent engaged in "make-work" activities such as inspections, parades, drill and sport. We were "stood down" at lunchtime. Service personnel who wanted to go home for the weekend had to apply for a "48 Hour Pass" and these were strictly rationed.

Legislation eventually caught up with common practice and the introduction of Working Time Regulations (2003/88/EC) placed a cap of 48 hours on the working week and workers had to opt out of the cap. This still allowed for a 6 day working week of 8 hours per day, but in practice this was ancient history in the UK.

Trades unions are still campaigning for shorter working hours and the current goal is a 30 hour working week, probably of 4 days.

29th August 2019

At the end of their song "Letter From America", The Proclaimers sing: 'Lochaber no more.' To what does this refer?

In 1987 the Proclaimers included the song "A Letter From America" on their debut album "This Is The Story". The song was later released as a single, reaching No2 in Ireland and No 3 in the UK. The song reflects Scotland's long history of emigration. The singer asks their departing loved one to send them back a letter from America in order to keep in touch, while also reflecting on the tragedy of so many Scots having to leave their native land.

In the singing of the song the departing loved one is reminded of the many places in Scotland that they will see no more. They depart from Wester Ross to arrive in Nova Scotia which, of course, is in Canada rather than America. About halfway through the song it specifically mentions Lochaber, the county of Sutherland and the isles of Skye and Lewis. These place names are reprised as the song fades out at the end.

Later the towns of Bathgate, Linwood, Methil and Irvine are all named. There is no clear connection between these towns, which span the central lowlands of Scotland from the Ayrshire coast in the west to Fife in the east.

Lochaber isn't a specific town or county but it is a geographic area in the north west of Scotland. It encompasses an area from the

Kyle of Lochalsh in the north, the stretch of water separating Skye from the mainland, to Fort William in the south. For political purposes it makes up six out of the 22 wards of the Ross, Skye and Lochaber corporate management area, which is also part of the Ross, Skye and Lochaber parliamentary constituency.

The departure point of Wester Ross is also a geographic area rather than a town or county, encompassing the towns of Ullapool, Gairloch and Lochcarron.

The origins of the name Lochaber are probably Pictish or Welsh, with "aber" meaning mouth, so the name would mean "mouth of the loch." Place names including the word "aber" are common in both Wales and Scotland.

The Proclaimers were formed by Charlie and Craig Reid in 1983, following various experiments with punk bands. The album "This is the Story" went gold in the UK, while their best known hit "I'm Gonna Be (500 miles)" appeared on their second album "Sunshine on Leith". Surprisingly, it only reached No 11 in the UK charts. The Proclaimers are still recording and touring.

30th August 2019

Why do so many football stadiums have a kop stand?

This harks back to the Battle of Spion Kop, which took place in 1900 during the Second Boer War. A kop is the colloquial name for a hill in South Africa.

The first reference to a 'kop' at a British football stadium was made in 1904 about the Woolwich Arsenal's Manor Road ground. A local newspaper reporter likened the silhouette of spectators standing on an earth bank to the soldiers ranked on Spion Kop. This analogy was repeated in the Liverpool Echo in 1906, giving Liverpool Football Club the name of the most famous Kop stand.

The idea of a bank of spectators being called a kop caught on and spread to many other football grounds.

The Battle of Spion Kop took place on 23rd/24th January 1900, on a hill 38 km to the south west of Ladysmith in Natal Province, South Africa.

Attempting to relieve the besieged town of Ladysmith, General Sir Redvers Buller had to cross the Tugela River in the face of well dug in Boer irregulars. Although the Boers were outnumbered, they were equipped with modern Mauser rifles and artillery. Buller launched a two pronged attack across the river. The objective of the force of General Warren, some 11,000 infantry and 2,200 cavalry, was to capture the 430 m high Spion Kop, which dominated the Boer line.

Attacking on the night of 23rd January, Buller's force quickly evicted a Boer picket and began to dig in. However, as dawn broke they discovered that they weren't on the top of the hill, but were only about half way up. Above them, well dug in, was a strong Boer force. The trenches that the British had dug during the night were inadequate to protect them. A force of 3,000 Boers began to attack the British from below, while artillery shells rained down at a rate of about ten rounds per minute.

Following a day of fierce fighting in hot, arid conditions, the British eventually captured the peak of the kop at around 5 pm. Casualties had been high with 243 British killed, several of them senior officers and 1,200 wounded. The Boers lost 68 dead and 267 wounded. Despite their victory, the British withdrew from the kop during the night of 24th January, leaving it in the hands of a small force of Boers. The reason for the withdrawal was given was a lack of water and ammunition. Buller withdrew his force back across the Tugela. Notwithstanding that, the Boers were unable to take advantage and Ladysmith was relieved four weeks later.

Winston Churchill was a war correspondent at the time, as well as being commissioned in the South African Light Horse. He acted as a courier during the battle, as well as providing many of the first hand reports of the fighting for the London newspapers.

26th September

Were sprats once so abundant off the east coast of England that they were ploughed into fields as fertiliser?

The use of fish as a fertiliser has been a common practice since at least 800 AD, when the Norwegians were known to use herring as a fertiliser. Sprats are known by many names, including the popular restaurant version: whitebait.

The North Sea was a great producer of the European sprat (*Sprattus sprattus*), which was part of the staple diet of the populations of the countries that have a North Sea or Baltic coastline. They were fished in such quantities that there was usually a surplus, Any fish not sold at market would be sold off to famers as fertiliser, but this was true of many common types of fish.

Sprats are still popular in northern Europe, where they are sold fresh, canned or smoked. The fish is also still popular in the Mediterranean and is still widely fished in the Baltic and Black seas.

Waste products of fish were turned into fishmeal for use as fertiliser and this included sprats that were too small to be saleable as food. In Britain sprats as a food cooked at home have fallen out of fashion, making their fishing unprofitable for all but the restaurant market. They have been replaced in agriculture by chemical fertilisers, though fishmeal fertilisers are available on the market for those who prefer an organic option. However, not all brands of fishmeal are purely organic.

Like many species of fish, sprats are subject to quota controls under the EU's common fisheries policy.

Is there evidence that one of the Titanic's coal bunkers was on fire days before she struck an iceberg?

Fires in the coal bunkers on steam ships weren't unusual. Coal dust has the ability to combust when exposed to a spark, which is why fire was a common danger in coal mines. Coal dust has also been known to combust spontaneously.

There was little air inside the bunkers so if there was a fire it would burn very slowly and the bunkers were made of steel, so the problem was contained. The bunkers were gravity fed, with the coal being extracted at the bottom to feed the furnaces. Eventually the coal below the fire would be consumed, exposing the burning layer and the stokers would just transfer the already burning coal into the furnaces.

If a fire in a coal bunker was threatening to become a danger, there was a standard procedure for dealing with it. The unburnt coal below the fire was moved to another bunker, exposing the burning coal which was then fed into the furnace in the normal manner. A fire hose could also be directed onto the burning coal from above, if necessary.

If there was a fire in one of the Titanic's coal bunkers it would not have been seen as a major concern and it would not have prevented the ship from sailing. If the fire was severe it would have been detected, as the heat would have been conducted through the steel bulkheads and would have been felt by crew members.

The coal bunkers extended through several deck levels and the bulkheads were exposed in several places, where the heat would have been detected. To affect the structural integrity of the ship, the bulkheads would have to have been glowing red to have caused any feeling of alarm. The paint on the bulkheads would have started to burn well before that point was reached.

In 2011 author David H Smith put forward the idea that the Titanic had been weakened by a fire in a coal bunker, in his book

"The Titanic's Mummy". He suggested that the fire had been burning for up to 10 days before the ship set sail. This claim was explored in a Channel 4 TV documentary entitled "Titanic: The New Evidence".

The only "evidence" of a fire Smith was able to cite was a dark mark on the exterior of the hull, in the region of one of the coal bunkers. The mark is detectable in photos taken at the time. The cause of the mark, Smith concludes, must have been fire in the coal bunker.

Most experts agree that Smith's findings aren't supported by any known facts and that a fire in a coal bunker, by itself, wouldn't be the cause of the Titanic's structural failures after it hit the fateful iceberg.

The inrushing water when the ship hit the iceberg would have extinguished any fire so, you know, swings and roundabouts.

9th October 2019

What is the origin of the girl's name Brenda?

Brenda is often thought to be the feminine form of the Irish saint's name Brendan (Brénainn in Irish), but linguistically this would not be the case.

The name Brenda is actually thought to be of Nordic origin with the name Brandr, meaning both flame and sword. This is where we get the word 'brand' meaning a burning bit of wood or a mark made by burning the skin. It arrived on British shores as a male name in the 8th century with the Norse colonisation of the Orkney and Shetland islands.

It is likely that a mishearing of the name Brandr resulted in it being heard as Brenda and was converted to a female name over time. Until the 19th century the name wasn't common outside of the northern isles, where the Nordic traditions were strongest.

The first recorded use of Brenda in the south is in Wales. It appears in the 12th century legend of Madoc, a tale that features the purported son of Owain Gwynedd and his wife, a Nordic Princess by the name of Brenda. This tale therefore supports the idea of a Nordic origin for the name.

In his 1823 novel "The Pirate", set in Orkney, Sir Walter Scott names his heroin Brenda and it is likely that this use popularised the name outside of Scotland.

There have been many famous Brendas. In the world of music there was Brenda Lee and Crystal Gayle was born Brenda Gayle Webb. In acting there is Irish actor Brenda Fricker, famous for her role as Megan Roach in Casualty and Brenda Blethyn, best known these days for her role as Vera. Brendas around the world have also made names for themselves in business, politics and the sciences.

Brenda as a name reached its peak of popularity in the 1940s, when it was in the top 20. In 2018 Brenda failed to make it into the top 100 names for new born baby girls.

15th October 2019

Was St Patrick, patron Saint of Ireland, born in Scotland?

There is no evidence that St Patrick was Scottish, but he may have visited Scotland during his ministry. Equally, there is no real evidence of where he was born.

The life of St Patrick is known through just 2 written works; the *Confessio*, which is a spiritual autobiography and his Letter to Coroticus, which was a denunciation of the way the British treated Irish Christians. Patrick's birthplace is thought to be a place called Bannavem Taburniae in Latin, but it can't be located on any contemporary maps.

St Patrick was born to a Romanised British family. His father was an official in the church, possibly a deacon. As Roman rule and Christianity didn't extend far into Scotland at this time, this would seem to suggest no Scottish family connections. Given the short sea journey from Northern Ireland to Scotland, Scottish birth can't be ruled out, but his family's religion would suggest otherwise.

Alternative birthplaces might include Somerset, Cheshire, Lancashire and Cumbria, to give them their modern names. All were raided by the Irish. Patrick's ministry undoubtedly started in central Ireland; the generally accepted location is Wicklow, south of modern Dublin, suggesting he had travelled by sea from further south.

At the age of 16 Patrick was kidnapped by Irish raiders and made a slave. The legend of Patrick suggests he was captured in Wales. There is no written evidence for this, though Wales was a Christian country by this time, especially in those areas of greatest Roman influence. On the other hand, it is thought that he was put to work in Antrim, which might suggest he had been captured in Scotland, only 21 miles away across the sea.

Patrick was already a Christian, in name, at the time of his capture and relied heavily on his faith to comfort him during the 8 years he was working for his captors as a herdsman. His *Confessio* states that "I did not, indeed, know the true God", suggesting he wasn't a true believer at the time of his capture, but became one during that time.

Following a dream that a boat was waiting to take him home, Patrick escaped and managed to get on board a boat that took him back to Britain. He was briefly recaptured before being reunited with his family.

Patrick is said to have had a dream which encouraged him to return to Ireland to take his Christian faith to the pagan tribes. Reluctant at first to heed the call, he did eventually travel to Ireland to undertake the ministry which earned him his fame. He was under constant threat of martyrdom from pagans who saw his teaching as a threat.

Patrick is also credited with taking Christianity to the Picts, a Scottish tribe and to the Anglo-Saxons who were starting their invasion of England at this time. His connection to the Picts may be where the suggestion of Scottish birth comes from.

It isn't known for certain when Patrick was born, but it is generally accepted that his ministry took place in the latter half of the 5th century. In his Letter to Coroticus, Patrick refers to the Franks (a Germanic tribe invading Roman Gaul and which would give France its name) as "still heathen" which must have been written between 451, when the invasion started and 496, when the Franks were baptised en-masse.

Contrary to popular legend, Patrick was not the first to take the Christian message to Ireland. It is thought to have arrived at the end of the 4th century with missionaries such as Palladus. He was a Bishop from Britain sent by Pope Celestine, but his name never gets a mention outside of the history books. An Irish academic, T.F. O'Rahilly suggests a "Two Patricks" theory, whereby some of Palladus's missionary work was attributed to Patrick in order to boost his reputation.

18th October 2019

Was Pontius Pilate born in Scotland?

It is highly unlikely that Marcus Pontius Pilatus, to give him his full name, was born anywhere other than Rome or one of its more secure provinces. Other than what appears in the Bible, so little is known about Pilate that it is impossible to say where he was born, but Scotland seems one of the most unlikely locations. There are a number of reasons for this.

Julius Caesar attempted full scale invasions of Britain in 55 and 54 BC, but both failed and got no further than the River Medway in Kent. It wasn't until 49 AD that an invasion was successful, and the Romans were able to start colonising the island they called Britain. As the Romans advanced further north, cross border trade would have started with the Scots, but it would have been very dangerous for Romans to travel north of the border.

It took until around AD 70 before the Romans attempted to invade northern England and Scotland. When Pilate was born isn't known, but for him to have been Prefect (not governor) of Judea during the ministry of Jesus, it would have had to predate the Roman invasion of Britain by several decades. Estimates for Pilate's term in office in Judea are between 26 and 36 AD.

A second reason is that it was rare for Romans to take their wives with them on campaign or on official duties into conquered territories that were less than stable. Roman wives generally stayed at home to raise their children in safety and groom them for their duties in adult life. This actually casts doubt on the biblical story of Pilate's wife intervening on behalf of Jesus, as Judea was a dangerous province at that time and it is unlikely that Pilate would have taken his wife there. For Pilate's mother, if she were Roman, to have travelled to Scotland prior to a successful Roman invasion would be unthinkable.

Finally, only Roman citizens could hold high office, which meant that Pilate's father must have been a Roman citizen. Roman citizens of high rank rarely married non-Romans because of the effect it would have on their careers.

For Pilate to have been born in Scotland, therefore, his father would have had to be a very brave but high ranking Roman explorer who travelled all the way to Scotland through hostile lands, then married a Scottish woman before returning to Rome through the same hostile territory with his wife and child. It isn't an impossible scenario, but it is highly unlikely.

Pilate appears to have gained his post of Prefect of Judea through the favour of Sejanus, the Eminence Gris behind Emperor Tiberius. At that time Judea was part of the Roman Province of Syria and only provinces had governors, who came from the senatorial class. Smaller areas within a province, such as Judea, were managed by Prefects. Pilate didn't even live in Jerusalem, as suggested in the Bible. The Roman seat of government in Judea was Caesarea, 70 miles away on the Mediterranean coast. What Pilate was doing in Jerusalem, with his wife, during the most sensitive Jewish religious festival in the calendar and at a time of high political tensions is something for Biblical scholars to explain.

Pilate's earlier history is a matter of speculation. As he was of "equestrian" rank, that would mean that he would have served as an officer in the army, probably as a Tribune (an aid to a general). Equestrians were one grade below Senators in the Roman class system and their position was dependent on their wealth initially and then on patronage.

After the death of Jesus, Pilate's relations with the population of Judea were somewhat stormy. Minor rebellions were constant as prophecies of the coming of a Jewish messiah (Jesus was just one of many) were enflaming the population and Pilate was instrumental in putting down those revolts.

Pilate was removed from office on the orders of Vitellius, the Governor of Syria and was recalled to Rome to stand trial for an attack on Samaritans (non-Jews who lived in an area between Galilee and Judea). There is a tradition in the church, stemming from the 4th century AD, that Pilate committed suicide after being recalled to Rome, but there is no evidence of that. He is barely known in Roman history and his name lives on mainly through the Bible.

Author's note: The appearance of two questions relating to the Scottish ancestry of figures associated with Christianity suggests some religious nationalist trying to "hitch their wagon to a star". But maybe that's just my interpretation. When my my letter about Pilate was published, it was heavily edited to remove some of the more contentious elements regarding the Biblical references to Pilate. But, as they said in the American TV series "Dragnet", I'm only interested in the facts, Ma'am.

24th October 2019

Are the Giza pyramids aligned with the stars?

The sides of the 3 pyramids at Giza are aligned almost perfectly with the four cardinal points: north, south, east and west. The accuracy is within 4 degrees of arc, or one fifteenth of one degree, a very small margin of error considering the methods of survey that were available around 4,500 years ago, when the Great Pyramid was built.

The two stars in the 'Big Dipper' constellation (Ursa Major) that point the way to the Pole Star would seem to be the most likely alignment for the north-south axis. The Pole Star itself would be very low on the horizon when viewed from Egypt.

The Ancient Egyptians believed that heaven lay in an area around the Pole Star marked by two stars that they called The Indestructibles. These were Beta Ursa Minoares in the constellation of the Ursa Minor and Mizar in Ursa Major or the Big Dipper. For this reason a vent pointing north was built from the burial chamber to the surface, to allow the Pharaoh to ascend into heaven. The angle of the shaft is such that The Indestructibles are always visible from the bottom.

By calculating the positions of The Indestructibles it is possible to date the building of Khufu's pyramid to 2,480 BC, plus or minus 5 years. This is more accurate than using Egyptian chronology based on its written history, which only has an accuracy of plus or minus 100 years.

In addition to being aligned north to south, the south west corners of the three pyramids are in a perfectly straight line. The north east corner of the smallest pyramid (Menkaure) aligns perfectly with the centre points of the two larger ones (Kufhu, the oldest and largest and Khafre). There are three much smaller pyramids in the shadow of the Khufu pyramid, known as the "Queen's pyramids".

All three pyramids at Giza share the same alignment, as do many others. There are 80 known pyramids in Egypt and there may be others hidden beneath the desert sands. The three pyramids at Giza are the most famous and receive the majority of visitors (14.7 million) each year.

The Ancient Egyptians had a great belief in re-incarnation and their construction of temples and graves reflected this. The east, where the Sun rises, was the side of birth.

For this reason all the major temples in Egypt were built on the eastern side of the River Nile. A Pharaoh, expecting re-birth, would expect to be re-born in a temple and therefore on the eastern bank. The west, where the sun set, was the side of death. All the major grave sites, such as the Valley of the Kings and the pyramids, are on the west side of the Nile.

The temple of Edfu is one of the few exceptions to the building rule. However, that was built during the reign of the Ptolemies, who were Greek. The first Ptolemy was one of Alexander the Great's generals. Therefore he and his descendants were not such great believers in the concept of reincarnation and paid little attention to its finer points.

24th October 2019

Could HHO gas, made from water, solve the energy crisis?

The idea of HHO gas is that water is separated into its three basic atoms, two of hydrogen and one of oxygen and then the three atoms are used for different purposes. The two hydrogen atoms, being combustible, would be used as a fuel.

The origins of the theory behind HHO is in Jules Verne's 1875 book "The Mysterious Island" in which he predicted that, one day, water would be used as a fuel. Since then the search has been on for this Holy Grail of fuels.

About a century later an Australian by the name of Yull Brown claimed to have found a way of separating water using electricity, paving the way for the water powered car. His "discovery" was called HHO gas or Brown's gas.

Since then there has been no working model of any vehicle that uses Brown's process to separate hydrogen from water to power an engine. The theory is simple enough, pass an electrical current through water containing an electrolyte such as salt; the electricity breaks the bonds between the three atoms in a molecule of water, releasing them as a gas. The hydrogen atoms are then fed to a combustion system to burn and provide motive power, much as petrol, diesel and LPG are used.

An American Department of Transportation report published in 2007 stated that a vehicle using the HHO system was feasible as a way of improving the efficiency of diesel power by increasing mileage and reducing emissions. This report was seized upon by proponents of alternative fuels as proof that the theory was valid, urging more research into the fuel.

However, the main issue is that it takes more energy to create the gas than is produced when the fuel is burnt. So, in energy terms you are robbing Peter to pay Paul. While it may be possible to reduce the amount of diesel that is used by the engine, far more energy would be required to produce the electricity used to split up the atoms in the first place.

Until that energy equation can be balanced or, better still, tilted in the other direction, there is no mileage to be gained from HHO fuel. However, were it to become a reality it really would be world changing. Four fifths of the Earth's surface is covered by water, giving us a huge source of energy. By re-combining the unused oxygen atoms with the hydrogen atoms at the point of combustion, water would be created, reducing the amount that is lost during the separation process and therefore making the fuel supply almost inexhaustible.

Author's note: Didja spot the puns in the last paragraph? They were, to my shame, deliberate.

24th October 2019

Would a Lancaster bomber have been capable of carrying either of the atomic bombs dropped on Japan to t end World War II?

The two bombs, called "Little Boy" (Hiroshima) and "Fat Man" (Nagasaki) weren't that big. Little boy was only 28 inches in diameter and ten feet long. It weighed 9,700 lbs and had a nuclear yield of 15 kilotons (kt). Fat Man was 60 inches in diameter and 128 inches in length. It weighed 10,000 lbs and had a yield of 21kt.

With a maximum bomb load of 14,000 lbs, both weapons would have been within the capacity of a Lancaster bomber to carry. It might have needed modifications to the aircraft to mount them, just as it did for the 'Upkeep' bouncing bomb used on the Dambusters raid, which was also 60 inches wide.

What was not possible was for a Lancaster bomber to complete the mission. The distance from Tinian Island, where the mission started from, to Hiroshima was about 1.500 miles, well within the range of a Lancaster. But the Enola Gay, the B29 Super Fortress aircraft that dropped both bombs, had to fly at a height of 31,000 ft in order to prevent it being damaged by the blast of its own bomb. The Lancaster's service ceiling was 21,400 ft with an 'all-up' weight of 63,000 lbs (all-up = aircraft + crew + fuel + weapon load). With a smaller bomb load and less fuel than usual this height could have been increased, but not by enough to reach the necessary safety height.

13th November 2019

Why does the new aircraft carrier, Queen Elizabeth, have two towers on its flight deck? And why is it commanded by a captain and not an admiral or commodore?

The rank of the captain of a Royal Navy ship is determined by the number of personnel employed on board, rather than by the size of the ship itself, although the two usually go hand in hand. A small ship with a small compliment, such as a minesweeper, might be commanded by a Lieutenant, a Frigate by a Lieutenant Commander etc.

An aircraft carrier, however, effectively has two crews, one to operate the ship and a second to operate the aircraft. Without its air complement, HMS Queen Elizabeth didn't have sufficient personnel on board to justify an officer more senior in rank than Captain. However, with the ship's aircraft, aircrew and associated technical personnel now arriving on board, the Captain has been promoted. The ship is now commanded by Commodore Steve Moorhouse.

Commodore is the normal rank for command of a fully operational aircraft carrier in the Royal Navy. However, an Admiral may use the carrier as his flagship when it is forming part of a "battle group", but the Admiral will command the battle group, not the flagship. In much the same way Captain Thomas Hardy commanded HMS Victory, not Admiral Nelson.

The Royal Navy experimented with aircraft carriers with twin islands, as they are called, in the 1920s, as they create a larger deck space on which to store and manoeuvre aircraft. However, it was found that the design caused turbulence and cross winds that affected the lightweight aircraft that were flown at that time. This was especially dangerous during landings, when most of the deck was in use. The design using a single island reduced the problem and that became the standard for aircraft carriers around the world, a tradition that was maintained until the arrival of the two new ships.

Turbulence is not such a problem for the much larger and heavier F35 aircraft, which lands vertically at the rear of the flight deck. This has allowed a break from traditional designs and the re-introduction of twin islands. Twin islands also allow the engine air intakes and funnels to be spaced further apart, which increases the distance permissible between the engines below decks, reducing the risk of them both being damaged by enemy action at the same time.

On board the Queen Elizabeth and its sister ship, Prince of Wales, the ship is commanded from the front island while air operations are commanded from the rear island.

16th November 2019

Why can't Britain ever be hit by a hurricane?

Hurricanes are caused by warm, moist air rising over the sea. High, cool air is sucked downwards to replace the warm air. The cooler air is then warmed and starts to rise, forming a donut shaped ring of rotating air, with the hole in the donut eventually becoming the "eye" of the hurricane. The moisture trapped in this cycle causes huge storm clouds to form.

The rotation of the Earth causes the clouds to start to spin around a central axis, which creates the winds that circulate around the eye of the hurricane. As energy is built up in the storm clouds the rate of spin increases causing the high winds associated with a hurricane. Once the wind speed reaches 64 knots (74 mph or 118 kph) it is officially classed as a hurricane rather than as a tropical storm. The winds in the strongest hurricanes (Strength 5) exceed 157 mph.

The motion of the wind causes the hurricane to start moving from its breeding grounds. In the Atlantic Ocean these are the area between the Colombian coast and West Africa and in the Pacific they are in the area off the western coast of Colombia to as far north as the Mexican border.

The spin of the storm dictates the direction of travel, which is typically a north westerly direction. In the Pacific Ocean this takes hurricanes away from the land, which is why we rarely hear of them, but in the Atlantic they are carried towards the Caribbean Sea and Central America. This is the main reason why Africa, the Iberian Peninsula, France and the UK aren't hit by hurricanes, as they all lie to the North East.

As a hurricane starts to drop its rain, two things happen. The first is that the strength of the wind decreases. The rate of decrease varies, which is why some hurricanes are quickly downgraded to "tropical storm" (wind speed less than 74 mph). The second thing is that the hurricane's direction of travel will change, caused by friction with the land.

Depending on exactly how much land is crossed, the hurricane can veer to the North and even North East. As the hurricane's first land fall is usually in the Caribbean, the amount of land crossed can be quite small around the smaller islands, introducing only small variations in direction of travel. If it hits Hispaniola or Cuba, it's direction will change significantly. The amount of change is also affected by whether all of the hurricane crosses land, or only part of it. Given that hurricanes can be up to 600 miles across, this can introduce considerable variations in direction of travel, which is why weather forecasters aren't always able to say where a hurricane will be 24 hours into the future.

Depending on the amount of direction change, the hurricane can then cross the American coast as far west as Texas, or miss the USA entirely on the eastern side, hitting places such as Bermuda and the Bahamas, as Hurricane Dorian did this year. Many hurricanes blow themselves out at sea, without ever crossing land.

There is an average of 6 officially classified hurricanes each year in the Atlantic Ocean, of which we only ever hear of the ones that cause significant damage and loss of life. "Hurricane Season" lasts from 1st June each year to 30th November. Outside of that window the weather conditions aren't right for a hurricane to form.

Our weather is affected by hurricanes, but not in a major way. As a hurricane travels up the eastern seaboard of the USA it can get caught up by the Jetstream and will be carried across the Atlantic to our shores. However, by the time it reaches us much of its power has been dissipated and it presents itself as a storm, rather than a hurricane. Some of these "hurricanes" are so minor by the time they reach us that we hardly notice them being any different from our normal weather.

One of the great myths to have grown up around hurricanes was the one that weatherman Michael Fish failed to forecast on 15th October 1987. In fact this wasn't actually a hurricane, because it didn't form as one or behave in the same manner. It did, however, contain hurricane force winds. It caused major damage to buildings and brought down thousands of trees. 19 people died as a direct result of it. Michael Fish did forecast high winds, but didn't describe them as a hurricane because meteorologically that would be incorrect.

Was Julius Caesar roundly beaten by the Britons in his second invasion of the British Isles, despite what his own histories say?

Julius Caesar invaded Britain twice, once in 55 BC and again in 54 BC. Both invasions had the potential to be successful, but Caesar was worried about leaving his province of Gaul unprotected during the winter months and withdrew his troops on both occasions, without suffering any significant military defeats.

Britain (as it would become known) was riven with tribal disputes, which assisted Caesar in his planning for his invasions. While it was possible that the British tribes might unite against his armies, the potential was there to divide them and conquer at least the southern part of the island. Caesar's own timidity is all that really prevented him from completing that conquest. Winter crossings of the English Channel were risky, threatening his supply lines. The dangers of newly conquered Gaul rebelling or being invaded by Germanic tribes from the north were ever present.

British tribes had allied themselves with the Gauls (the tribes of the country we now call France) to whom they were kin, which was (partially) his motivation for invading. He wished to prevent such alliances from being formed again. But Britain was also rich in minerals, particularly tin, lead and copper, so there was a lot of money to be made there.

Worried by a possible invasion, the nearest tribes of Britain sent ambassadors to Caesar in Gaul, promising non-alliance if they were left alone. Caesar had an ally in Commius, King of the Atribates tribe (they inhabited what we now call Hampshire, Wiltshire and Sussex) and he used him to try to win over other kings. For his first invasion Caesar is said to have taken 800 ships carrying two legions and cavalry. He seems to have been in a hurry because the legions left most of their baggage and all of their siege artillery behind. Caesar set sail on 23rd August (according to the modern calendar).

Having intended to land at Dover, he found the cliffs defended against him so he looked for a new landing site. Archaeological evidence suggests this may have been Pegwell Bay, near Ramsgate. The landing was opposed but the skilful use of slingers and archers drove the Britons back, allowing a beachhead to be secured. The cavalry had been delayed at sea so weren't available to pursue the retreating Britons and capitalise on the victory.

Caesar was taken by surprise by the strong British tides, which caused many of his ships to be damaged and prevented the cavalry from landing. This meant that Caesar was unable to consolidate his beachhead and any significant distance inland. The Britons attacked again, twice, but were driven off both times. After negotiating for tribute to be paid and hostages to be handed over by the cowed Britons, Caesar withdrew to Gaul for the winter. In order to save face, he classified the adventure as a reconnaissance in his reports, rather than as an invasion.

The second invasion, the following year, went better as Caesar took 5 legions with him. Fighting some battles along the way, notably at the River Stour in Kent, he reached the Thames at its first viable crossing point (near Brentford, London) but found the northern bank held against him by Cassivellaunus, king of the Trinovantes tribe from what we now call Essex, Middlesex and Hertfordshire. Some accounts state that a "war elephant", carrying slingers and archers, was used against the defenders and routed them. Whether this is true or not can't be verified. If so, it would have been the first time such an animal would have been seen on our shores and one wouldn't be seen here again until 1255 AD.

Following this defeat, the Trinovantes sent ambassadors to Caesar offering tribute, hostages and food. Five other tribes surrendered completely. Technically Caesar had negotiated a peace treaty which would have allowed his soldiers to remain in Britain, but with unrest growing in Gaul, the province for which Caesar was governor and therefore his primary responsibility, Caesar decided once again to withdraw from Britain. He didn't leave a single soldier behind to maintain Rome's claim to the islands and he never returned.

Britain would remain independent until 49 AD when 4 legions, under Senator Aulus Plautius, would mount a successful invasion, turning Britain into a Roman colony for a further four centuries.

However, Caesar wasn't defeated in battle and there don't appear to be any contemporary accounts to suggest that he was. His reputation as a soldier was boosted by his successes in Gaul and, to some extent, in Britain which propelled him through the Roman hierarchy until he was able to seize power and make himself effective dictator, the act that led to his assassination.

26th November 2019

Is there any record of what Jesus did between childhood and his late 20s?

Of the 4 gospels, only that of Luke mentions Jesus in the years between his birth and his baptism. The baptism of Jesus was at the start of His ministry, estimated to be when He was about 30 years of age.

After the birth of Jesus, fearing Herod might kill their son, Mary and Joseph are said to have fled with Him to Egypt (Matthew 2:14). Matthew 2:19-21 reports the return of the Holy Family to Israel, but not Jesus's age at the time.

Luke Chapter 2 refers to Jesus, as a boy, being taken to the Temple in Jerusalem, where Simeon declares Him to be the Messiah. (Luke 2:29-32). The same chapter records that Mary and Joseph took Jesus to Jerusalem every year, to dedicate His life to God. On one occasion they accidentally left Jerusalem without Jesus (a strange thing for devoted parents to do) and discovered he had been left behind in the Temple and was found three days later debating theology with the Temple elders (Luke 2:43-48). These are the only two stories of Jesus as a child.

There is something of a problem with this account. The first thing is that Luke wasn't an apostle. His gospel was written several years after the death of Jesus, so any account of Jesus's life would be regarded as "hearsay" rather than direct observation. Who told Luke the story isn't recorded. The second is that of the four gospel writers, he is the only one to mention these incidents. If the story originated with Mary and Joseph, as could be expected, then the two apostles, Matthew and John, who knew Jesus's parents, haven't recorded the event in their gospels.

As well as the two gospels written after Jesus's death, Mark and Luke, another gospel also contains "hearsay" evidence.

Matthew, who provides the best known account for the birth of Jesus, must have based his gospel solely on what he was told by Mary and Joseph as he wasn't present at the birth. Luke's account can only be the re-telling of the stories of others. The actual witnesses to the birth of Jesus, the shepherds and the wise men, left no physical account of what they saw and neither Matthew nor Luke make any subsequent references to either group. Mark and John don't mention Jesus's birth at all, which is a strange omission considering that John, as an apostle, was at least acquainted with Mary.

This is something of a problem throughout the gospels. No two accounts of events can ever be expected to be identical, but some of the omissions from Matthew and John's gospels suggest that, at times, they were witnessing different events entirely.

Only John tells the story of the raising of Lazarus from the dead, for example (John 11:1-44). Such a momentous event has been left out of the gospel of Matthew. Jesus's seminal speech, the Sermon on the Mount, in which he lays out most of what would become Christian doctrine, is only retold in Matthew's gospel (Matthew 5 – 7). John mentions the gathering of the great host to hear Jesus preach (John 6:1-15), but only refers to the miracle of the loaves and the fishes, not to what Jesus actually said. Matthew, on the other hand, doesn't refer to the feeding of the five thousand. Given its miraculous nature, this is a major omission. Instead, Matthew tells of another miracle, the curing of a man with leprosy (Matthew 8:1-4) which John doesn't mention. John then jumps ahead (John 6:16-21) to that evening, when Jesus walks on water to join the apostles in a boat, which Matthew, who was in the boat, neglects to mention.

If these differing accounts were to be placed in front of a court of law, it must be wondered what a jury would make of the testimony of the two eyewitnesses, as they don't seem to agree on much.

Of the four books of the Bible on which the whole Christian faith is based, two were written by people who weren't witnesses to the events they describe and the other two fail to corroborate each other's accounts of many of the events the authors witnessed.

Author's Note: When the Daily Mail published the answer to this question, they used another Correspondent's answer, restricting it to the account of Jesus at the temple, making no mention of the many anomalies contained in the gospels. I wonder why?

1ˢᵗ Deecmber 2019

Which political party was the first to issue an election manifesto? Were the promises kept?

The word "manifesto" comes from the Latin *manifestum,* meaning clear or conspicuous. Given the language used in some political manifestoes, they may not be described as either.

Manifestoes have been around for a long time, but don't necessarily relate to politics. There have also been spiritual and religious manifestos. A Christian might regard the Sermon on the Mount as a manifesto, as it lays out Christ's promises to his followers.

One of the earliest manifestos on record is the "Baghdad Manifesto" of 1011 AD. It questioned the legitimacy of the ruling Fatimids based on their lineage.

The United States Declaration of Independence (1776) and the French Declaration of the Rights of Man and Citizens (1789) can both be regarded as manifestoes.

The earliest British political example is The Tamworth Manifesto (1834) issued by Sir Robert Peel on which historians believe the current Conservative Party is based.

The manifesto broadly set out ideals of reform for the Conservative Party, in particular the acceptance of the 1832 Reform Act and made promises to review "institutions, civil and ecclesiastical". The basic message of the manifesto was that the Conservatives had to reform in order to survive.

The passing of the Reform Act two years earlier was key to the manifesto. The major plank of the Act was electoral reform which would get rid of "rotten boroughs" in which there were no, or few, voters and which gave the landowner automatic ownership of the seat. In exchange for this, new constituencies were set up based on the population of eligible voters.

The Reform Act also increased suffrage by giving more people the right to vote. However, the right to vote was still based on property/land ownership or amount of rent paid. There was a rental threshold of £50 per year in rural constituencies and £10 per year in cities. Given the legally binding nature of the Act, the Conservative Party had no option but to deliver on its provisions.

Given the vagueness of the other promises, it isn't really possible to say whether or not they were kept. Certainly reform of institutions took place in the country during the 19th century and on into the 20th century, but how much of that would have happened anyway, isn't clear.

The Tamworth Manifesto, named after the town in which it was written, opposed perpetual change, fearing it would create a "climate of agitation". Given the state of modern politics, he may have had a point.

Robert Peel became Prime Minister in December 1834 (no problems with holding a winter lection that year, it seems), lost the election of 1835 and won again in 1841 before losing again in 1846 to the Whig (Liberal) Lord John Russell. Peel is most often remembered as the founder of the police force, to which the public attached his name, calling the police officers "Bobbies".

Today, manifestos have a semi-legal basis. Under the Salisbury Convention, a party winning an election should not have its manifesto promises opposed by the House of Lords following the second and third readings of Bills based on those promises. This convention came into being following Labour's victory in the 1945 general election. At that time Labour held only 16 out of 761 seats in the House of Lords, which meant the Lords could block all of Labour's manifesto promises on the creation of the welfare state. Lord Salisbury, a Conservative peer and Leader of the Conservatives in the Lords, brokered a lasting commitment for the Lords not to block manifesto promises so long as the House of Commons voted in favour of them.

If manifesto promises are now broken, it is down to a lack of political belief in them by the party who made the promise and then won the election, or the cost of implementing them has made them prohibitive.

Author's note: This question was posed just before the General Election of December 2019, when questions were being asked about the affordability of Labour's promises in their election manifesto. Labour lost the election in a spectacular manner, but Brexit may have played a bigger part in that than their manifesto promises.

4th December 2019

We have vitamins A to E and K; why aren't there vitamins F, G, H, I and J?

Our knowledge of vitamins is relatively new in scientific terms. It started in the 1920s with a Polish chemist, working in London, by the name of Casimir Funk. He came up with the notion of "vital amines", which became contracted to "vitamins". Study into this area then flourished.

An amine is derived in nature from ammonia, to which atoms of hydrogen are attached to create organic groups which have nutritional value.

Each vitamin serves a different purpose within our body. Vitamin A helps our immune system to function; Vitamin C helps in the maintenance of blood cells, bone and cartilage, etc.

Vitamins were named alphabetically as they were discovered, which started at A and continued as far as U. Some vitamins had two letters, such as PP. However, it was soon found that mistakes had been made. Firstly, it was discovered that not all vitamins are amines. Some are other chemical compounds.

Then it transpired that Vitamin B wasn't just one vitamin, it was 12. Later it was found that not all 12 B vitamins were essential and so we are left with B1, B2, B3, B6, B7 and B12. Other vitamins were discovered to play no real part in our health and so they were also dropped from the inventory. These were called "ghost vitamins" and account for the missing letters of the alphabet. Vitamin K was named for Koagulante, the Polish word for coagulant, which is its main purpose. It could have been renamed vitamin F to maintain the alphabetical sequence, but wasn't.

There are considerable myths about vitamins. Vitamin C, for example, is consumed in vast quantities to ward off colds and flu, but several scientific studies have shown that it is no more effective in that role than taking nothing at all. The best way to avoid catching colds and flu is to wash the hands after contact with foreign objects, surfaces and other people.

Vitamin supplements are multi-billion pound business, but they are largely a waste of money. Vitamins are extracted from food very late in the digestive process; vitamins B and K as late as the large intestine, also known as the bowel. Supplements in pill or liquid form are broken down in the stomach and extracted early in the small intestine, where they are sent to the liver, which treats them as a waste product and expels them via the kidneys and bladder. All that most vitamin supplements do is provide the user with expensive urine.

The best way to make sure we get enough vitamins is to eat a balanced diet and if that can't be achieved, eat high fibre breakfast cereals which have been fortified with vitamins and minerals. The fibre in those makes an ideal transport system for vitamins because it isn't digested by the body and passes right through us, carrying vitamins to the right place to be extracted by our body.

One vitamin supplement can be helpful. Our main source of vitamin D, essential for good bones and teeth, is sunlight. In winter, taking a vitamin D supplement helps to compensate for our shorter days. But you can also get vitamin D from oily fish – such as salmon, sardines, herring and mackerel, red meat, liver and egg yolks all of which make a supplement unnecessary.

Author's note: Although this answer was published, a lot of the comments made about the efficacy of vitamin supplements were edited out. Given that the Daily Mail attracts considerable advertising revenue from supplement manufacturers, this came as no surprise.

9th December 2019

Gunther Toody and Frances Muldoon had a song written about them, but who were they?

On 17th September 1961 the first episode of a new TV sitcom aired on TV in the USA. It was called "Car 54 Where Are You?". The series ran until 14th April 1963, with 60 episodes.

Gunther Toody and Francis Muldoon were the two hapless police officers who rode in the eponymous car, suffering various disasters each week. The characters were played by actors Joe E Ross and Fred Gwynne respectively.

Because the TV series was made in black and white, the cars used were actually painted in bright red and white, so that they appeared to be in the correct shades of grey for New York Police Department cars of the period.

Although the show only ran for 2 years it won an Emmy. The series was shown in the UK in 1964 and 65. The series was recreated as a film in 1994, but flopped at the Box Office.

Joe E Ross had appeared previously in the Phil Silvers vehicles featuring the character of Sgt Bilko. He had played the part of the timorous Ritzik, who always got himself roped into Bilko's schemes. After Car 54, Ross was better known for voicing cartoons, featuring in "Hong Kong Phooey" and "Help! …It's Hair Bear Bunch." He died in 1982.

Fred Gwynne had started out as a straight actor and appeared in the 1954 film "On The Waterfront" with Marlon Brando. After Car 54 he became much better known as Hermann Munster in the horror spoof sitcom "The Munsters". Having become typecast, however, he returned to the theatre, appearing in several Broadway productions. As well as acting, Gwynne was also a talented painter and illustrator and wrote and illustrated several children's books. Fred Gwynne died in 1993.

9th December 2019

Does the universe have a shape?

The answer is yes, but what that shape is depends on assumptions about other aspects of the nature of the universe.

According to Einstein's General Theory of Relativity, space itself can be curved by mass. Because of this, the shape of the universe is governed by its density, which is one of the two components of mass (the other is volume).

Scientists have calculated the "critical density" of the universe, which is proportional to the square of the "Hubble Constant", which is used in measuring the expansion rate of the universe.

If the actual density of the universe is less than the critical density, there is not enough mass to prevent the expansion of the universe and it will continue to expand forever. This produces a shape like a horse's saddle.

If the actual density of the universe is greater than the critical density, then there is enough mass to stop the expansion of the universe at some point. It will form a spherical shape and once it reaches its maximum point of expansion it will start to contract once again.

If the actual density of the universe is equal to the critical density, in other words it contains exactly enough mass, then it won't curve at all and will be flat, like a pane of glass and is infinite in size.

Some of the current thinking is the universe is flat and therefore infinite, but scientists are unable to view the outer limits because of the speed of light. The universe is thought to be 13.8 billion years old, so scientists can only see objects at distances of 13.8 billion light years or less. By definition, infinity is more than 13.8 billion light years away.

It must be said that scientists are not in agreement with this interpretation of the universe, with some suggestions that it may be rolled up like a scroll or even donut shaped and many scientists believe that it is more balloon like in shape.

12th December 2019

What does short-selling a stock or share mean?

Going "short" is a speculative transaction carried out on stock markets. It relies on the ability to forecast what is going to happen to share prices at some point in the future and acting accordingly.

The difference between a stock and a share is a minor technical one. Stock refers to ownership certificates in general while a share is the ownership certificate of a specific company.

For short selling to work, it depends on a traditional time lag between selling a share and having to deliver up the share certificate to the new owner. On many markets this time lag was up to two weeks

Going "short" means selling shares you don't own, in the hope that you can buy them at a cheaper price in time to deliver them to the buyer, pocketing the difference between sale and purchase prices as profit. Think of it as selling apples you don't have at 20p per apple, because you know that the price of apples is going to drop and you will be able to buy apples at 15p each next week so that you can deliver them. You then make a 5p profit on each apple. It is called "short selling" because at the time of the sale you are short of apples.

In these days of instantaneous computerised stock market transactions, it isn't possible to use the traditional time lags for these speculations. Instead, the person making the gamble will borrow the shares in order to sell them, in the hope of buying them back at a cheaper price and returning them to their original owner.

Most on-line share trading accounts don't permit short selling. It has to be done through a broker, as it is the broker that guarantees the delivery of the shares. Brokers are bound by the motto of the stock market "My word is my bond", meaning they will honour any trade in which they are involved. That, in turn, means they have to trust their clients' integrity and ability to meet any debts that might be incurred. A short seller who gets it wrong could have quite a bill to pay in order to purchase the shares they have already sold.

Short share dealing relies on a thorough knowledge of the companies that are being traded, so that rises and falls in share prices can be predicted with a reasonable degree of accuracy. Not surprisingly, illegal "insider dealing" using information gained from company employees, is sometimes a feature of this sort of trading.

People known to be short sellers are watched like hawks by other traders, as their actions can influence market behaviour. If a short seller is known to be shorting a specific share it can have a downward pressure on the price, even though it isn't justified by the company's performance. Unsurprisingly, short traders are quite voluble about their trading so as to capitalise on this sort of behaviour.

There is also a transaction known as "going long" where people borrow money to buy shares in the expectation that they will rise in price and deliver a profit in time to repay the loan. This is really just a variation of the old stock market gambit of "buy low, sell high".

Who was Tom, the man lending his name to acts of foolery, and what did he do to earn this?

This appears to stem from a jester by the name of Tom Skelton. A synonym for a jester was "fool", so Skelton would have been known as Tom the jester or Tom the fool.

The Pennington family has lived in Muncaster Castle, near Ravenglass in Cumbria, for more than 800 years. Like many in the nobility, they employed a jester to keep them amused. It was they who are supposed to have employed Tom Skelton.

Tom's name may have been passed down to us not because he was funny, but because of a tragedy. Tom's story may have given us another bit of vernacular, the "fool's errand", which also relates to the tragedy.

The story goes that Sir Alan Pennigton's daughter sneaked out to attend a dance, attracting the attention of two village lads, Wild Bill of Whitbeck and Dick, a carpenter's son and servant at Muncaster Castle. The unnamed girl favoured Dick, which caused Wild Bill to tell tales on her to a local knight, who wished to marry the girl.

The knight engaged Tom Skelton to exact revenge against Dick, by beheading the boy with his own axe. Believing Dick had also stolen money from him, Tom became a willing accomplice. He succeeded in Dick's murder and is said to have boasted of it to other servants in the castle.

What became of Skelton isn't recorded, but if his crime was discovered he would have been tried and executed. There is no record of Tom Skelton having stood trial for murder. Certainly, after Tom Skelton, the Pennington family no longer employed a jester.

There are said to be no records of Tom Skelton as he was "just a servant" and of no account. However, that is unlikely. The stewards of all households kept meticulous accounts of employees' wages and other expenditure. Similar sets of accounts are held in most grand homes and are often on display to the public. The lack of any historical evidence such as that suggests the story may be made up.

There is a portrait of Tom Skelton in the collection of the Shakespeare Institute, purchased from the Haigh Hall collection of the Earl of Crawford and Balcarres, which is said to prove Skelton's existence, but that portrait could be of anyone. The painting is titled "Tom Skelton" but the artist is unattributed and the painting is dated between 1620 and 1668.

When Tom Skelton is supposed to have lived is quite vague. Some say around the time of the battle of Bosworth (1485) while other sources place him during the reign of Henry VIII, some fifty years later. A writer by the name of John Brigg tells the tale of Skelton in the Westmorland Gazette and Lonsdale Magazine published in 1895 and places Skelton around 1600, which would mean he was alive at the time of Elizabeth I, but his story doesn't refer to any sources for his tale.

Shakespeare is supposed to have used Skelton as the inspiration for the character of Fool in King Lear. The Pennington family have now revived the post of jester in the form of an annual competition. This year's winner was Martin Soan, a comedian.

16th December 2019

Did an Elizabethan law restrict the colour of clothing depending on rank?

These were the "sumptuary laws" and stem not from Queen Elizabeth but from her father, Henry VIII. The root of the word is the same as for "sumptuous", which we associate with luxurious living.

Sumptuary laws were made on religious grounds to prevent extravagance, usually in food or clothing. English monarchs had a record of trying to limit who could wear what and Henry VIII also introduced laws with this in mind. Generally, they served to keep the poor and middle classes "in their place".

Under Henry's laws, introduced during his first Parliament (1510), The Acts of Apparel prohibited anyone beneath the rank of Knight of the Garter from wearing velvet of crimson or blue. The wearing of velvet of any colour was prohibited below the rank of Knight, except for the sons of judges and some other dignitaries. These are just a few examples of the laws. The acts were extended in 1514, 1515 and 1533 to cover more items of clothing

Amongst other rules was that only the Royal Family could wear "cloth of gold" and only members of their household could use gold thread on their clothing. The laws were graded according to rank, with Dukes having more privileges than Earls and Marquises, for example. Generally, any expensive fabric, such as silk, satin or damask, was forbidden to be worn by the majority of the population, who were limited to wool and linen, both of which had to be died in drab colours

Elizabeth I extended the laws laid down by her father and her sister Mary to include things such as ruffs, hose and the length of swords. These laws travelled across the Atlantic Ocean to the American colonies and there are records of sumptuary laws being passed in Massachusetts as late as 1651.

Enforcement of the sumptuary laws included the confiscation of the garment, which represented considerable wealth, perhaps half a year's wage for most people. Fines were also imposed. The enforcement of sumptuary laws was difficult and as social changes resulted in the laws being ignored they gradually passed into history.

17th December 2019

Has it finally been proven that the chicken came before the egg?

The answer is the opposite, the egg came first.

Birds evolved from dinosaurs, specifically flying dinosaurs such as the Archaeopteryx. Dinosaurs were egg laying, so the egg came before the chicken. At some point two birds that were not quite chickens laid an egg that included the genetic mutation that evolved to become the chicken.

If you were to ask which came first, the dinosaur or the egg, the answer would still have to be the dinosaur or, more likely, some earlier species. Procreation has to take place before the product of that procreation can exist. At some point evolution gave up on cell splitting as a way of procreating certain types of life and produced a genetic mutation that resulted in egg laying.

There is one form of the question which results in the egg being first: "Which came first, the chicken or the chicken egg?" Then the chicken came first, because only a chicken can lay a chicken egg.

19th December 2019

Who invented bitcoin?

Bitcoin is a "crypto" currency created in 2008 by an unknown individual or group of people using the pseudonym Satoshi Nakamoto, which suggests a Japanese origin, but that is speculation. Anyone could be behind that name. Crypto in this sense means that it is protected against replication by encryption systems.

The word first appeared as a website, bitcoin.org, followed in 2009 by a paper proposing a peer-to-peer electronic currency system. The paper was published under the name of Satoshi Nakamoto, inextricably linking the name with the currency.

Bitcoin operates through an autonomous software that "mines" the currency. It consists of about 30,000 lines of code. By using the code, people enter a lottery system to gain control over the 21 million coins that will be released over a 20 year period. Once they own the coins they are free to exchange them or trade them. Bitcoins are held in an electronic "wallet" that only the owner can access.

The popularity of Bitcoin was caused by an American games designer by the name of Hal Finney, who offered to "mine" the first Bitcoins when the software was released in 2013, earning 10 coins from "block 70" of the release. His blogs on the subject started to stimulate interest in the currency, with financial journalists writing about it and speculating on its viability as an alternative currency that is not dependent on any government to back it.

Finney describes his impressions of Satoshi Nakamoto as being a young man of Japanese extraction who was "smart and sincere". But he never met him and his sole dealings with Satoshi Nakamoto appear to be by electronic means. Finney died a year later from natural causes, having never discovered Satoshi Nakamoto's true identity.

Bitcoin is supported by "blockchain" technology that creates accounting ledgers that can't be tampered with. This allows the currency to be traced back to the source code and therefore ensures the currency can't be forged. But given its "virtual" nature, its trading can be the subject of fraud, as no physical currency is ever held to prove it exists.

A currency is only a currency if people treat it as such and can agree its value. The value is created by trading the currency on financial markets. Over time the trading in Bitcoin has created a value for it and there are a number of businesses that now accept it in exchange for goods or services. Whether that is just a fad or is here to stay can't yet be determined as the currency is so new.

For large scale businesses Bitcoin is not a viable means of exchange as its price is subject to widescale fluctuations, which means agreeing a price in Bitcoins today could result in a financial loss when the product is eventually delivered and paid for. Conversely a buyer might have to pay considerably more for goods than they had planned, for the same reason.

At the time of writing the Bitcoin was being traded at £5,428 per coin. Speculation in the currency has resulted in it trading as high as £10,000 and as low as £2,500 this year alone. It is not an investment for the faint hearted.

In 2017 Bitcoin reached its peak of $20,000, or £15,000 at today's exchange rate. Many people lost money by speculating on the price of Bitcoin during that period and it is thought that a single speculator may have been behind the rise in the price, walking away with several million dollars when they cashed in their stake. The losers were the smaller investors who saw the currency as a "one way bet" and lost money when the price dropped. It halved in value over a period of a few days as more and more speculators sold their holdings and took their profits, forcing the price down even further.

Since its inception the Bitcoin has been responsible for the creation of up to 1,600 new crypto currencies, but how many of those are genuine and how many are scams it isn't possible to tell unless you are an expert on blockchain technology. Trading in crypto currencies is not protected by any legal framework or financial compensation schemes, which means that investors are not protected against fraud. Generally, the people who make money from Bitcoin and other crypto currencies are the people who act as brokers for the currency, as they charge a commission on every trade and therefore can't lose when the value of the currency changes.

The fact that once they have been "mined" Bitcoins can't be traced and are international in their nature makes them popular for criminal activity. But the effect of that is to legitimise Bitcoin to some extent. If criminals are willing to trust their ill-gotten gains to it, why shouldn't the rest of us trust it?

Author's Note: The answer to the question was published wasn't mine and omitted all of the detail about the manipulation of Bitcoin prices by unscrupulous traders and the use of the currency by criminals.

20th December 2019

What is the origin of the phrase 'up the spout'?

This term, meaning that something is ruined or lost, gone forever, has its origins in the 19th century with a reference to pawnbrokers. The spout referred to was the device used to send goods that had been pawned to an upper level of the pawnshop for storage. The likelihood of the pawned item ever being redeemed was remote, so its owner tended to consider the item lost and gone forever.

The term is explained by Pierce Egan in his 1821 book "Real Life in London" which means it must have been in common use before that. Pawnbroking was illegal in Britain and even when permitted it was a profession that was looked down upon, being seen as a way to get rid of stolen goods for cash. An 18th century law prohibited publicans from acting as pawnbrokers. However, the Pawnbrokers Licence Law of 1785 allowed a pawnbroker to set up business for £10 in London and £5 elsewhere – a considerable sum of money.

Modern pawnbroking started with an Act of Parliament passed in 1800, which legalised pawnbroking and set maximum interest rates that could be charged, setting them at one and two thirds percent per month or 20% per year. This would suggest an origin for the term "up the spout" of sometime between 1800 and 1821.

The Act was put forward by Lord Eldon (John Scott, created 1st Earl of Eldon in 1821), who would go on to become Lord High Chancellor in 1801. He had admitted to using pawnbrokers on occasion. For many years afterwards, pawnbrokers toasted the health of Lord Eldon at their dinners.

Colloquially, being "up the spout" was also a reference to becoming pregnant and may refer to the loss of a girl's "honour" if she was unmarried at the time. Like an item that had been pawned, her honour was unlikely to be redeemed. The term was most commonly used in London.

23rd December 2019

Why is it illegal to wear yellow clothes in Malaysia?

This stems from political demonstrations in 2015.

On 29th/30th August of that year, protesters took to the street demanding the resignation of Malaysian Prime Minister Najib Razak, who had been accused of embezzlement and corruption. The protestors chose to wear yellow as a symbol of their solidarity, much as the "gilet jeune" movement wears yellow hi-viz jackets in France.

The protests were organised by the movement known as "Bersih", meaning clean or fair, which had been active in Malaysia from 2005 when it was formed as the Joint Action Committee for Electoral Reform. The movement held a series of rallies in major Malaysian cities between 2006 and 2016.

Although originally supported by people from across all three of Malaysia's ethnic groups (Malays, Indians and Chinese) it is now seen as being predominantly backed by the minority Indian and Chinese communities.

Unable to stop the protests, the country's equivalent to the Home Secretary, Ahmad Zahid Hamidi, banned the wearing of yellow. The move had no obvious effect on the protestors. Although leaders of the Bersih movement were arrested, it wasn't specifically for the wearing of yellow clothing, but more part of the government's counter to the demonstrations.

At their 2016 rally, Bersih were opposed by counter demonstrators wearing red shirts. That group was made up mainly of supporters of the United Malays National Organisation (UMNO), the Malaysian governing party. Police prevented any serious disorder by keeping the two factions apart.

Najib Razak left office in May 2018 when his party suffered an unexpected defeat in the Malaysian general election. Razak was prevented from leaving the country after his electoral defeat and is now under police investigation for crimes alleged to have been committed while he was Prime Minister.

It is not illegal for people going about their normal daily lives to wear yellow clothing, however, support for Bersih might be inferred by their opponents if someone were to be seen wearing a yellow tee-shirt.

30th December 2019

Were family names routinely changed when immigrants arrived at Ellis Island in New York?

There are several factors relating to this, but the main ones were confusion over identity, illiteracy and language barriers.

Many passengers, especially those arriving before World War I, weren't in possession of travel documents such as passports, so there was nothing that names could be copied from by immigration officials.

Although each ship had a manifest to show the names of its passengers, the tickets for travel were often bought by distant relatives on behalf of family members, leading to mistakes in family names caused by changes on marriage, or changes of the actual passenger as tickets were sold on. This resulted in the migrant giving a different name to that on the ship's manifest. The immigration officials insisted the immigration documents matched the names on the ship's manifest, so the immigration records recorded the wrong name.

Even when the problem of misidentification had been overcome, illiteracy was another problem, where passengers didn't know the spelling of their own names, or language difficulties where the correct spelling was misunderstood. There are many ways that letters of the alphabet are pronounced differently in the many different European languages (I is often pronounced as e, etc), or the sound they make is altered by such devices as umlauts and cedillas.

Finally, impatient immigration officials, faced with long queues, would make a 'best guess' at what the name might be and how it was spelt, sometimes anglicising it in the process, so 'stein' in a name might become stone.

Once a name had been recorded on immigration documentation, it was almost impossible to get it corrected, so most migrants just accepted their new name.

Because of the high numbers of migrants passing through Ellis Island and other immigration centres, there was also a lot of duplication in names, especially the more common ones. For this reason, the US immigration authorities insisted on including a middle initial in all documentation in order to remove some of the duplications. If a person didn't have a middle initial, they would be allocated one, but it wasn't the initial of an actual name. Even today you can ask some Americans what their middle initial stands for and they won't be able to answer. The initial has just been passed down through the family as a matter of tradition.

Ellis Island had held the name of several owners before being bought by Samuel Ellis in the 1770s. It was then bought by the US government in 1808 for use as a military fort, guarding New York harbour, before becoming the official immigration centre for the city in 1890, relieving the pressure on the overcrowded immigration offices at Castle Garden on Manhattan Island.

Unfortunately the new buildings on Ellis Island were made of Georgia Pine and burnt down in 1897, destroying all the New York immigration records going back to 1855. The buildings were rebuilt and re-opened in 1900.

First and Second Class passengers had their documents checked on board ship when the ship docked. The thinking was that if you could afford the higher ticket prices, you were unlikely to become a burden on the US taxpayer. These passengers only went to Ellis Island if they were clearly sick or their documents weren't in order. The Third Class, or 'steerage' passengers were transferred to Ellis Island from the port and would undergo health checks as well as checks on their identification and sponsorship to enter the country.

Despite being nicknamed as the 'island of tears', the vast majority of migrants were treated courteously and spent only a few hours on the island before starting their new life in America.

Between its opening and its closure in 1954 Ellis Island handled over 12 million migrants. It is now a museum of immigration and thousands of visitors go there each year to look up the arrival records for their families. Because of the issues described earlier, this is not always an easy task. Nowadays immigration records can also be accessed via the internet.

31ˢᵗ December 2019

Who invented the Ouija Board?

The Ouija board has its origins in China around the year 1,100, where it was known as planchette writing. People believed it was a way of talking to the dead. It found its way into the west in the 19ᵗʰ century, when spiritualism was popular and a better way of "talking to the dead" was desired.

American businessman Elijah Bond patented a method of planchette writing that was combined with a board, on which was inscribed the letters of the alphabet and the words "yes" and "no". His patent was filed on 28ᵗʰ May 1890, thus crediting him as the inventor of the Ouija board, though it wasn't called that at the time. That name wasn't used until an employee of Bond, William Fuld, took over production and created the name.

Fuld claimed to have come up with the name by using the board to talk to a dead Egyptian, but it is in fact a combination of the French and German words for "yes". Fuld changed his story several times and even claimed to be the board's inventor.

Ouija boards enjoyed their heyday between the 1920s and 1960s. Fuld's estate then sold the patent to Parker Brothers, makers of board games. Parker Brothers in turn sold the company to toy makers Hasbro in 1991.

In the 1960s British toy and board game manufacturer Waddingtons did produce a Ouija board as a child's toy, but Fuld and Parker Brothers had already been marketing the board for children in the USA.

Science regards the phenomenon of the Ouija board as an ideomotor response (IMR). This is an involuntary muscular response created by the subconscious mind. Whatever words are spelt out are therefore the common denominator of what is going through the minds of the group of users.

The belief that Ouija boards actually work may stem from the condemnation of its use by Christian groups early in its history, though no evidence is offered to support that any spirits had ever been summoned. The idea that Ouija boards are capable of channelling evils spirits is mainly the work of popular film and fiction.

Author's Note: This question had been asked on a previous occasion in a slightly different form, when I also submitted an answer. So, if you have read this response in one of the earlier volumes of answers, you aren't suffering from déjà vu.

1st January 2020

What is the cylinder or box found on computing or charging cables?

Although it is comparatively rare these days, there are occasional surges in voltage on mains electricity that can cause damage to delicate electronic equipment. Short transients in voltage, less than 3 nano seconds in duration, are called spikes and longer transients are called surges. To protect against damage, the equipment is fitted with a surge suppressor or surge protector, which is the cylinder or box like shape seen on the cable.

Where larger electronic equipment is kept permanently connected to the mains, such as TV sets or PCs, the surge suppressor is usually built into the equipment and therefore isn't visible. In many types of battery charger, the surge suppressor is also built in.

Visible surge suppressors are usually only fitted to cables that can be detached from their original equipment, ensuring that whatever equipment the cable is re-attached to, it is protected against surges. This can result in some equipment having double protection – both built in and as part of the cable. This is common where the equipment is manufactured by one company but the mains cable is provided by a sub-contractor. It is cheaper to manufacture just one type of cable, fitted with surge suppression, rather than manufacturing one type with and one type without.

The important bit of the battery charger is the plug assembly, which contains the components that convert 230 volts of alternating mains current (ac) into low voltage (typically 5 volts) direct current (dc) which is used to charge the battery of a tablet or mobile phone. The charger will usually have in-built surge suppression.

Within the little black cylinder or box that is visible is are components called a metal oxide varistors (MOVs) which diverts the spike or surge in electricity and prevents damage from occurring.

These semiconductor varistors (variable resistors) have a variable resistance which is dependent on the voltage applied. Under normal circumstances, when the supply voltage is at the correct level, they apply a high resistance, preventing significant current flow through them. When a surge occurs their resistance drops and the excess voltage is diverted to earth, reducing the danger of damage. As soon as the surge has passed, the resistance of the varistors returns to normal.

There is a second type of surge protector called a gas discharge arrestor. In those an inert gas is ionised by the surge, allowing it to pass the excess voltage through it to earth.

On older equipment, toroidal choke coils were used to smooth out variations in voltage. These rely on the variations in magnetic field produced by an electric current passing through a coil to "smooth out" surges. However, the coils could be quite bulky and aren't well suited to modern electronic devices, where compact sizes are needed.

It is possible to install "whole house" surge protection, which is applied to the domestic mains electricity supply and will reduce the risk of damage to all the electrical equipment in a single residence. However, as most electronic equipment is supplied with surge protection devices, this would seem to be a bit redundant. White goods (washing machines, fridge's etc) don't generally require surge protection.

8th January 2020

What is free with regard to pubs described as free houses?

A Free House is a pub that is not tied to a specific brewery for its supply of beer. Typically, the pub will be owned by the landlord, or will be rented from a private owner. This means that the licensee can source their beer from wherever they wish, making them "free" of a beer tie.

As the 20th century arrived, large breweries came to dominate the business. Small brewers were forced out or were bought up by the larger brewers. This process continued into the second half of the century, with many regional and county-based breweries disappearing. Some of those old brewery names are still to be found in the brand names of some beers. The brewers also bought up a lot of pubs so that they had a guaranteed market for their beers. This control of the beer supply led to a gradual loss of quality that wasn't addressed until the re-introduction of "real ales", created by independent brewers, in the 1980s and 90s.

What emerged was three business models for pubs. The first was the managed house, where the brewery employed a manager and also supplied the beer. Then there was the tenancy, where the licensee rented the pub from the brewery and the brewery supplied the beer. Finally there was the "free house". In practice many free houses negotiated supply contracts with breweries in order to get the best price, but the contracts weren't necessarily exclusive to a single brewer.

During the late 1980s Prime Minister Margarette Thatcher concluded that a handful of breweries controlled too many pubs and decided to break up what amounted to a cartel. At that time 6 breweries in England owned 75% of all the pubs. The biggest breweries were ordered to make a choice between brewing beer or managing pubs – but they couldn't do both. Smaller brewers with fewer pubs weren't required to make such a radical change.

From 1990 onwards some breweries countered by "spinning off" pub ownership as a separate business, but brand new pub chains, such as Punch Taverns, also started up, providing new tenancies for pub owners. It didn't change the method of supply, as the new pub chains dictated what beers could be sold in the pubs and they negotiated the supply contracts. They then sell the beer to the landlord at a profit. Whole independent chains of managed houses also appeared, such as J D Wetherspoons.

Tenants were allowed to provide "guest beers" of their own choice, but even this is generally managed by the owners of the chain, as they can negotiate the best prices for the beers.

Effectively the three-way split of business between managed houses, tenancies and free houses is still in place, only the ownership of the premises has altered in the first two types.

10th January 2020

Why do so many male footballers wear a garment resembling a bra?

In the topflight of football, the majority of players wear this garment.

It is a harness that contains sensors that measure the players various bodily functions eg, their "vital signs" such as heart rate, breathing, body temperature and blood pressure. In this way a player who is tiring can more readily be identified. allowing the club's coaching team to make recommendations to the head coach about the timing of substitutions. The data is sent to the coaching team in "real time" via satellite and is displayed using specialist software on their laptops or tablets.

After the match the data can be analysed to help with decisions regarding the player's fitness training regime and even their diet.

The harness also incorporates tracking telemetry to allow coaches to analyse the player's movements around the pitch, either in real time or after the match.

In a sport where even the minutest change in a player's performance can make the difference between winning and losing, technology such as this is playing an ever-larger role. The same technology is also used in other sports, such as rugby.

Author's note: I had previously answered this question in regard to the rectangular bulge that can be seen on the back of the shirts of topflight rugby players. Obviously the reader, being a football fan, wasn't able to extrapolate from that answer. Just joking – no need to e-mail with complaints.

10th January 2020

Do all artificial satellites travel in the same direction and at the same speed?

Most satellites follow the rotation of the Earth and travel from west to east. However, the path doesn't have to exactly follow the Earth's rotation. They can take a more diagonal orbit. The optimum orbit for a satellite is to follow the path of the equator. If a mapping or observation (spy) satellite were to do that, it would only be able to view the ground beneath it, not that to the north or south. For this reason, some satellites sometimes take on a diagonal orbit. This allows the satellites to cover the whole of the Earth's surface over the duration of a number of orbits. This would make the orbit approximately northwest to southeast, or southwest to northeast. The extreme examples of these sorts of satellites actually rotate at such a diagonal that they orbit from pole to pole.

In order to remain in orbit, the satellite must balance two forces. The first is the force of gravity, which is trying to pull the satellite back to Earth. The second is centrifugal force, which is created by the satellite's own speed. If the speed of the satellite is too slow, it will fall back to Earth; if it is too fast it will shoot off into deep space.

To maintain an orbit at a height of 150 miles, a satellite must maintain a speed of approximately 17,000 mph. In practice there are no modern satellites in such a low orbit so higher, but slower, orbits are the norm.

Once in orbit the satellite needs no additional power input to keep it there. The Earth's gravitational force is weak enough to prevent it slowing the satellite down significantly. However, over many years the satellite will slow down bit by bit and it will be dragged back to Earth. On-board fuel reserves can be used to maintain altitude for a bit longer, but there wouldn't be enough fuel to keep the satellite aloft forever. The rate of decay of the satellite's orbit is predictable, so a replacement satellite can be launched in plenty of time. The satellite's electrical systems are powered using solar energy.

The exact speed of travel varies according to distance above the Earth. This is particularly relevant for satellites which are in geostationary orbit, ie they are always at a fixed point above the Earth's surface. This is a requirement for TV satellites, communications satellites and navigation satellites.

To maintain a geostationary orbit at a height of 22,233 miles, the satellite must travel at a speed of 7,000 mph. This will allow it to make one orbit every 24 hours. As the Earth is also rotating once every 24 hours, it means the satellite remains above a fixed point on the Earth's surface. If you vary the height of the satellite, you must also vary the speed, getting slower the higher you go.

Early TV satellites didn't have this geostationary capability, so when they were used to relay live sporting events, such as the World Cup in Mexico in 1970, matches could only be viewed if the satellite was at the right point in its orbit. Some viewers around the world saw the beginning of the match but not the end, while others saw the end but not the beginning. If the satellite was on the wrong side of the Earth when a match was played, nobody could watch any of it elsewhere in the world.

Imagine shining a torch on a wall. The closer to the wall the torch is, the smaller the area that is illuminated. So it is with satellites. The lower they are, the less ground they can "illuminate". This is known as the satellite's "footprint". If a communications satellite is only required to relay signals from London to Paris, it can have a small footprint, which means it can remain in a lower orbit and travel at a faster speed. If it is required to relay signals across the Pacific Ocean, it must have a large footprint and therefore a higher orbit, which means it must travel slower.

Satellites required to communicate around the world work in relays. The first satellite will receive the signal from Earth, then relay it to a second satellite which is in its "line of sight", which may beam it back to Earth or relay it on to a third satellite, and so on.

So, all satellites travel in roughly the same direction, but at different speeds according to their altitude.

13th January 2020

If all the money in the world was shared equally with every person, how much would each of us get?

There is approximately $90.4 trillion in terms of money in the world. $4.7 trillion of that is currency in circulation and the rest is held in bank or savings accounts.

The current population of the world is given as approximately 7.53 billion. Dividing one by the other would give us $12,000 or just over £9,000 per person. In the UK that is less than one third of the national average wage.

However, there is a considerable difference between money and wealth. A lot of wealth is held as property, stocks and shares, bonds, art, precious metals, jewellery and other alternatives to money. Vintage cars, antiques and certain bottles of wine can all be classified as wealth.

The current estimate of the value of wealth and money combined is about $280 trillion. This would increase the individual "share" to about £27,000, which is still a little bit below the national average wage

The main beneficiaries of this share out would be those who have the least; the people of the world's poorest countries in Africa, Asia and South America. The majority of the population of the UK would become poorer as a result of such a re-distribution of wealth, because homeowners and anyone with savings would have to hand it all over to be shared out. Only those with combined cash and wealth less than £27,000 would benefit.

With so many more "poor" people in the UK, they will spend less because they have less to spend, which would force many businesses to collapse, creating unemployment, which creates more poverty. To give just one example, if no one can afford to buy a house, then no one will be able to employ builders. That new poverty couldn't be compensated because the cash and assets have already been shared out. The collapse of the economy in this way means less tax income, so public services suffer, leaving everyone poorer.

Converting wealth into cash that could be distributed is fraught with problems. Many objects that are held to be valuable become valueless if no one has the money to buy them. A work of art may be valued at £1 million, but if no one has £1 million with which to buy it then it is worthless in financial terms. If we take the wealth from those who have it, then there is no one who could afford to buy most of the assets that represent wealth in non-monetary terms. Much of the £280 trillion in wealth is illusory because of that, which means the actual share of wealth would be far less than £27,000 and much closer to £9,000.

But what happens when that wealth is shared out? Money can only be spent once, so when the recipients of their share spend it on food, rent or whatever, it is gone. The money goes into the pockets of those who provide what has been purchased. This means that wealth starts to become concentrated once again, into the hands of those who can provide things that other people want.

The origins of many of our wealthy families in the UK was in agriculture, because they provided for our staple needs: food and clothing. Those that owned the land on which food could be grown and sheep reared, employed those that didn't. Later this accumulated wealth funded the growth of industrial revolution, destroying many artisan trades, such as spinning and weaving, in the process. Sharing out wealth will simply restart this process to create a new group of wealthy people.

Sharing out the world's wealth provides only a temporary respite. Some people would again be as poor as they are today, only a year after receiving their share of the wealth. Many who are only slightly better off now would suddenly find themselves much poorer.

Author's note: My answer to the question wasn't published and I assume it is because of the later economic discussions included in my response.

15ᵗʰ January 2020

During World War II at White Waltham airfield, what did the letters MORU stand for?

MORU stands for Mobile Operations Room Unit. It was aimed at providing air forces in the field with the same level of operational support as RAF squadrons received while operating from fixed airfields in the UK. As armies in the field manoeuvred, the RAF aircraft that supported them were required to move with them, to keep flying distances as short as possible. These mobile wings were known as "tactical air forces" to distinguish them from the strategic assets such as Bomber Command and Fighter Command.

The most important post in a MORU was Forward Bomb Control. That person controlled all fighter, bomber and light bomber wings in their area of operations. MORU was run primarily in conjunction with army commanders.

A commander in the field would pass requests for air support to his Air Liaison Officer (ALO) in the MORU, usually an army officer, who would then liaise with his RAF counterparts in the

MORU to set up fighter and/or bomber missions to meet that request, using whatever aircraft were available. When planning major battles, the MORU would be directly involved so that they could deliver whatever air support the battle plan required, but at the same time provide ad hoc missions as new tasking was requested by commanders on the ground.

A MORU was housed in seven 3 ton trucks, which were equipped as offices and communications centres. Each truck was allocated a separate function: Ground Controller, Air Controller, Intelligence, Forward Bomber Control, Air Liaison Officer, Ground Operations Room and Plotting Table.

The ground controller and ground operations room was responsible for supply chain issues such as weapons and fuel supplies, plus aircraft maintenance, while the "air" side covered the battle planning, meteorology, crew briefing and battle management. The plotting table showed the location of force elements, their tasking and their readiness states.

The MORU at White Waltham was probably the UK base for a number of teams who could then be deployed in support of ground operations. For example, a MORU would have gone to Normandy following the D Day landing as RAF units moved to France, but during the planning for the landings they would have needed a UK base from which to operate.

As Commander in Chief of 21st Army Group for D Day, General Montgomery had been impressed by the way MORUs had worked for the Desert Air Force in North Africa and then Italy. He was determined that they should be part of his organisation for D Day and onwards.

Author's note: Despite having served in the RAF for 23 years, I had never heard of a MORU either, though I had heard of Forward Air Controllers. So, the answer was as new to me as it was to many of the readers of the Daily Mail.

31st January 2020

How are Dukedoms allocated? Why are some attached to cities (York, Cambridge and Edinburgh) and others to counties or areas (Sussex, Cornwall and Wessex)?

Duchies (or Dukedoms) were introduced to England in 1337 by Edward III, who created three of them: Cornwall, Lancaster and Clarence. As it was Edward's three eldest sons who were granted these titles, they held a higher position in the order of precedence than Earls.

Of these titles, only the Duchy of Cornwall still exists, held by Prince Charles.

After the Wars of the Roses the Duchy of Lancaster reverted to the Crown and, because the Yorkist faction was victorious, has never been bestowed again. The revenue from the estates forms part of the national income and an MP is often appointed to be Chancellor of the Duchy of Lancaster to give them a place in Cabinet. Michael Gove is the current incumbent. Officially it is the monarch who appoints the Chancellor, not the Prime Minister, because they become a Privy Counsellor, though it is clearly a political appointment.

The last Duke of Clarence was Prince Albert Victor, the second son of Queen Victoria. After his death the title fell into abeyance but could be used again.

There seems to be no logic in the selection of the names. From the first three created we can see that one was a county, one a city and the third is thought to originate from the manor and castle of Clare in Suffolk, which was named after the de Clare family.

Earls (from the Norse word "Jarl", meaning Lord) had been the traditional pinnacle of the aristocracy of England since Anglo-Saxon times. William the Conqueror confiscated the titles and the land that went with them and handed them to his closest supporters. They remained second in order of precedence to the Royal Family until the creation of Duchies.

The purpose of a Duke was to govern a large portion of land on behalf of the monarch. They had the power to dispense justice, collect taxes and raise armies on the monarch's behalf. For this reason they were the most trusted of the monarch's Court. Many Dukes that were created were direct relations while others were relations by marriage. By the time of the Battle of Bosworth (1485), 31 Duchies had been created.

On the creation of a Duchy, the incumbent was granted large portions of land. But because the title had been bestowed by the monarch, it could also be stripped from them by the monarch. This was common right up until the time of Charles I, usually for acts of treason or rebellion. Any Duchy that has remained in the same family for any length of time points to a family that has successfully avoided upsetting the monarch or has been forgiven for their crimes. If there is no surviving heir for the title, it reverts to the Crown.

The title of Duke of York wasn't created until 1385 when it was awarded to Edmund of Langley, the fourth son of Edward III, who was already Earl of Cambridge. Since the 15th century it has been the title of the second son of the monarch. Consequently, it hasn't always existed. Its first use as the title for the second son was for Richard, the son of Edward IV, one of the two "princes in the tower" whose disappearance remains a mystery to this day.

Once the title of a Duke was back in Royal hands, it could be bestowed on a new favourite, usually with the lands that went with it if they hadn't already been sold off to raise money for the Royal treasury. The titles of the Dukes of Sussex, Edinburgh and Cambridge were recreated, having been out of use since 1843, 1899 and 1904 respectively.

New Duchies were also created from time to time as new Royal favourites rose up, but these didn't have the traditional lands attached to them. The title gave the incumbent a seat in Parliament, what we now call the House of Lords, but not much more. A smaller grant of land was sometimes given. This was the case with John Churchill, the 1st Duke of Marlborough, who was granted land in Oxfordshire by Queen Ann on which he built Blenheim Palace. He was given his title for his successful leadership of the army during the War of the Spanish Succession. Arthur Wellesley, who we know as the Duke of Wellington, gained his title in a similar way.

Prince Edward is Earl of Wessex, not a Duke. The title was recreated, having not been used since the Norman Conquests because the house of Wessex was the ruling family of England, defeated by William the Conqueror. William's good friend William FitzOsbern was granted the title but on his death it was incorporated into the holdings of FitzOsbern's son, the Earl of Hereford in 1071. The title was recreated by our current Queen for her youngest son in 1999, having been out of use for over a thousand years.

Author's note: Surprisingly there was a similar question published in the Daily Mail a few days after this one, asking why there was no longer a Duke of Clarence. I pointed out that I had already answered that question within this one, but the Daily Mail published another answer anyway. Column inches to fill, I suppose.

4th February 2020

Did Sikh soldiers fight in the British Army in World War I?

The Indian Army, comprising all ethnic and religious groups from the sub-continent, served in the European, Mediterranean, East African and Middle Eastern theatres of conflict during World War I.

Early in 1914 it became apparent that if war was to break out in Europe, the Ottoman Turkish Empire would be a threat to British interests, particularly those relating to the oil fields of the Middle East and access to the Far East via the Suez Canal. The Government in India was instructed to prepare plans to deploy Indian troops in the defence of those interests.

At the start of World War I the Indian Army had 150,000 trained men. Two Divisions of Cavalry and two of Infantry, known as Expeditionary Force A, was sent to the Western Front as soon as war broke out, arriving in Marseille on 30th September 1914. They saw their first action at the Battle of La Bassée between 10th October and 2nd November.

A further six expeditionary forces were assembled from India, serving in East Africa, Palestine, Mesopotamia (Iraq) and in the Gallipoli campaign. They were regularly reinforced as casualties mounted.

Thirteen members of the Indian Army were awarded Victoria Crosses, the first of these going to Darwan Singh Negi of the 39th Garhwai Rifles, for action in France in November 1914. Given the inclusion of Singh in his name, it may be assumed that he was a Sikh.

In all, 62,000 Indian Army soldiers were killed during World War I and a further 67,000 wounded.

In the recent film 1917, a Sikh soldier is shown travelling in a truck with British soldiers. However, the truck is transporting "casuals", who were soldiers who had become separated from their units and had been attached to another unit to fill gaps in the ranks. This accounts for the wide variety of accents heard during those scenes.

It is known that Indian Army units fought alongside British troops in some battles and there are photographs in existence of soldiers from both armies standing side by side.

Soldiers of Afro-Caribbean heritage served in British Army units (Northampton Town footballer Walter Tull was just one of them) so there is no reason to suppose that men of Indian ethnicity didn't also serve in the British Army if they were living in Britain at the time.

Author's note: This question followed hot on the heels of actor Lawrence Fox claiming on the BBC TV programme Question Time, that Director Sam Mendes had been "politically correct", rather than factual, by including a Sikh soldier in his award winning film "1917". Fox was then accused of being racist for assuming that Sikhs hadn't served in the British Army on the Western Front in World War I. Personally I don't think Fox was being racist, he was just displaying his ignorance of British military history.

Which British monarch was the lowest down the royal line of succession?

This would be Henry Tudor (1457 – 1509), who defeated Richard III at the Battle of Bosworth (1485) to become Henry VII.

Several monarchs were the grandsons or granddaughters of Kings, because they had no direct heir or the direct heirs hadn't survived to inherit the throne. Both George I and Queen Victoria became monarchs that way. But Henry Tudor was the great great great grandson of a King, with no English monarch in his family tree until we get as far back as Edward III (1340 -1377). How Henry Tudor became King is a consequence of the very complex and deadly politics of the Plantagenet dynasty.

On the death of Edward III, his grandson Richard II ascended to the throne. Richard II's father, the heir apparent Edward the Black Prince, had died of the plague in 1376. Richard II's throne was usurped by his cousin Henry IV, the son of John of Gaunt (1st Duke of Lancaster), who was Edward III's second son.

Through Henry IV we get Henry V and Henry VI. But Henry VI was considered an unsound King, suffering from what we would call mental health issues, allowing the House of York to contest the throne, which ultimately went to Edward IV during the "Wars of the Roses", also known as "the Cousins' war".

Edward IV was the great grandson of Edward III through his father, Richard of York. Richard was, in turn, descended from two of Edward III's other sons, Lionel of Antwerp (the 1st Duke of Clarence, on his mother's side) and Edmund of Langley (the 1st Duke of York, on his father's side). Edward IV's lineage died out with the mysterious disappearance of both of his sons, the 'Princes in the Tower'. His son was Edward V but was never crowned. after Edward IV's brother Richard seized the throne on his death to become Richard III. There was never any consideration given to any of Edward's several daughters inheriting the throne.

The lineage of Henry Tudor is through John of Gaunt's second son, John Beaufort, 1st Earl of Somerset (grandson of Edward III), then his son John Beaufort, 1st Duke of Somerset (great grandson) and finally his daughter Margaret Beaufort, Countess of Richmond and Derby (great great granddaughter), who was Henry VII's mother.

Henry VII's father was Edmund Tudor, Earl of Richmond, who was half-brother to Henry VI. Henry VI and Edmund had the same mother, Catherine de Valois, but Edmund's father was Catherine's second husband, Owen Tudor, who wasn't of Royal blood; at least, not Plantagenet Royal blood. This meant that Edmund wasn't in line to inherit the throne, but Henry could because of Margaret Beaufort's ancestry, however thin the bloodline might have become by that time. But first Henry had to fight Richard III in order to claim the crown.

If Edward IV's sons hadn't disappeared, it is unlikely that the Tudor dynasty would have arisen to seize the throne as Henry Tudor had such a weak claim. If Richard III had won the Battle of Bosworth, it is his second son, John of Gloucester, who would have inherited the throne. Richard III's first son, Edward of Middleham, had died in 1484 aged 10.

Author's note: Trying to describe the familial relationships involved in the above answer in a way that wasn't confusing was something of a challenge. I don't know if I succeeded. Drawn as a "family tree" the relationships are much easier to trace, but that isn't the form that the daily Mail uses in its Answers to Correspondents' Questions feature.

How accurate have Baba Vanga's predictions been to date?

This is a difficult question to answer as many people who knew Baba Vanga claim she never made some of her predictions and Baba Vanga herself denied making some of them. However some studies of all those that could be attributed to her have concluded that about 80% were accurate.

Vangeliya Pandeva Gushterova (née Dimitrova), known as Baba Vanga (Baba means Grandmother and Vanga is a diminutive of Vangeliva), was born on 3rd October 1911 in the country now known as North Macedonia but which was at various times part of Serbia, Bulgaria and Yuogoslavia. According to local legend she was a sickly child and not expected to live so the family didn't name her. Instead the midwife went out into the street to ask passers-by to give her a name.

According to her own account Baba Vanga didn't have any special powers until a "tornado" lifted her off her feet and threw her into a field, where she lost consciousness and was later found injured. As a result of her injuries she suffered a loss of vision which continued to deteriorate through the rest of her lifetime. At the age of 25 she attended a school for the blind in Zenum, which is now part of Belgrade.

It was during World War II, when her hometown of Sturmica was ceded to Bulgaria, that she first started to gain a reputation for prophecy and soothsaying. On 8th April 1942 the Bulgarian Tzar, Boris III, visited her assuring her reputation.

After World War II Baba Vanga was particularly popular with Russian leaders, having been consulted by Leonid Brezhnev and Sergey Medvedev (on behalf of Boris Yeltsin). She is said to have predicted Yeltsin's second term as Russian President. In July 1992 he won the general election that gave him his second term.

Amongst claims made about her abilities are that she foretold the break-up of the Soviet Union, the Chernobyl disaster, the date of

Stalin's death, the sinking of the Russian submarine *Kursk*, the September 11 attacks, Topalov's victory in the world chess tournament and the tensions with North Korea.

On the other hand, Bulgarian sources say that the people who were close to her claim that she never prophesied about *Kursk* or other subjects circulating the internet and that many of the myths about Baba Vanga are simply not true, which ultimately hurt and crudely misrepresent her and her work.

Two of her accepted predictions appear to be verifiable. The first relates to Yugoslavian actress Silvana Armenulić who met her in August 1976. The meeting didn't go well, with Baba Vanga sitting with her back to her guest and ignoring her. Armenulić was just leaving when Baba Vanga stopped her and told her to return in three months. She then corrected herself and said *"Wait. In fact, you will not be able to come. Go, go. If you can come back in three months, do so."* Two months later Armenulić died in a car crash.

The second prediction relates to 9/11 and was made in 1989. "Horror, horror! The American brothers will fall after being attacked by the steel birds. The wolves will be howling in a bush, and innocent blood will be gushing."

With hindsight this prophecy is easy to interpret, but in 1989 it would have been much harder to understand.

Baba Vanga died on 11ᵗʰ August 1996.

Author's Note: Questions about the accuracy of predictions made by seers and fortune tellers (Nostradamus, Mother Shipton etc) are a regular feature of the questions in the Daily Mail. I guess people just love to believe in fortune tellers. None of the answers I have researched has convinced me that there is any basis for these predictions having been accurate. Soime of them may never even have been made in advance of the events. However, Baba Vanga's two predictions, mentioned above, have come closest to convincing me.

Have the Americans landed a C-130 Hercules aircraft on a moving aircraft carrier?

On 30th October 1963 the United States Navy made history when a Marine KC-130 landed on board the aircraft carrier USS Forrestal. It was the first of four evaluation operations of the aircraft type on a carrier.

The Captain of the aircraft was Lt James H Flatley III and he was accompanied by Lt Cdr "Smokey" Stovall and Machinist's Mate (Jet) 1st Class Ed Brennan.

The purpose of the trials were to determine whether or not the C-130 was capable of operating as a "COD" (carrier on board delivery) aircraft. It was already established that the basic C-130 was a very capable long range freight carrying platform, but could it be used to deliver to ships at sea?

The Navy couldn't find two regular C-130 pilots willing to carry out the tests, so they chose two fighter pilots as being the only ones willing to undertake the risky operation. They had one four hour familiarisation flight with a Lockheed test pilot before carrying out 100 test landings at the Naval Air Station at Patuxent River, Maryland.

The test landings on the Forrestal were conducted 500 nautical miles out in the Atlantic Ocean. The aircraft itself actually belonged to the United States Marines and had its markings painted over with those of the US Navy.

With a load of 25,000 lbs the aircraft required only 295 ft to land and 745 ft to take off, which was within the parameters of the Forrestal's flight deck. The forward motion of the ship produced a head wind which helped to add extra "lift" for the Hercules. On 30th October the crew carried out 29 "touch and go" landing and take offs, which were repeated on 8th, 21st and 22nd November.

They also carried out a total of 21 "full stop" landings without the aid of the normal arrester gear, followed by take offs from a standing start, without the aid of a catapult.

Film of the trials is available on the internet.

The US Navy concluded that by using the C-130 it was possible to deliver 25,000 lbs of cargo at a range of 2,500 miles, to an aircraft carrier. However, the idea of using the aircraft as a COD was still considered too risky and it never became an operational tasking. The aircraft's size meant it couldn't fit onto the carrier's elevators or on her hanger deck, which would impede other operations while the aircraft was on board. It also risked the aircraft sliding off the deck in heavy weather.

The aircraft did set the record for the largest aircraft ever to land on a carrier, which remains unbroken today.

In place of the C-130, the Navy embarked on developing the Grumman C-2 Greyhound to fill the COD role. This is a two engine cargo plane which entered service in 1965 and the C-2A(R) version remains in use today, alongside the V-22 Osprey. The V-22 has tilting engines to allow it to take off and land vertically, like a helicopter. This aircraft has been selected as the long term future COD aircraft.

* * *

The last letter of 2020 brings to an end this volume of my answers, however I doubt if I'll stop answering the questions that are posed in the Daily Mail, so be on the lookout for Volume 4 in about 3 years' time.

And Now

Both the author Robert Cubitt and Selfishgenie Publishing hope that you have enjoyed reading this book.

Please tell people about this eBook, write a review on Amazon or mention it on your favourite social networking sites. Word of mouth is an author's best friend and is much appreciated. Thank you.

Find Robert Cubitt on Facebook at https://www.facebook.com/robertocubitt and 'like' his page; follow him on Twitter @robert_cubitt

For further titles that may be of interest to you please visit the Selfishgenie website at **http://selfishgenie.com/index.html** where you can optionally join our information list.

Printed in Great Britain
by Amazon

51803143R00153